Campground Management

How to Establish and Operate Your Campground

Rollin B. Cooper

SP

SAGAMORE PUBLISHING

Champaign, IL 61824-0673

ISBN: 1-57167-382-2
Library of Congress Catalog Card Number Pending

Cover Design and Photos: Charles L. Peters

Interior Design: Janet Wahlfeldt

Sagamore Publishing, Inc.

P.O. Box 647

Champaign, IL 61824-0647

Web Site: http//www.sagamorepub.com

This book is dedicated to my wife, Nancy, without whom I would have not even contemplated this project. I deeply appreciate her encouragement throughout the entire project, and especially her many critiques of each chapter.

Contents

Acknowledgments

Acknowledgments are sincerely owed to the many people who have made this book possible. Mike Byrnes, editor of *Woodall's Campground Management,* provided the initial encouragement to write this book several years ago. Joe Bannon, President of Sagamore Publishing, provided the encouragement to complete the manuscript.

Special thanks are due to Don Schink of Chartwell Business Planning, who reviewed the entire manuscript and provided substantial contributions in the financial management section. Appreciation is also due to Jack Gray, retired marketing specialist, University of Wisconsin-Extension, for substantial contributions in the marketing chapter.

I also thank Professor Robert Espeseth, Department of Leisure Studies, University of Illinois, for his input in the design and risk management chapters, plus a critical review of the entire text. Thanks are also due to Michael Schink, transportation planner, Jefferson County, Colorado, for several design and campground layout drawings.

Also, I very much appreciated the efforts of several campground owners who took time out of their busy schedules to read the manuscript. They include Paul Hagen, Pride Of America Campground, Portage, WI; *Charlie Van Treese, Yogi Bear Jellystone Park,* Knightstown, IN; Robert Ludwig, Bakersfield Palms Park, Bakersfield, CA; Grace Carlson, Cheerful Valley Campground, Geneva, NY; Al Daniels, Normandy Farms Family Campground, Foxboro, MA; and Ron Meinholz, Pine-Aire Resort and Campground, Eagle River, WI. And many thanks to all the campground operators whose examples and accompanying contributions enhanced the book.

Special thanks are also extended to David Gorin, executive vice-president, and *Dawn Mancuso, former executive director, National Association of RV Parks and Campgrounds,* for coordinating the campground owner review, and for reviewing the manuscript and making useful comments. Thanks also to David for encouraging the publication of this manuscript.

Gratitude is also due to Bill McKnight, Jim Calfee Insurance Agencies, Inc., for reading and making very useful suggestions for the risk management section.

Last, and certainly not least, thanks to *David Weizenicker, Wisconsin Department of Natural Resources,* for encouraging, coordinating, and reviewing the manuscript in his department, and to Rodney Nelson and Thomas Ellingson of that department for reviewing the book and making useful suggestions.

For the revised edition, thanks to Paula Martell, Neshonic Lakeside Campground, West Salem, WI; Connie and Dan Agnello, Baraboo Hills Campground, Baraboo, WI; John Imler, Imler Consulting and Publishing, Inc., Sacramento, CA; Jane Nordstrom, Vice President of the National Association of RV Parks and Campgrounds, Falls Church, VA; and Robert Hartford, Evergreen USA, Lewiston, ME.

Foreword

I first met Rollie Cooper in 1980 when I attended the Campground Operators' Short Course at Camp Upham Woods in the Wisconsin Dells. This four-day course, taught by Rollie and other extension personnel from Wisconsin and Illinois, covered the basics of campground management for neophytes and veterans of campground operations alike.

At the time, the short course was one of a few systematic programs that provided beginners with the simple tools and techniques they needed to survive in the business. Those basics were sorely needed, because 20 percent of the private campgrounds in the United States were changing hands annually due to low profits.

Generally, people become campground operators now for the same reasons they did then (1) they love camping and believe that running a campground would prove to be an ideal life, or (2) they are retiring or retired and want a source of income. Most don't have business backgrounds, and not much in life's experiences prepares a person for this small business that demands more dedication per dollar of return than almost any other business in the world.

That combination of a need for a quick education to acclimate people to the industry so they could survive in their chosen work, and the lack of educational opportunities drove home to all of us involved in providing camping opportunities how precious every ounce of practical knowledge was.

That's why the short course was treasured, and that's why one of the most popular educational tools in our industry remains the crackerbarrel. This informal gathering of campground operators usually has a moderator, but beyond that, the crackerbarrel's structure is amorphous. Someone asks a question or describes a problem, and anyone who wants to contribute tells how he or she did it, or solved it at his or her campground.

Rollie has worked with campground operators and campground associations for over 25 years, and those basics of campground management he's been teaching have been refined and enhanced by all their experiences. In that sense, this book has been very long in the preparation stage, and each element in it has been field tested by ordinary people who one day decided that owning a campground was the life for them.

His starting the book by exploring the question: "Have you got what it takes?" is no editorial nicety that leads into the main text. Both of us have heard over the years the complaint from experienced campground owners that the newcomers don't realize how much work a campground demands from its owners; therefore, Rollie wisely decided to put a warning label at the beginning: "Running a campground isn't for the leisure class."' He then explains what's required for success before discussing the beginning steps to campground ownership.

He explores the "I love New York" campaign not because the campaign won awards, but because this successful hospitality training program was presented, through the generosity of New York state's Division of Tourism, by Holly Nolan to campground operators in many other states besides New York. Its principles have been working for people in the campground industry for a number of years.

The chances of success in our industry are much better today than they were in 1980, and, with the publication of the short-course-plus-more in book form by Sagamore Publishing, they've improved even more.

Mike Byrnes, Editor
Woodall's Campground Management

Preface

The opportunities facing the independent business person in today's society are seemingly limitless. More and more consumers place demands on business for an endless list of products and services provided to make their lives easier, happier, or more fulfilled. With this opportunity, however, come ever-increasing pressures, demands, and risks—pressures to follow certain legal and ethical guidelines; demands for more and more capital; and personal, financial, and professional risks.

Common knowledge tells us that one way to reduce the risks inherent in operating an independent business is to learn from others' experiences. Collecting that experience and putting it into book form is not an easy task for an industry in which much of the history is still anecdotal. Furthermore, the profession requires a range of information and understanding rarely matched in other fields.

Campground and RV park operators must wear many hats. At times, they are called on to be electricians and plumbers. They must be good hosts to their guests. They are responsible for maintaining the environmental quality on the grounds, which often demands some background in horticulture, engineering, and environmental science. They often oversee the management of lakes, creeks, or other bodies of water. They are entertainers, hosts, psychologists, and friends to their guests and employees. They must be marketers, constantly looking for new campers. They must be financial wizards who know what it takes to keep their businesses running profitably and be constantly aware of their financial situation. They must be employment agencies that hire, fire, and manage staff relations that are often complicated by interactions between family and nonfamily members. The list goes on and on.

Clearly, no book on campground management could possibly cover all these functions completely in one volume. However, Dr. Cooper presents all the basics in a thorough, easily readable, and understandable way. He has included discussions on feasibility studies and business plans, marketing, personnel management, park design, budgeting and finance, and retail operations, among others. For the university student or someone new to the industry, this book provides the information needed to understand the key aspects of park management and a framework with which to pursue further study. For the experienced campground operator, the book will be an enjoyable refresher that offers numerous innovative ideas that can directly be put to use. It is an integral part of the Certified Park Operator program, the professional certification program developed by the National Association of RV Parks and

Campgrounds (ARVC) to encourage ongoing educational opportunities and recognition to those park operators who strive for personal and professional excellence. This book is also destined to become an industry classic that should be on the bookshelves of every park operator, university library, and recreation student.

In his introductory chapter, Dr. Cooper describes the relative youth of the camping industry, and says that this youth accounts for the small amount of statistical and managerial data currently available on the subject. *Campground Management* is part of an on-going program ARVC has established to address this industry need. In cooperation with Sagamore Publishing, ARVC is offering this book as the third in a series on various aspects of park and recreation management. The two previously-published books focus more closely on recreation programming and campground marketing. Additional titles will also be published in the coming years.

Special recognition must go to Dr. Cooper for sharing the great wealth of knowledge on campground operations he has accumulated over the years through his relationship with the Wisconsin Association of Campground Owners, the Great Lakes Midwest Campground Associations, ARVC, and the University of Wisconsin's Recreation Resources Center. This book is a testimony to a man who has dedicated himself to assisting and improving the campground and RV park industry.

Credit also goes to David Bennett, Grace Carlson, Blaine Forrest, Paul Hagen, Bob Ludwig, Leon Rye, Candy Scarlett, Wayne Schramm, and Charlie Van Treese who served on the editorial board that helped produce this book, and to the many campground owners/operators. Those who took the time to write down and share what they've learned through trial and error, so that their colleagues would not have to, helped to make this book possible.

ARVC also wants to express its sincere appreciation to Sagamore Publishing for helping the organization fulfill one of its most important missions—to provide educational and informational materials germane to campground and RV park enterprises.

Part

I

ESTABLISHING YOUR CAMPGROUND

Camping as an activity has existed in many forms for centuries. It probably originated out of necessity when people traveled, and no other lodging facilities were available. Native Americans camped as they roamed the forests and grasslands in search of food. Early explorers camped as they explored and mapped the United States. Pioneers camped as they moved across the country to build new homes and find fortunes. Today, armies camp as they conduct field operations.

A Brief History of Recreational Camping

Camping as a recreational activity in the United States is a relatively recent event. In 1890, President Theodore Roosevelt founded Yellowstone National Park, and in 1910 the first camping facilities in the park were developed. Recreational camping probably began in the east, where fishing and hunting camps served the needs of a burgeoning urban population.

Most private campgrounds were developed after World War II and were essentially rustic, primitive facilities with few amenities. As profits became available for upgrading facilities and grounds, and camping equipment became easier to use, recreational camping became more popular.

As camping gained in popularity in the late 1950s and into the 1960s, the demand increased for privately-owned camping facilities that offered more extensively developed facilities and grounds than those available at most public parks. This book will focus on the two basic forms of campgrounds that help meet the needs of these campers: overnight or transient campgrounds, and destination resort-type campgrounds. However, much of the material applies to public campgrounds as well, because they too are under budget pressure to operate efficiently.

Public campground facilities, as stated, are usually less elaborate than private facilities, with fewer services and amenities. On the other hand, the investment made in preservation of the natural resources of the park may be considerable and may require regulation and management by numerous park officials.

In the later 1960s and early 1970s, much recreational land development focused on lake lots purchased for weekend cabins, second homes, and retirement homes. Supply (availability), inflation, increased government regulation, advertising, and associated development costs increased the price of such lots to the point that few could afford to purchase them, to say nothing of having enough capital left over for building. This price factor added to the attractiveness of using privately owned campgrounds for recreational enjoyment.

The Maturing Campground Industry

The relatively young campground industry is still growing and maturing. The National Association of RV Parks and Campgrounds (ARVC) is only in its 32nd year. Youth accounts for several industry characteristics. First, there are few standard industry-wide management practices. For example, campground rate structures follow almost every form possible. Reservations and registration procedures and policies vary widely as well.

Second, there is limited industry financial data available for making management decisions. Nor is there sound marketing information to assess the effectiveness of various marketing activities. Large certified public accounting (CPA) and consulting firms usually do not have small campgrounds as clients, and so do not have databases from which to generate financial standards and other industry data. Although university trade association (ARVC) and Department of Natural Resources recreation agencies are conducting applied research on the industry, this is a relatively recent development and is spotty at best.

Finally, the varieties of equipment and vehicles used for camping change constantly, resulting in evolving demands for campsite facilities. These changes in demand include the size of campsites, increasing power requirements, sewer hookups, telephone, and TV service. Such new demands require substantial capital outlays for upgrading campgrounds.

High-quality camping facilities require a greater capital investment than most people realize. I have counseled dozens of would-be campground owners or developers who were shocked to learn that campground development costs can range from $2,500 to over $10,000 per site for a well-developed campground.

Recreational camping is perceived as such through an entire spectrum of attitudes, activities, and expectations by the camping public. There are the wilderness walk-in backpackers; campers who carry all food and equipment with them. There are the fully self-contained motor home and travel trailer campers, who prefer the amenities and services provided in a modern motor home.

Woodall Publications Corporations 1999 data show 7,003 U.S. enterprises that offer camping to the public. These businesses offer 884,965 campsites. In addition, national, state, county, and municipal agencies offer thousands of camp- sites to the public. This book is intended to offer advice and information to the operators and owners of the widely diverse campground styles represented by these numbers.

Chapter

1

HAVE YOU GOT WHAT IT TAKES?

There are many reasons why people want to run a campground. Unfortunately, there is sometimes little correlation between people's motives for entering the campground business and their potential for financial success.

This chapter deals with the reasons many people have for going into the campground business, and the characteristics required for success in the campground business. Many of these characteristics are not specific to the successful operation of a privately-owned campground but apply to the successful operation of small businesses in general—especially small home-based businesses. The chapter concludes with common pitfalls in the campground business.

Why the Campground Business?

As mentioned above, the reasons given for entering this industry are as diverse as the people who wish to enter it.

Dream fulfillment. A very common reason people start a business is to fulfill a dream. A typical person considering the campground business is someone who has camped a great deal and has found it enjoyable. He or she has seen many campground operators who enjoy operating their campgrounds and whose lifestyles seem enviable. Of course, what is observed is only the guest-related behavior of the campground operator and the rest of the staff. Operating a campground looks like fun and seems exciting—like taking a camping vacation every day of the year. There is a lot of fun and satisfaction in operating a campground, but these dreamers don't see what goes on the rest of the time in the lives of the campground operator and the staff.

Independence. Many people dislike working for someone else and punching a time clock every day. Being in business for oneself eliminates that feeling of obligation to another person or organization. For some it provides almost as much freedom as retirement. The promise of being one's own boss is a compelling reason for many who would like to operate a campground.

Retirement security. Some people see the campground business as an activity for their retirement, especially early retirement. They sell their house, and/or they cash in their retirement annuity and make a down payment on a campground.

A rewarding lifestyle. Many decide to become campground operators so they can live the campground lifestyle. An example is a couple with children whom they want to raise with work responsibilities. Others just want to get away from city life.

Location. For some, operating a campground is the only job they can find that they like, or feel qualified to do, in the particular geographic area in which they prefer to live.

Profit potential. Others see owning a campground as a good investment, as a business in which to earn a profit above the returns for labor and capital committed to the business.

There are, no doubt, other reasons for going into the campground business. These might include having grown up in a campground, having inherited a campground, or owning land for which a campground seems to be the best use. Whatever the reason, there are characteristics essential for success that should be seriously considered before making a commitment of money, time, and family energy. These characteristics are discussed in the following section.

Which Characteristics Promote Success?

Business success is usually the result of a good idea, common sense, and much hard work. More specifically, the following characteristics are thought to be essential for success. Not all of them are necessary in each individual operator for him or her to be successful, but the odds are better if most of them are present in at least one member of the management team.

Drive to achieve. Do you have a strong desire to be successful in a small business? This feeling may give you the necessary drive, the toughness, and the perseverance needed to overcome the stress and the emotional pressure of campground management.

Sound judgment. Are you able to make sound decisions in a timely manner? Can you make a major family decision such as the purchase of a new home or a new car without difficulty? Do you think logically? Can you distinguish between emotional and rational decisions, choosing the rational answer?

Ability to plan. Can you think ahead? Are you adept at anticipating trends, problems, and opportunities? You can't hope to hold a successful campground owner's workshop, build a house, or achieve a career goal without sound planning. Nor can you operate and manage a successful campground without it. You need the willingness and ability to plan and visualize achieving almost any long-term goal.

All areas of campground management must be studied, including financial management, personnel management, marketing, and customer relations and operations. There are no shortcuts. It may take a long time, perhaps years, to succeed. You must have a written business plan, an example of which is described in Chapter 2.

Willingness to take risks. You must be relatively comfortable in taking risks, because owning and operating a campground certainly carries a fair degree of risk. Bad management decisions can lead to some degree of failure. Many events outside the operation and management of the campground can also be disastrous. These risks might include an economic recession, a gasoline crisis, bad weather, or a sudden shift in camper preferences.

Self-discipline/determination. Being the operator of a campground makes you the boss. There's no one around to tell you what to do. You must be a self-starter. Equally important is the ability to keep going when circumstances are difficult. The axiom, "When the going gets tough, the tough get going," is especially applicable to campground management.

Credibility, honesty, and integrity. These qualities are the basis of success. You wouldn't perform an operation if you weren't a surgeon. The same principle applies to business. Don't attempt to start an enterprise if you don't know anything about it. Learn everything you can about it before proceeding. It is vital to business success to develop a reputation for being trustworthy. Otherwise, your dealings with campers, suppliers, and staff will be difficult at best and nonfunctional at worst.

Ability to organize. Are you able to look at a job and determine the most efficient and effective manner in which to complete it? The inability to do so will make your labor and material costs exorbitant.

Good health and stamina. Good health is required, because there are times when being laid up with an illness could spell disaster for your campground. Late in a busy season, when the urge to throw in the towel is the strongest, stamina is essential to keep things going.

Enthusiasm and optimism. These characteristics are important in selling the campground to others, both campers and staff. Enthusiasm and optimism are contagious. When you talk enthusiastically to a prospective camper, he or she feels welcome, and ideally more like camping at your campground than at your competitor's. Likewise, your staff will feel more like pitching in. They'll tend to have more fun, and campers who see and talk to them will have a more enjoyable camping experience.

Labor skills. Some member of your management team needs to be a fairly good carpenter, electrician, plumber, landscaper, gardener, painter, and so on. This is true especially when you are starting out, when hiring people with these skills would raise expenses higher than campground receipts. It is necessary to hire certain professionals, because laws require that some jobs be completed by certified plumbers or electricians, for example. Often, you can work out arrangements with such craftsmen that will allow you to do much of the work on a project.

People management and hosting skills. One of the most important sets of skills needed are people-related skills. You must be able to manage people in your campground—employees as well as your camper guests. If you like inviting friends into your home and entertaining them, you will probably enjoy having campers in your campground while helping them to have a good camping experience. If, on the other hand, you tend to be on the quiet, reserved side, you may find hosting camper guests difficult.

Managing employees is also important. You may start out with a small operation and not have to manage anyone, but as you expand, you'll no doubt find it necessary to expand your staff. Leadership ability is essential to manage your employees so that they perform as you desire. You need to set an example for them to follow.

Ability to raise capital and handle credit. You almost certainly will need to borrow money to get started. Chapter 9, Financial Management, discusses the substantial financial capital needed to buy or develop a campground. This is one of the major obstacles for people who want to go into the campground business.

Does your personality coincide with some of the characteristics discussed above? Appendix A contains a test that will give you further insight into your ability to run a campground.

Family Considerations

Many small campground operations are family-operated small businesses. It is important for you and your spouse to agree on how business management decisions will be made.

If you or your spouse currently leaves the home to work daily, you may find it a difficult adjustment to be with each other all day long, day after day in the operation of your campground. Combine this with having your children around when your campground is filled with campers, and you can see why management skills become critical to smooth, happy campground operations.

Can you, your spouse, and other family members honestly discuss your relative strengths and weaknesses regarding the management of your campground? Can you agree on who is to perform each of the necessary tasks?

Will everyone agree to forego family vacations during the peak camping season? Are all family members willing to work at the campground over the weekends, especially the holiday weekends?

Common Pitfalls

Delusions of grandeur. A common problem is the inability to see your campground as it really is, which is the way it appears to others. People fall in love with a dream, an idea, or a campground and lose all sense of reality about acquiring and managing it. Overassessment of the appeal of the site location is a common pitfall.

Inability to assess the market. Some people believe that people will come from miles around to visit their campground. These campground operators often multiply the number of sites in the campground by the days in the camping season times the site rate to arrive at the gross site rental income. They never consider that their occupancy might be something less than 100 percent!

Inability to manage and organize. Some people simply aren't good managers, planners, or organizers.

Lack of human relations skills. Lack of people management and hosting skills can drive away customers and employees.

Insufficient means to generate capital. When planning the financial start-up of a campground, the operating capital necessary for the first season is often overlooked. New owners may get so carried away paying for the campground itself, that further operating capital is not available, so they are unable to get started. A large part of the first season's operating capital must be spent before campground income is received.

Inadequate or no record keeping. Nothing is more critical to sound campground management than accurate records. Financial records tell you where you are and where you've been in the financial management of your campground. Marketing records tell you the same information with regard to your market, and so on.

Failure to face regulatory problems. The various regulatory agencies play a key role in determining whether or not a campground will be successful. Failure to attend to these details before purchase or development can spell disaster.

Lazy behavior. There is no substitute for plain hard work. If you aren't willing to work long hours, sometimes at very tedious or dirty jobs, you will have problems.

Take an honest look at yourself and the rest of your management team. See how you match up to the characteristics discussed in this chapter. Then realistically decide whether you and your management team have what it takes to be successful campground managers. Remember, it isn't necessary to have all the favorable characteristics and none of the pitfalls.

Appendix A

Test Your Success Characteristics

Under each question, check the response that most closely fits your honest reaction to the question.

Are you a self-starter?

_____I do things on my own. Nobody has to tell me to get going.

_____If someone gets me started, I keep going all right.

_____Easy does it. I don't put myself out until I must.

How do you feel about other people?

_____I like people. I can get along with just about anybody.

_____I have enough friends. I don't need any more.

_____Most people irritate me after awhile.

Are you a leader?

_____I can get most people to go along when I start something.

_____I can give orders if someone else tells me what we should do.

_____I let someone else get things moving. Then I go along if I feel like it.

Can you take responsibility?

_____I can make up my mind in a hurry if I have to. It usually turns out OK.

_____I don't like to be the one who has to decide things.

_____I can if I have plenty of time. If I have to make up my mind quickly, I often second guess myself later.

Are you a good organizer?

_____I like to have a plan before I start. I'm usually the one who gets things lined up when the group wants to do something.

_____I do all right unless things get confusing. Then I quit.

_____I get all set, and then something comes along and presents too many problems. So I just take things as they come.

Are you a hard worker?

_____I can keep going as long as I need to. I don't mind working for something I want.

_____I'll work hard for a while, but when I've had enough, that's it.

_____I can see that hard work gets me anywhere.

Can you make decisions?

_____I can make up my mind in a hurry if I have to. It usually turns out OK.

_____I don't like to be the one who has to decide things.

_____I can if I have plenty of time. If I have to make up my mind quickly, I often second-guess myself later.

Can people trust what you say?

_____You bet they can. I don't say things I don't mean.

_____I try to be on the level most of the time, but sometimes I just say what's easiest.

_____Why bother if the other guy doesn't know the difference?

Can you stick with a long-term project?

_____If I make up my mind to do something, I don't let anyone stop me.

_____I usually finish what I start—if it goes well.

_____If it doesn't work right away, I quit.

How good is your health?

_____ I never run down!

_____ I have enough energy for most things I want to do.

_____ I run out of energy sooner than most of my friends seem to.

Now count the checks you made as follows:

How many checks are there beside the first answer to each question?_____

How many checks are there beside the second answer to each question?_____

How many checks are there beside the third answer to each question?_____

If most of your checks are beside the first answers, you probably have what it takes to run a business. If not, you are likely to have more trouble than you can handle by yourself. You need a partner who is strong on your weak points. If many checks are beside the third answer, not even a good partner will be able to shore you up.

(This survey was contributed by A. Charles Wise, Area Recreation Business Agent, University of Wisconsin–Extension, West Bend, Wisconsin.)

Chapter

2

THE FEASIBILITY STUDY AND BUSINESS PLAN

How can you tell in advance if your campground will be successful? How do you even measure success? Wouldn't you like the answers to these questions before you make a major commitment of your financial assets and your lifestyle to a particular campground business? The answers to these important questions are derived from a market feasibility study and cash flow analysis. These two analyses, along with other studies, make up a business plan.

Certainly no rational person would make a major investment in a development project such as a campground without attempting to get the best possible information beforehand. This chapter explains how to find relevant information in a logical way, and how to organize and analyze it. You can obtain and analyze the information yourself or hire a consultant to do it for you. In either case, you need to know what should be included in a business plan or business analysis.

The Keys to Success

There is no absolutely certain way to know in advance if your campground will be successful, but it is possible to improve the odds. In the previous chapter we looked at personal characteristics that are keys to success. Equally important are major keys to financial success in the campground business.

Location, Location, Location

Proximity to one's camping market is definitely important to success. Campers prefer to travel a limited distance to their camping destinations. This is especially true when short duration camping trips are taken, such as regular or extended weekend trips.

Scenic Areas

Success is also affected by location on or near a site rich in natural and scenic resources. Many campgrounds are located near oceans, lakes, rivers, and streams. Others are located in beautiful terrain, and still others are located near unusual rock formations and natural waterfalls. Good examples are the campgrounds located next to or within the national and state parks. Man-made attractions can also be excellent spots for nearby campground locations. For example, amusement parks attract large numbers of tourists, some of whom like to camp.

Highway Access

Being located near or in clear view of a heavily-traveled interstate highway is clearly a key to success, especially if such visibility occurs just before an inter-change. This type of location will automatically attract transient (overnight) camping business. These are campers who just stop for an overnight rest and continue on their trip the next morning. A few recreation activities and ameni-ties are needed for these campers. The same type of location can also attract those who go camping without a specific destination or reservation, with only a general area in mind. Being in a visible location will attract such campers.

Such a location may have a negative effect on destination campers, those campers who come and stay for a period of time, such as a week. These camp-ers don't want the noise or sight of traffic on an interstate highway and are willing to seek a remote location.

Known Recreation Area

The probability for success is greater in areas that are well-known recreation and tourism areas. However, you must still be competitive from a quality stand-point. Tourists are already coming to such an area. Often, many other camp-grounds in the area are enjoying large camping volumes. As another new campground, you would likely capture your share of that established camping market.

On the other hand, if you decide to develop a campground in a remote area where there are no other campgrounds or attractions, you alone will have to attract campers to the area and to your campground.

Sound Management

Certainly, good management is a key to success in a campground, as in any other business. Sound financial management, personnel management, and the presence of quality facilities are required. Also required is the manage-ment of the day-to-day operations of the campground. These are often as-sumed in business plans and stated as such.

Effective Marketing

While often thought of as part of campground management, marketing is singled out in this book to highlight its importance. Attracting the desired volume of campers is perhaps the biggest challenge of all to campground operators.

Reputable Hospitality and Service Attitude

Being in the campground business is being in the people business. Once campground guests are invited through advertising and promotions, they have to be made to feel welcome during their stay so they'll come back, tell other campers about their wonderful camping experience, and bring others with them. Repeat business is necessary for success in most campgrounds, and proper hospitality and service practices are a necessary key to repeat business.

Adequate Capital

Not only is capital needed to buy an existing campground or to develop a new campground, capital is also needed to operate the campground for the first couple of years. Advertising and promotions need to be carried out before income can be generated. Debt service payments, wages, store inventory, operating supplies, and taxes must be paid at least once before income is received.

Proper Planning

This discussion would be incomplete without stressing the importance of adequate and proper planning. As was stated in the previous chapter, it is necessary to plan and to think things through beforehand in order to be successful. If you don't have a plan, you probably won't achieve your business objectives. Failure to plan is planning to fail.

A Campground Business Plan Outline

All of the planning you need to do can be summarized in a business plan. The plan should be written so that you can refer to it over time. A written plan also can help you review your original objectives and help you remain true to them, or when necessary, revise them. The plan should be written down so you can show it to others, primarily to your lender. Loan officers need to know how you plan to earn enough money from your campground business to pay back the money you borrowed from them. They also need a business plan to get a loan guarantee, such as a Small Business Administration guarantee. Further, they need it to syndicate, or share, the loan with other banks.

Most importantly, writing a business plan helps you to make decisions. It is a guide for you to use in managing your business. You may not follow it all the time—in fact, many successful business managers don't follow every detail in their business plans. Rather, they deviate from them when conditions change, when such deviations are necessary.

When you prepare a business plan, you should first gather all the information you'll need, then write a draft of it. Next, you may want to take it to someone to review for you who will give you suggestions on how it can be improved. Then you should review it again yourself and write a final draft.

The following section outlines a typical business plan for a private campground. A campground business plan doesn't have to look exactly like this outline, but it should contain most of this information in some logical form. Many of the segments included in the following outline are more fully developed in later chapters.

Description

The physical description is your introduction. Create a general statement that briefly describes your campground. Tell how many acres it includes, and give a physical description of the site. Let the reader know the number of sites you would like to have when running at capacity. Briefly describe the stages of development, including the planned size and facilities at each stage. Use site maps, drawings, and/or pictures. If you are buying an existing campground, describe what physical changes you plan to make.

Location

Explain your campground's exact location: state, county, nearby city, and so on. Use road maps and plat maps to show the location.

Development Concept

Describe specifically what kind of campground you plan to develop. Will it be transient or destination? Rustic or highly developed? Family oriented or group oriented? Perhaps all the campgrounds in the area are rustic. If so, there may be a need for a high-quality, full-service campground. Describe the market niche or market segments you plan to attract. Examples of camping market segments include: rustic or wilderness, overnight, bare bones, family, young family, adult, resort campground, seasonal, and activity-centered campgrounds, those which provide activities such as golf, tennis, and horseback riding.

Highway Linkages

Tell how easy it is to get to your campground—how far off the interstate or major state highways it is, and how far on county trunk roads. Describe the traffic flows on the major highway linkages.

Plans for Facilities, Activities and Amenities

You should be specific about bathrooms, laundry facilities, camp store offerings, recreation activities, recreation buildings, swimming pools, waterfront development, fitness centers, nature trails, and so on.

Financial and Nonfinancial Objectives

In this section you should state exactly what you want to achieve with your business. If you're starting your campground just to make money, how much do you want to earn? If you're making an investment, what return do you want to get from this investment? Financial objectives can be described in terms of a percentage rate of return on your investment, or a net profit of so many thousands of dollars.

Nonfinancial objectives should be detailed also. As mentioned in the previous chapter, some people want to create a job for themselves or other members of their family. Others go into the campground business because they want to live in a certain part of the country. There are many nonfinancial reasons for wanting to operate a campground.

Market Analysis

Describe your major market areas. How do you determine your major market areas when you're starting from scratch? Often the major tourism markets for a given geographic location are commonly known—a campground consultant will have this information. As a general rule, consider everyone in a 25-to 150-mile radius to be potential campers in your market area. Determine the population size, the consumer spendable income, and lifestyle profiles, including recreation and leisure preferences of the population in that particular area.

Market potential is often overestimated by enthusiastic campground developers. Keep asking the question: *"Why would campers want to come to my campground, rather than go somewhere else?"*

If you are considering the purchase of an existing campground, request past camper registrations. Previous campers are likely to return if they have had a good camping experience. Tabulate these by origin, type of camping party, and any other available information to develop a profile of previous campers. Also ask for occupancy and income records to help you determine the volume of site rentals.

Population

This is a more detailed description of the area in which your campground is located. Describe the population of the area in which your campground will be located, not the population of your market area(s). That comes later.

Employment and Income

Who are the major employers? How many people do they employ, and what type of employment predominates in the area—skilled or unskilled, blue or white collar, and so on? A discussion of employment is important, because the people in the labor force comprise part of your potential market and perhaps part of your future staff. Such information is important in planning your marketing programs and in staff recruitment.

Consumer Spendable Income

Include this only if you view your area as one part of your market area. What is the average spendable (after taxes, etc.) income in your campground area? This is an indicator of the level of economic prosperity of the area. People's ability to spend is an important determinant of your potential market. Campers must have the money as well as the desire to buy something, such as a camping experience.

Tourist Attractions

Briefly describe the recreation or tourism attractions in the area. What reasons are there for people to come to your area, other than to camp at your campground? Include fishing, boating, sight-seeing, golf, antique centers, and attractions such as museums, amusement parks, casinos, and so on. Well-known national, state, and county parks should also be described. Shopping centers and factory outlets should also be included. Special events in your area should be noted, as well as a description of fall color in your area.

Traffic Counts

Traffic count data are useful in describing the potential for off-road business. This is especially true if you plan to operate a transient park. The difference between in-season and off-season traffic counts is important. Although only approximations, projections made from traffic counts are useful.

Hotels and Motels

These are significant in analyzing campground potential for several reasons. First, the number of rooms available indicates the size of tourism development in an area. It obviously tells how many visitors can stay overnight.

Also, when camper parties come to your campground, some members may prefer to stay in a motel room. Grandpa and Grandma may be past their camping years and yet still want to be with their children and their children's family, so they'll stay in a nearby motel. Likewise, you may have a chance to book a family reunion. Not everyone may want to camp. Motels in the area allow them to stay nearby and enjoy the reunion activities at your campground.

Restaurants and Supper Clubs

Camper studies show that campers do much of their dining away from the campsites. Dining establishments need to be identified. These are known as complementary businesses, because they complement your business or make your business better.

Area Campgrounds

The competition, or supply of campgrounds in your area, needs to be listed in your market analysis. However, campgrounds may be considered assets as well as competitors, because they are also in the business of attracting campers to the area. As stated earlier, it's easier to capture a share of a market that already exists than it is to create a new market. In addition, you may cooperate with other campgrounds in advertising, sport shows, and referrals of overflow campers. Eventually, however, there is a limited number of campers, and if the supply or competition is larger, your chance of attracting a certain volume will be smaller, all other things being equal.

Sales Volume of Area Campgrounds

The success of other campgrounds in your area is a good indicator of the potential success of your campground. If other campgrounds enjoy a substantial sales volume, yours has a good chance of doing well also. Unfortunately, the reverse may also be true.

How do you acquire such information? Camper registration records for public parks are public information and are easily attainable. Another method is to ask area operators. Of course, they may not tell you if they suspect that you're planning a competing campground. You may want to observe other campgrounds during the week and on weekends, or you may ask someone else, such as a private consultant, to do the research for you.

Demand Estimation/Camper Volume Projections

These are the most difficult sections of the feasibility study to complete. However, they are also important keys to estimating your gross income and consequent net profit. Given all the previous information you've gathered, you need to estimate how many campers you think you'll attract. There are several approaches to this important task. They are described below.

Threshold Analysis

Estimate the number of visitors coming to your area and how many of them will want campsites. If there is no more specific information available, use the percentages of campers in the general population.

Note. The National Sporting Goods Association estimated that in 1995, 18 percent of the population seven years old and older went camping overnight at least once in the previous 12 months. *(Statistical Abstract of the United States, 1997, p. 259).*

Market Share

In this procedure, estimate the number of campers camping in your area, and divide that number by the number of campsites in your area, including the number of campsites in your campground when completely developed. Then multiply the result by the number of sites in your proposed campground to get the number of campers that will be your share of the total. This assumes that every campground will attract a camper volume proportionate to the number of campsites owned.

Compare with other enterprises: You may find one or two campgrounds that are similar to the campground you plan to develop. Each campground doesn't need to be in your market area, as long as its market area is also similar to yours. You first determine the occupancy and sales volume of each one. You then assume your performance will be similar to that of the comparable campground. Your performance may be slightly above or below the performance of the comparable campground, based on certain differences.

State and Area Industry Occupancy Averages

Also useful are state and national occupancy averages. For example, an RV Park and Campground Industry Education Foundation study reports a median occupancy of 51 percent for 222 ARVC campgrounds reporting (*National Operations Survey of the RV Park and Campground Industry*, 1998, National Foundation for RVing and Camping,).

Expert Opinion

Find a knowledgeable person, describe your campground to him or her, and ask what he or she thinks your camper party volume/occupancy will be. Lack of information will likely prevent you from using all the above approaches. However, you or your consultant should use at least two of these approaches.

If you're considering the purchase of an existing campground, find out what the occupancy rates have been for the past two or three years. Then, by looking at the current physical features, the former marketing expenditures, and other indicators of how well the campground was operated, consider how you might do better in terms of occupancy.

Marketing Plan

In your marketing plan, explain how you plan to attract campers by reviewing your total marketing program—including your marketing objectives, strategies you plan to use, budget, and evaluation. Information in later chapters on marketing deals with this very important subject.

Financial Analysis

If you buy a campground, you will know what the investment is going to be, based on the price you must pay for it. What you offer to pay should be influenced by an appraisal that you and your realtor arrange to have completed on the property.

Most people are surprised to find out what it costs to develop a campground. Perhaps this is because much of the development is underground, in the form of water, electric and sewer lines, and sewage and septic systems. These items are much more costly than most people realize.

If you develop a campground from scratch, your costs are much more difficult to estimate. Development costs vary considerably. Factors that cause such variation include the land cost, the quantity and quality of amenities and services to be provided, how much of the work you complete yourself, and the labor market in your area. A checklist helpful for estimating the costs involved in developing a campground is located in Appendix A of this chapter. The categories listed will help you to determine an estimate of what each of these items will cost you. It is suggested that you establish estimates on major items at this stage, even though you may not be sure if you are going to go forward with your campground.

You need to decide what rates to charge for your campsite rentals because of the impact on your campground income. You must also remember that rates affect the image and the positioning of your campground. This will be discussed later in Chapter 18, Product and Market Identification.

Financial Projections

This is the cash flow section of your business plan, and it will show your projected bottom line, or net profit. It will also tell you how much cash you'll need each year or each month. It is a projection of your income, expenses, and net profit (or loss) for at least three years.

In this section you should restate your objectives, your development concept, and your marketing plan. These projections should include the occupancy for the first three to five years and the number of sites to have developed ready to use for each year.

A three- to five-year cash flow analysis should follow. Three years is perhaps the most common number of years used for a relatively small campground development. Projecting longer than three years is not very meaningful. To explain the rationale for the projections, there should be a set of notes following the cash flow projections. They can be summarized as follows.

Items that fluctuate proportionately to sales. For example, sales and related costs of sales from the various profit centers will increase roughly proportionately to the increases in camper volume. Liability insurance premiums for some recreation activities are based on gross income from the activity.

Categories that are fixed. Some expense categories are relatively fixed, such as legal and accounting, dues and subscriptions, and office expenses, although they will also increase occasionally. The mortgage, the amount of interest, and the terms of repayment will remain constant unless there is a clause in the contract that allows for renegotiation or unless further borrowing is needed.

Expenditures with annual increases. Some expense items increase a certain percentage every year. Examples include:
- five percent increase in insurance, energy, utilities, and so on;
- five percent increase, plus the percent increase in occupancy for operating supplies, maintenance repairs, and supplies; and
- two and one-half percent increase for taxes and labor.

Known relationships. Examples of these relationships include:

- cost of goods sold—about 75 percent of store sales, depending on pricing policies.
- marketing expenditures of five percent of total sales is recommended, with more at start up; and
- payroll expenses—11 percent of payroll.

Projections for campsite rentals. This is the major item in the cash flow and the one on which most of the other income and expense items depend. It can be estimated using the following methods:

Past Operations

If you've been in business, or if you're buying a campground that has been in business of the general type that you plan to operate, you can extend the trend of sales into the future based on past trends, modified by significant changes you plan to make.

Industry Averages

Using state or national averages, per-site income, and expenses, multiply each by the number of sites in your operation.

Best Estimate

If no better information or rationale can be found, campsite rental income can be determined by using your best judgment or that of someone experienced in the campground business.

Computation

Using industry occupancy averages, you can compute site rental income by multiplying the length of season in days by the average site rate, times the number of sites, times the average occupancy rate.

You may want to do three different sets of projections, using an optimistic, a pessimistic, and a realistic scenario. If you are a new campground operator, it's advisable to do the cash flow on a monthly basis for the camping season. A sample financial management worksheet is found in Appendix B of this chapter. It is intended to assist in projecting income and expenses.

Legal Considerations

You may want to consult with your attorney and accountant regarding which form of business organization is best suited for your campground. Common forms of business organization are sole proprietorship, partnership, limited partnership, corporation, and sub chapter "S" corporation. There are tax, liability, and transfer of ownership considerations involved in the choice of business organization, so become familiar with each type as it relates to your particular situation. The form you choose should be indicated in your business plan. A further discussion of this is presented in Chapter 5, Business Organization Options, Concepts, and Agreements.

In recent years, managing risk has become important because of escalating liability insurance premiums and a lawsuit happy society. A plan for managing or minimizing the exposure to risk should be developed and included in your business plan. Doing this will minimize your liability insurance premiums. The coverages that you decide to carry should be summarized in your business plan. Refer to Chapter 16, Campground Risk Management, for more information.

Personnel Plan

In this section, you need to describe how you plan to manage your campground. This essentially means explaining what needs to be done and who is going to do it.

Many operations are family-run enterprises, with a spouse and one or more children involved. Outside help may need to be hired as well. Each member of any management team has unique skills and usually other responsibilities outside the campground. The campground tasks that need to be performed vary in the skills required. As an operator, you will need to list all responsibilities and decide which member of your management team is going to do each of them. More discussion of this is included in Chapter 13, Staff Management.

Generally, the campground management plan consists of one spouse running the office and the front desk and performing most of the marketing functions. The other spouse may do the outside work, including maintenance, building repairs, camper assistance chores, and so on.

You also need to create a set of campground rules or policies that cover the following questions and others.

- When are your quiet hours?
- What is your refund policy?
- What are you going to do about pets?
- What hours will your store be open?
- What reservation policy will you have?

Rules and policies do not have to be specifically spelled out in this section, but some general statements to this effect should be stated in order to satisfy the reader that you've given these issues consideration.

Summary, Conclusions, and Recommendations

In this section, the entire plan is very briefly summarized. The conclusion is drawn whether the project, if developed, will be successful or whether it should be undertaken at all. A private consultant will make a recommendation regarding alternatives, to increase the potential for success.

Your Assets and Liabilities

When you take your business plan to the bank to get a loan, the loan officer will want information about your assets and liabilities. The officer will request a statement of your personal financial condition. Assets include:

- property, real and personal;
- securities;
- retirement plans;
- savings accounts;
- life insurance policies and their current cash values; and
- any other businesses you may own.

You will have to tell him or her about your liabilities—all the debts that you have, such as mortgages, loans, and outstanding credit card balances. Your spouse will have to provide the same information.

You should also provide the loan officer with a resume of your educational and work experience. Include the same for your spouse and children who will be assuming management positions.

Should You Hire a Consultant?

Should you try to write the business plan yourself, or hire a business consultant to write it for you? The more you do yourself, the more you'll learn about the campground business, and of course, the less the plan will cost you. It's a little like calculating your own income taxes, because you have to provide much of the information to the accountant anyway. A good consultant will be knowledgeable about business ratios, loan requirements, and other information specific to the campground industry.

There are often adult education workshops available on starting a small business. While they aren't specific to campgrounds, they can be very helpful, because many of the business principles that you'll learn are the same for starting and operating any small business.

Consultants base their fees on the amount of work that they do for you. They estimate the length of time it will take them, based in part on how much research is necessary. Reputable consultants will perform a cursory examination of your campground business concept, and if it doesn't look feasible, they'll tell you at that point, and won't proceed any further, nor charge you for further work unless you request it. Lending institutions generally require an outside or neutral business analysis. In this case, you must hire a consultant.

Appendix A

Campground Investment Estimate

A Checklist for Building a Campground

Land	$_____
Construction of lake/pond	_____
Swimming pool	_____
Roads and trails	_____
Camper pads	_____
Electric hookups to sites	_____
Water hookups to sites	_____
Sewer hookups to sites	_____
Telephone and TV cables	_____
Dump station, septic tanks, drainage fields	_____
Well and equipment	_____
Tennis court	_____
Playground equipment	_____
Volleyball court	_____
Basketball court	_____
Mini-golf course	_____
Bikes and boats	_____
Shuffleboard, horseshoe courts	_____
Building construction	_____
Office	_____
Store	_____
Recreation building	_____
Shower, toilet, laundry	_____
Pit toilets	_____
Storage and maintenance building.	_____
Home	_____
Other _____	
Other _____	

Landscaping   _____

Washers and dryers   _____

Cash register(s)   _____

Computer   _____

Store fixtures and coolers   _____

Recreation building furnishings   _____

Store inventory   _____

Garbage cans   _____

Picnic tables   _____

Campsite signs   _____

Highway and directional signs   _____

Front entrance sign, lighted   _____

Planning, legal and contingency   _____

Permits and licenses   _____

Other _____

Other _____

Total   _____

Appendix B

Financial Management Worksheet

Projections of Income and Expenses

Income	Gross Sales	–	Cost of Sales	=	Departmental Gross Profit
Site rentals					
Daily/weekly	_____		NA		NA
Seasonals	_____		NA		NA
Cottage rental	_____		NA		NA
Trailer/tent rental	_____		NA		NA
Day use receipts	_____		NA		NA
Campground store					
Groceries	_____	–	$ _____	=	$ _____
Camping supplies	_____	–	_____	=	_____
Gifts/souvenirs	_____	–	_____	=	_____
Vending machines	_____	–	_____	=	_____
Wood/ice	_____	–	_____	=	_____
Bottled gas	_____	–	_____	=	_____
Beer, wine	_____	–	_____	=	_____
Other _____	_____	–	_____	=	_____
Recreation income					
Marine (bait, tackle)	_____	–	_____	=	_____
Watercraft rentals	_____	–	_____	=	_____
Bike rentals	_____	–	_____	=	_____
Mini-golf	_____	–	_____	=	_____
Other equipment rentals	_____	–	_____	=	_____
Game room	_____	–	_____	=	_____
Other services income	_____	–	_____	=	_____
Laundromat	_____	–	_____	=	_____
Coin-operated showers	_____	–	_____	=	_____
Honey wagon/ dump station fees	_____	–	_____	=	_____

Bar	_____	–	_____	=	
Snack bar/restaurant	_____	–	_____	=	_____
RV storage	_____	–	NA	=	
RV repair	_____	–	_____	=	
RV sales	_____	–	_____	=	

Other
Interest on
  bank accounts _____   NA   _____

Total Gross Income _____

Total Cost of Sales _____

Total Gross Profit
(gross sales less cost of sales) _____

Expenses	$ Amount	Your % Last year	Industry % of gross sales
Payroll	$_____	_____	13.5
Payroll taxes, unem- ployment benefits	_____	_____	3.0
Ads and promotions	_____	_____	3.1
Office, postage, printing	_____	_____	1.2
Utilities	_____	_____	6.3
Telephone	_____	_____	1.3
Operating/cleaning supplies	_____	_____	3.7
Maintenance/repair	_____	_____	5.2
Legal/accounting	_____	_____	1.2
Licenses/permits	_____	_____	0.7
Dues/subscriptions	_____	_____	1.0
Vehicle expenses	_____	_____	1.7
Travel/education	_____	_____	0.8
Insurance	_____	_____	3.7
Taxes—real estate	_____	_____	4.3
Garbage disposal	_____	_____	2.2
Machine hire	_____	_____	1.9
Miscellaneous	_____	_____	4.8
Interest on short- term loans	_____	_____	1.4
Other	_____	_____	0.5

Total Operating Expenses _____

Net Profit (before depreciation, owner's draw, income taxes, and debt service) _____   _____

Chapter

3

INFORMATION, ASSISTANCE, PERMITS, AND LICENSES

Government bureaucracies are sometimes looked upon as endless generators of red tape that must be cut through before necessary permits or licenses are issued. All of the tax reports and accompanying money that campground operators must pay the IRS and their state Departments of Revenue, as well as unemployment compensation, licensing and regulations, can seem like an impossible maze through which few can find their way. On the other hand, government agencies can be an excellent source of information and assistance.

This chapter reviews most of the various permits, licenses, and zoning-related assistance that may be required in your state. This chapter also provides information about universities and private enterprises, which are also sources of information to the industry. Be aware that states vary in the amount of assistance they offer as well as in the strictness of their regulations.

The Regulatory Bureaucracies

Remember that people working in bureaucracies at all levels of government are human beings. If you approach them with an attitude of cooperation, a sincere desire to learn about the regulations, and the intention to comply with all the rules, you will likely receive greater cooperation than you would otherwise. Most of our laws and regulations arose out of attempts to solve problems encountered at all levels of government.

Unfortunately, many small business people treat regulatory agencies and their staff like the enemy. A few agency regulators may appear hostile, but most are generally only doing their jobs. They may have a fair degree of latitude in their interpretation of the regulations, so it certainly doesn't hurt to approach such people in a sincere, honest, and friendly manner.

This may be especially true if you need a local zoning variance. Local zoning officials are more apt to grant variances to hard-working individuals trying to make an honest living than they are to grant such variances to rude and impatient individuals.

Existing Properties

If you are considering purchasing an existing business property, be aware that all grandfathered conditions falling short of existing code requirements cease at the time of sale. Codes and regulations that have to be met in full by the new owner include building structural codes, septic, water, and electrical codes. This can involve considerable expense and should be considered in purchase negotiations.

Helpful Agencies, Workshops, and Publications

Knowing what you need to do and where to get the permits can save you endless time and frustration, as well as money. Some permits and approvals require considerable processing time. You will need to initiate such processes well in advance of the time that you need the permit.

Most regulatory agencies have the ability to provide information. Remember, the degree of cooperation you receive will vary depending on the personality of the person you contact, the administrator of the regulatory unit, and your approach. In addition to the regulatory agencies, agencies have been established specifically to provide assistance to small business enterprises.

Small Business Development Center (SBDC), Small Business Administration (SBA)

The Small Business Development Center (SBDC) is a branch of the Small Business Administration (SBA), which in turn is a branch within and funded by the U.S. Department of Commerce. Present in many but not all states, the SBDC is usually housed within the state's Department of Economic Development or a similar government agency. In a few states, it is administered through the state university extension service. The SBDC provides information on small business start-up through individual counseling services, adult education workshops, and seminars. SBA provides an educational service to SBA borrowers.

State Department of Economic Development

State Departments of Economic Development usually have a form of information assistance. Your state may even have a one-stop permit information center where anyone can go for information on all the permits needed for starting a small business. The state may also provide an information hotline or a small business ombudsman office to help deal with its respective permit processes.

Cooperative Extension Service

There is a nationwide network of county-based Cooperative Extension Service offices. These offices often have information that can be very helpful, especially on local zoning regulations, where local businesses can go for information.

The National Association of RV Parks and Campgrounds (ARVC)

The National Association of RV Parks and Campgrounds (ARVC) is the national trade association of the privately-owned campground and RV park industry. It conducts a variety of education programs, including the Certified Park Operator (CPO) program, which includes educational courses offered at its national convention, and at its state associations, conventions and meetings. National Campground Owners Association offers a complete catalogue of educational and informational materials about campground and recreational vehicle (RV) park operations and management. ARVC also offers a trade show in conjunction with its national convention. Operators can view and purchase products needed in the operation of their businesses.

Also, campground operators gain a great deal of knowledge at these conventions by visiting with other operators from around the country and by attending informal discussion sessions (cracker-barrels), where common concerns are raised and discussed. ARVC can be contacted at 113 Park Avenue, Falls Church, VA, 22046-4308. The telephone number is (703) 241-8801, and the fax number is (703) 734-3004.

ARVC has a national network of affiliated state associations and two regional groups comprised of several geographically convenient state associations. The Northeast Association holds an annual conference and trade show. Information on the dates and locations of regional shows and conferences can be obtained from the ARVC headquarters.

The School of RV Park and Campground Management is held every year in January at the Oglebay Resort in Wheeling, West Virginia. Completion of the school program requires attendance over a two year period. The school curriculum emphasizes business management skills necessary to successful business operations. Topics include Basic Business Planning, Developing a Marketing Plan, Personnel Management, Tax Planning, Effective Recreation Programs, Food Services, Emergency Planning, and Profitable Store Management. The program is aimed at operators with at least one full year of park experiences. In 1998 the school added optional electives to the base curriculum. Students receive both CPO (Certified Park Operator) and CEU (Continuing Education Units) credits for participating in the school. Successful completion of the two-year program earns a participant more than half the points needed to qualify for the CPO designation.

Students arrive on Sunday; classes begin on Monday and run daily through Thursday afternoon. Graduation ceremonies are held Thursday evening, and students depart Friday morning. *Contact ARVC for more information.* To register directly, you may call the school at (800) 624-6988, extention 4019. The National Foundation for RVing and Camping, the educational arm of ARVC, awards a number of scholarships for the school each year. For information, contact ARVC.

State Campground Trade Associations

There are 46 state campground associations that provide educational programs and other services to their respective memberships. A list of these associations is included in Appendix A of this chapter.

Recreational Land Development Association

The American Resort Development Association is an association of companies and individuals who own, sell, and develop residential, recreational, and resort real estate, as well as those who provide products and services to this industry. Part of the association's annual conference is focused on RV park and camping resort development. The address and phone number are: 1220 L Street N.W., Fifth Floor, Washington, D.C. 20005, (202) 371-6700.

National Campground Franchisers

Included in national franchisers or chains are Leisure Systems, Inc. (Jellystone Parks) and Kampgrounds of America (KOA). These are listed in Appendix B at the end of this chapter. With a substantial national advertising and promotions program, these companies offer considerable management assistance and provide education and information programs.

Workshops and Short Courses

The Campground Design, Rehabilitation, and Programming workshop is held annually in the fall at Martin, Tennessee. For information, contact Phil Lavely, Park and Recreation Administration, University of Tennessee at Martin, Martin, TN 38238, phone (901) 587-7261, or Richard Cottrell, phone (502) 753-6902.

Advanced campground design and redesign is a course taught in Auburn by Richard L. Cottrell, a campground design consultant who also teaches at the Tennessee workshop. For information you may contact him at 104 N. 18th Street, Murray, KY 42071, phone (502) 753-6902.

Two real estate brokers conduct courses on buying campgrounds. Subjects covered include income and expenses, owner fringe benefits, amenities, lifestyles unique to campgrounds, how much to pay, what to expect financially, a suggested purchase contract, the search process, structuring price and terms that allow the buyer to be successful while keeping the seller happy, and closing process problems and solutions. The brokers who conduct the courses are: Dale S. Bourdette, Campground Data Resources, P.O. Box 889, Lake Wales, FL 33853, phone (941) 676-0009, and Darrell Hess, Darrell Hess & Associates, P.O. Box 1381, Lake Junaluska, NC 28745, phone (828) 452-1535.

The National RV Park Institute, located at P. O. Box 5578, Auburn, CA 95604, phone (530) 823-1076, trains people seeking employment in, prospective buyers of, and current employees and owners of RV parks and campgrounds. Among the courses offered are the following: Hospitality, Inspection of Facilities, Risk Management, Legal Obligations of Employers and Employees, Legal Aspects of Operating and Building a Campground, Marketing, Promotion, and Electrical Repairs and Maintenance. The institute conducts two sessions a year, both in working campgrounds.

Publications

Woodall's Campground Management is a monthly tabloid newspaper with helpful news and feature articles covering every aspect of campground operation and development. In January, it contains a buyers' guide to products and services for campgrounds. Write to *Woodall's Campground Management*, 13975 West Polo Trail Drive, P.O. Box 5000, Lake Forest, IL 60045-5000.

Concerning park practice, the National Recreation and Park Association (NRPA) consists of park and recreation professionals who publish a wide variety of educational materials. Write to this association at: 2775 S. Quincy St., Suite 300, Arlington, VA 22206, or phone (703) 820-4940. In Appendix C you will find publications for campers and RV owners and dealers.

John Imler, a former park owner, operates Imler Consulting and Publishing, Inc., 2445 Harvard St., Sacramento, CA 95815, phone (916)920-0166, which specializes in the RV park industry. He is also the author of *The RV Park Business*, a discussion of buying, building, and operating campgrounds and RV parks and resorts; *Designing RV Parks and Resorts for the 21st Century;* and *Being a Successful Manager of an RV Park, Resort, or Campground*. Prices for the books are $30, $60, and $40, respectively, and include shipping and handling. (California residents must add 7.75% sales tax.)

The Foresight Management Group, 79 James Young Dr., Georgetown, ON L7G 5S5, Canada, phone (800) 851-6676, sells two books written by its manager, Ed Brooker: *Campground Entrepreneurship: Getting into and Successfully Operating a Campground/RV Park* ($59) and *Strategic Marketing for Campgrounds and RV Parks* ($45). Prices include shipping, handling and taxes.

Outdoor Hospitality, a magazine sponsored by the National Foundation for RVing and Camping and the National Association for RV Parks and Campgrounds, began in 1997 as a quarterly and became a bimonthly in 1999. Published by Imagination Publishing of Chicago, Illinois, its editorial supports ARVC's mission of "Outdoor Hospitality Excellence Through Industry Unity." For more information, you may contact ARVC.

City Libraries

Your local city library is an excellent source of information for getting started in business. There are many reference books and periodicals in this area. Depending on the size and completeness of the library, there may well be sources of data needed for developing your business plan, including census data reports.

Licenses and Permits

This section covers most of the licenses and permits you will need to run a full-service campground.

Zoning Permits

Before you make a commitment on a parcel of land for a campground, make sure the local zoning ordinance will allow such a use. After discovering if a zoning ordinance is in place, find out what uses are permitted. It probably isn't zoned for recreation, so you'll have to get a variance or have the ordinance changed.

Making such a change almost always requires a public hearing, at which local residents can appear and voice their approval or disapproval. Some of the people living in the area are apt to object to a campground being developed in their neighborhood. This is largely because they don't want to have campers recreating in their neighborhood. Likewise, if your land is on a body of water, the neighbors see campers as strangers coming in and using their lake or river.

Property Restrictions

Property restrictions can involve the issue of floodplain restrictions, in which case buildings cannot be erected within so many feet of the designated high water mark. However, recreation fields can usually be located in the floodplain areas. Try to look at the land when it is not frozen and covered with snow. If the land under consideration is low and or wet, it may be in a designated floodplain. If this is the case, be sure to get a qualified environmental specialist to look into it for you. Otherwise you may lose the right to develop such land. There are also building restrictions in many areas, which define what buildings can and cannot be built and how they are to be built.

Soil Evaluation and Septic Tank Approvals

If you plan to install a septic system, approval is required by the Division of Health or a similar agency. Many counties have an Agricultural Stabilization and Conservation Service (ASCS) office, where you can obtain a soil survey map that shows the suitability of the site for a septic system. Such information is often available from county or regional planning commission offices. If it looks favorable, then you can have a percolation (perk) test done. This entails digging a hole to a certain depth, pouring water into it, and timing the absorption rate of the soil. This test is often done by the county sanitation official or other appropriate official. You'll probably have to pay for the equipment used to dig the hole. The county extension office can be useful in providing information on how to get this done.

Well Permits

Approval of plans for well and pump installation is required by the Department of Natural Resources (DNR) office or similar agency in your county. Have each well tested at least annually, if not more often, during the camping season. It's also a good idea to have them tested prior to purchase.

Building Permits

New construction or alteration of existing structures usually requires a permit. In some states, plans—including plumbing and heating plans—must be submitted to the Chief Building Inspector of the Department of Industry, Labor, and Human Relations or similar agency for approval. Local building inspectors can be identified by contacting your local county Cooperative Extension Service office.

Swimming Use License

Approval for swimming pool installation or alteration may be required from the Division of Health office in your district.

Campground License, Recreational and Educational Camp License

Most states require licensing to operate a campground, educational, or recreational camp. Contact the Division of Health office in your district.

Restaurant License

If you want to prepare and serve food on your premises, you'll no doubt need a restaurant license from the Division of Health office in your district. Be sure to check on the requirements and costs for acquiring such a license, before purchasing food service equipment.

Confectioner's License

You may need a confectioners license to sell cotton candy and other snacks. Check with your county extension office or other county administration offices to find out where to get a license application.

Bait Dealers' License

Some states require a license from the Department of Natural Resources (DNR) for minnow sales. Check with your nearest DNR district office for further information.

Cigarette, Beer, Soda, Liquor Licenses

These are typically obtained through your local municipality. Beer and liquor licenses are often difficult to obtain. In some states, for example, such licenses are allocated on the basis of the permanent residential population. It doesn't matter if there is a large transient summer tourist population. Campground operators have been known to purchase taverns just to get these licenses.

Boat and Snowmobile Licenses

In order to provide boat and snowmobile rental services, a license from the DNR is often required.

Worker's Compensation Coverage

In some states, if you have three or more employees you must get worker's compensation coverage. In addition, several states require worker's compensation coverage if you have a quarterly payroll that exceeds $500. For information and forms, contact the Worker's Compensation Office in the state agency that handles this.

Unemployment Compensation Coverage

Contact the Division of Unemployment Compensation or the respective agency in your state for help in this area. If you are taking over an existing business, contact the Successorship Department or similar office, depending on your state.

Work Permits for Minors

Minors need work permits in most states. Proof of age (birth certificate) and written consent are needed from their parents or legal guardians. This information should be presented to the Work Permit office. This office is sometimes located in the area high school.

Sellers' Permit

States that collect sales tax will require some sort of permit to conduct sales so they can collect the tax. The state Department of Revenue issues these permits. Depending on sales volume, you may have to report and submit payments monthly, seasonally, or annually.

Incorporation Papers Registration

The Secretary of State or similar office registers corporations. Sole proprietorship and partnerships do not need to be registered.

Name Protection

If you want to prevent others from using your campground name, you must register it with the Secretary of State's Office. If you desire national protection, you must register your name with the U.S. Office of Patents and Trademarks. These offices will let you know if someone else is already using the name you chose.

Doing Business as

Some states require the filing of "Doing Business as" notices in papers of record, regardless of the type of ownership. Check with your Secretary of State's office.

Appendix A

State Campground Trade Associations

Alabama Association of RV Parks & Campgrounds
P.O. Box 70
Springfield, TN 37174
(931) 487-9871

Alaska Campground Owners Assn.
Cheryl Brown, executive director
P.O. Box 101500
Anchorage, AK 99510
(907) 277-4603

Arizona Travel Parks Assn.
G. Michael Williams, executive director
Williams and Associates
3030 North Third Street
Suite 200
Phoenix, AZ 85012
(602) 241-8554

California Travel Parks Assn.
Tug and Judy Miller, executive directors
P. O. Box 5648
323 Nevada St.
Auburn, CA 95604
(530) 885-1624

Colorado Campgrounds and Lodging Owners Assoc.
Sally Harms, executive director
17486 Weld Country Road 8
Brighton, CO 80601
(303) 659-5252

Connecticut Campground Owners Assn.
Allen Beavers, Jr., executive director
14 Rumford St.
West Hartford, CT 06107
(203) 521-4704

Delaware Campground Owners Assn.
727 Country Club Rd.
Rehoboth Beach, DE 19971
(302) 227-2564

Florida Assn. of RV Parks and Campgrounds
Joe Striska, executive director
1340 Vickers Dr.
Tallahassee, FL 32303-3041
(850) 562-7151

Georgia Assn. of RV Parks and Campgrounds
Bull Sullivan
Brookwood RV Resort
1031 Wylie Road
Marietta, GA 30067
(770) 427-6853

Idaho RV Campgrounds Assn.
Knute Blodger
P.O. Box 7841
Boise, ID 83707
(208) 345-6009

Illinois Campground Assn.
Shari Weber, president
Geneseo Campground
22978 Ill. Hwy. 82
Geneseo, IL 61254-8319
(309) 944-6465

Indiana Campground Owners Assn.
Colin Johnstone
c/o Hidden Lake Campground
11460 S. Strawtown Pike
Fairmount, IN 46928
(317) 948-4862

Recreation Vehicle Indiana Council
c/o Indiana Manufactured Housing Assn.
3210 Rand Rd.
Indianapolis, IN 46241
(317) 247-6258

Iowa Association of RV Parks and Campgrounds
Amana Colonies RV Park
P.O. Box 400
Amana, IA 52203
(319) 622-3344

Kansas Campground Association
Larry Olson, president
Pinehaven Retreat
Route 2, Box 1408
St. Johns, KS 67576
(316) 549-3444

Campground Owners of Kentucky
Eben Henson
c/o Pioneer Playhouse
840 Stanford Road
Danville, KY 40422
(606) 236-2747

Louisiana Campground Owners Assn.
Danny Young
P.O. Box 4003
Baton Rouge, LA 70821
(504) 346-1857

Maine Campground Owners Assn.
Dan Billings, executive director
P.O. Box 61
Lewiston, ME 04243-0061
(207) 782-5874

Maryland Assn. of Campgrounds
Debbie Carter, executive director
Buttonwood Beach RV Resort
170 Buttonwood Road
Earlville, MD 21919
(410) 275-2108

Massachusetts Assn. of Camp ground Owners
Mellisa Boynton, executive director
P.O. 548
Scituate, MA 02066
(781) 544-3475

ARVC Michigan
Dave Kuebler, executive director
9700 M-37 South
Buckley, MI 49620
(616) 269-4068

Minnesota Assn. of Campground Operators
c/o Sandy Lien, director of education
Minnesota Resort Assn.
871 Jefferson Ave.
St. Paul, MN 55102
(612) 222-7401

Mississippi Campground Owners Assn.
Bill Mooney
c/o Biloxi Beach Campground
1816 Beach Blvd.
Biloxi, MS 39531
(601) 432-2755

Missouri Association of RV Parks and Campgrounds
John Westonberger, executive director
P.O. Box 70
Spring Hill, TN 37174
(931) 487-9871

Montana Campground Owners Assn.
Jack Clarkson
c/o The Madison Arm Resort
P.O. Box 40
West Yellowstone, MT 59758
(406) 646-9328

National Assn. of RV Parks and Campgrounds
Jane Norstrom, vice president
113 Park Avenue
Falls Church, VA 22046-4308
(703) 741-8801

Nebraska Assn. of Private Campgrounds
Lee Ross
c/o Fort McPherson Campground
HC 01, Box 142
Maxwell, NE 69151
(308) 582-4320

New Hampshire Campground Owners Assn.
Ron Brown, executive director
P.O. Box 141
Twin Mountain, NH 03595
(603) 846-5511

New Jersey Campground Owners Assn.
Jay and Marji Otto, executive directors
29 Cook's Beach Rd.
Cape May Court House, NJ 08210
(609) 465-8444

Campground Owners of New York
Robert Klos, executive administrator
32 Ossian St.
P.O. Box 497
Dansville, NY 14437
(716) 335-2710

North Carolina Association of RV Parks and Campgrounds
c/o Charlene Barbour, president and CEO Management Concepts
1418 Aversboro Rd.
Garner, NC 27529-4547
(919) 779-5709

Northeast Campground Assn.
Dave Tetrault, executive director
P. O. Box 146
Stafford, CT 06075
(860) 684-6389

Ohio Campground Owners Assn.
Sammi Suter, executive director
5310 Main Street, Suite 104
Columbus, OH 43213
(614) 552-8368

Oklahoma Assn. of RV Parks and Campgrounds
David Miller
Rockwell RV Park
720 S. Rockwell
Oklahoma, City, OK 73128
(405) 787-5992

Pennsylvania Campground Owners Assn.
Beverly Gruber, executive director
P. O. Box 5
New Tripoli, PA 18066
(610) 767-5026

Ocean State Campground Owners Association (RI)
510 Gardiner Road
Richmond, RI 02892

South Carolina Campground Owners Assn.
Kelly Smith
P.O. Box 1184
Irmo, SC 29063
(803) 772-5354

South Dakota Campground Owners Assn.
Jack and Cherrylee Bradt, executive directors
c/o Rushmore Resort and Campground
Box 124
Keystone, SD 57751
(605) 666-4605

Tennessee Assn. of RV Parks and Campgrounds
John Westenberger, executive director
P.O. Box 70
Spring Hill, TN 37174
(931) 487-9871

Texas Assn. of Campground Owners
Brian Schaeffer, executive director
6425 S. IH-35, Suite 105-110
Austin, TX 78744
(800) 657-6555

Utah Campground Owners Assn.
Mark Menlove
c/o Salt Lake VIP Campground
1370 W. North Temple St.
Salt Lake City, UT 84116
(801) 364-3320

Vermont Campground Assn.
Neil Maurer,
c/o Vermont Magazine
P. O. Box 800
Middlebury, VT 05753
(802) 388-8480

Virginia Campground Assn.
Bob Ramsey, executive vice president
2101 Libbie Ave.
Richmond, VA 23230-2621
(804) 288-3065

Washington Assn. of RV Parks and Campgrounds
Rob Linderman, executive director
12819 S.E. 38th St., Ste. 323
Bellevue, WA 98006

Wisconsin Assn. of Campground Owners
Barney Bernander, executive administrator
P.O. Box 580
Pardeeville, WI 53954
(608) 429-3061

Wyoming Campground Assn.
Marshall Hood
c/o Foothills Motel and Campground
P.O. Box 174
Dayton, WY 82836
(307) 655-2547

Appendix B

Franchise Resource Information

Campground Franchise Contracts

KOA (Kampgrounds of America)
P.O. Box 30558
Billings, MT 59114
(406) 248-7444

Leisure Systems, Inc. (Yogi Bear's Jellystone Park Camp Resorts)
Rob Schutter, president and CEO
6201 Kellogg Ave.
Cincinnati, OH 45228
(513) 232-6800

Appendix C

Publications for Campers and RV Owners

Broker's Newsletters with Lists of Campgrounds for Sale

Broker's Bulletin, Darrell Hess & Associates, P. O. Box 1381, Lake Junaluska, NC 28745, (828) 452-1535

CampgrounData, Campground Data, P. O. Box 889, Lake Wales, FL 33853, (941)676-0009

Camping and RV Magazines and Newspapers

Camping and RV Magazine, Box 1341, Eagle, ID 83616-1344, (715) 373-5556

Camperways, see Woodall Publications.

Camper's Monthly, P. O. Box 260, Quakertown, PA 18951, (215) 536-6420

Camping Canada's RV Lifestyle, 7/yr., (Canadian) CRV Publications Canada, 2585 Skymark Ave., Ste. 306, Mississauga, ON L4W 4L5 Canada (905) 624-8218. Formerly *Camping Canada, Canadian RV Dealer, Camping Canada and RV Dealer.*

Camping Today, 10/yr., Family Campers & RVers, 4804 Transit Rd., Bldg. 2, Depew, NY 14043, (716) 668-6242, $25 membership in group.

Camp-Orama, see Woodall's Publications.

Chevy Outdoors, quarterly, Aegis Group Publisher, 30400 Van Dyke Ave., Warren, MI 48093, (810) 574-9100, formerly *Chevy Camper.*

Coast to Coast, monthly, Coast to Coast Resorts, 64 Inverness Dr. E., Englewood, CO 80112, (800) 368-5721.

Disabled Outdoors Magazine, quarterly, John Hopchik, Jr., HC 80 Box 395, Grand Marias, MN 55604, (218) 387-9100.

Family Motor Coaching, monthly, Family Motor Coach Association, Famoco Corp., 8291 Clough Pike, Cincinnati, OH 45244, (513) 474-3622.

4WD and *Off Road* are publications for off-road vehicle users.

Highways, the magazine of the Good Sam Club, published in five regional editions, 11/yr. Affinity Group, Inc., TL Enterprises, 2575 Vista Del Mar Dr., Ventura, CA 93001, (805) 667-4100 Formerly *Good Sam's Hi-Way Herald.*

Midwest Outdoors, monthly, 111 Shore Dr., Burr Ridge, IL 60521-5885, (630) 887-7722.

Motorhome, monthly, Affinity Group, Inc., TL Enterprises, 2575 Vista Del Mar Dr., Ventura, CA 93001, (805) 667-4100.

Northeast Outdoors, see Woodall Publications.

RV Times, Sheila Jones Publishing, Ltd., 945 Alston St., Victoria, BC V9A 3S5, Canada, (250) 475-8860. RV and camping information and events in Alberta, British Columbia, Montana, and Washington.

RV West, monthly, Vernon Publications.

Trailblazer, 10/yr., Thousand Trails/NACO, 2711 LBJ Freeway, Suite 200, Dallas, TX 75234, (214) 488-5021.

Trailer Life, monthly, Affinity Group, Inc., TL Enterprises, 2575 Vista Del Mar Dr., Ventura, CA 93001, (805) 667-4100.

Trails-A-Way, name changed to *Woodall's Midwest RV Traveler.* See Woodall Publications.

Western RV News, 42070 S. E. Locksmith Ln., Sandy, OR 97055, (503) 668-5660.

Woodall Publications Corp., 13975 W. Polo Trail Dr., Lake Forest, IL 60045, (800) 323-9076. Company produces the following newspapers for campers:

• *Woodall's Camperways*, monthly, covers the mid-Atlantic states of Delaware, eastern Pennsylvania, Maryland, New Jersey, lower New York, and Virginia;
• *Woodall's Camp-orama*, monthly, covers Florida;
• *Woodall' Carolina RV Travelers*, monthly, covers North and South Carolina;
• *Woodall's Midwest RV Traveler*, monthly, covers Michigan, north central Illinois, and the Chicago metro area and northern Indiana;
• *Woodall's Northeast Outdoors*, monthly, covers the New England states of Connecticut, Maine, Massachusetts, New Hampshire, New York, Rhode Is land and Vermont;
• *Woodall's Southern RV*, monthly, covers Florida and Georgia; and
• *Woodall's Texas RV*, 6/yr., covers Texas.

   Workamper News, job listings for RVers, 6/yr., 201 Hiram Rd., Heber Springs, AR 72543-8747, (501) 362-2637.

RV Buyer's and User's Guides

Van Conversion Blue Book Official Market Report, quarterly, National Market Reports, Inc., 29 N. Wacker Dr., Chicago, IL 60606-3297, (312) 726-2802.

Recreational Vehicle Blue Book, 3/yr., National Market Reports, Inc., 29 No. Wacker Dr., Chicago, IL 60606-3297, (312) 726-2802.

RV Buyer's Guide—both Woodall Publications and Affinity Group, Inc., TL Enterprises produce RV buyer's guides. See previoius listings for contact information.

RV Lifestyle Publications Catalog, Recreation Vehicle Industry Association, Dept. POF, P. O. Box 2999, Reston, VA 20195-0999. Lists many helpful RV/camping publications that can be ordered by mail.

RV Repair and Maintenance Manual, Affinity Group, Inc., TL Enterprises, see previous material for contact information.

RVRA Rental Directory, Recreation Vehicle Rental Association, 3930 University Dr., Fairfax, VA 22030.

Woodall's RV Owner's Handbook. Vol. 1: Introduction to RV basics. Vol. 2: The Operation of major RV systems. Vol. 3: Covers emergency and money-saving repairs and preventive maintenance. See previous Woodall listing for contact information.

Campground Directories

American Automobile Association, 1000 AAA Dr., Heathrow, FL 32746-5063, (407) 444-8200, produces regional RV and tent site campbooks for its mem bers. They cover: California–Nevada; Eastern Canada; Great Lakes; Mid eastern; North Central; Northeastern; Northwestern; South Central; South eastern; Southwestern; and Western Canada and Alaska.

Anderson's Campground Directory, Drawer 467, Lewisburg, WV 24901, (304) 645-1897.

KOA Directory/Road Atlas/Camping Guide, Kampgrounds of America, Inc., P. O. Box 30558, Billings, MT 59114-0558, $3 by mail; free at any KOA camp ground in North America.

Wheelers Recreational Vehicle Resort and Campground Guide, Print Media Services, 13110 Jarvis Ave., Elk Grove Village, IL 60007, (847) 981-0100.

Woodall Publications Corp., produces the following campground directories:

- North American Campground Directory;
- Eastern Campground Directory;
- Western Campground Directory;
- Regional Camping Guides;
    - New York and New England—covers Conn., ME, MA, NH, NY, VT and ON;
    - The South—AL, FL, GA, KY, LA, MS, NC, SC, and TN;
    - Great Plains and Mountain States—CO, MT, NE, ND, SD, UT, and WY;
    - Far West—AK, AZ, CA, ID, NV, OR, WA, BC, Yukon and MX;
    - Mid-Atlantic—DE, Washington D.C., MD, NJ, PA, VA, and WV;
    - Great Lakes—IL, IN, IA, MI, MN, OH, and WI;
    - Frontier West—AR, KS, MO, NM, OK, TX, and MX;
    - Canada—all provinces and territories.
- Tenting Directory;
- Go & Rent . . . Rent & Go;

Yogi Bear's Jellystone Park Camp-Resort Directory, free, Leisure Systems, Inc., 6201 Kellogg Ave., Cincinnati, OH 45228, (513)232-6800

RV Trade Publications

CampgroundData, see Broker's Newsletters.

Canadian RV Dealer, see Camping Canada's RV Lifestyle listing.

MH/RV Builders News, 6/yr., P. O. Box 72367, Roselle, IL 60172, (847) 891-8872.

Outdoor Hospitality, 6/yr., published by Imagination Publishing for the National Association of RV Parks and Campgrounds, 8605 Westwood Cen ter Dr., Suite 201, Vienna, VA 22182, (703) 734-3000.

RV Business, Affinity Group, Inc., TL Enterprises, see previous listing for contact information.

RV News, monthly, D & S Media Enterprises, Inc., 408 E. Southern Ave., Tempe, AZ 85283, (602) 784-4060.

RV Park and Campground Report, the newsletter of the National Association of RV Parks and Campgrounds, 8605 Westwood Center Dr., Suite 201, Vienna, VA 22182, (703) 783-3000. Formerly NCOA News.

RV Trade Digest, Continental Comm, Inc., P.O. Box 1805, Elkhart, IN 46517, (219) 295-1962.

The Resort Trades, The Trades Publishing Co., 20 Our Way Dr., Crossville, TN 38555-5790, (931) 484-8819.

Standards of Recreational Vehicle Parks, RVIA, P.O. Box 2999, 1986 Preston White Drive, Reston, VA 22090, (703) 620-6003.

Western RV News, see listing in "Camping and RV Magazines and Newspapers."

Woodall's Campground Management, monthly, 13975 W. Polo Trail Dr., Lake Forest, IL 60045, (847) 362-6700.

Chapter

4

CAMPGROUND DESIGN

How do you design your campground? How does a professional campground designer approach the design of a campground? What is involved in planning, designing, or redesigning a campground? Can you do it yourself, or should you hire a professional? These and other questions are discussed in this chapter.

Reading this chapter won't make you a professional campground designer, but it will help you understand what goes into the planning and design process, what information is needed, and what to look for in a good campground design. This chapter also includes practical tips on bathroom floor plans, campsite layout, and low-cost landscaping practices.

The Three Preliminary Design Steps

Many campgrounds have been built with little, if any, planning and design, resulting in mistakes that operators have had to live with. Some operators make the mistake of getting into the planning and designing of their campgrounds before they make some important preliminary marketing and management decisions. Such decisions can influence many aspects of the physical plan. For example, whether a campground is intended to be a transient or a destination campground influences the site size and the amenities needed for the campground. Whether or not you plan to have a year-round campground in the snowbelt is another example of an important design consideration.

Therefore you need to decide first which of the camping market segments you want to attract. Then you will decide what kind of recreation activities and amenities to offer them. Following these decisions, you will plan the roads, campsites, buildings, and other physical facilities.

Overall preliminary work involved in campground planning can be divided into three steps:

- research,
- site selection, and
- site analysis.

Research

The quality of the final design depends in large part on the quantity and quality of information available for analysis. Much of the information needed is available from various government agencies. Such information varies in quantity and quality from one geographic area to another. Most of this information is usually available at little or no cost.

Actual physical inspection of the site is vital. The person or team doing the analysis should spend enough time visiting the site to become completely familiar with it.

Site Selection

Site selection is important to the overall success of the business enterprise. As was stated in the feasibility chapter, location is one of the most important determinants of financial success. Accessibility to campers and visibility from a major highway are closely related considerations. An attractive and appealing natural site is of high priority.

Land already owned needs to be carefully considered as well. All too often land is developed because it is already the operator's property. It would often be more advisable to sell such land, and buy land that would be more desirable for campground development.

Site Analysis

Included in the site analysis are the following considerations.

Accessibility/Location Analysis

As stated above, the site must be easy to reach, not only in terms of being a short distance from a federal or state highway on a good public road, but also in terms of ease in getting off the highway into the campground entrance. Good visibility, assured by adequate frontage, and the absence of a hill or sharp curve near the entrance is an asset. It should also be easy for campers to get from the campground to nearby attractions, such as recreation, sight-seeing, shopping, and restaurant sites.

Physical Analysis

All features, both natural and developed, that might affect the final plan should be mapped and recorded in writing. Aerial photos, topographic maps and soils maps are excellent tools to use in analyzing the physical features of the site. Physical features that need to be analyzed follow.

Soils and Geology

Soil information can usually be obtained from the Natural Resource Conservation Service, located in every county. Such information will describe the suitability of soils for different types of recreation use. Problematic soils must be identified so that such areas can be restricted to limited types of development or recreation use. Soils data relates to geology, drainage, vegetation, and other physical features.

Topography and Drainage

Topographic information is used to identify potential use areas and significant elevations. It also identifies slope problems, including potential erosion, drainageways, and susceptibility to flooding. Variations in elevation enhance the aesthetic attractiveness of the site. However, excess topography can also cause problems, such as a lack of level area for site development and costly road building.

Water (for Drinking and Recreation)

Water is critical to the operation of a campground. Losing the water supply on a hot day in a full campground is a nightmare for most campground operators. Many campgrounds have two wells so that one will work in the event the other fails. With groundwater contamination becoming more common, site analyses must include a careful examination of the potential water supply. Soils, geologic formations, and water tables are indicators of the quality and quantity of available potable water. Land and mineral filters and softeners can be very costly.

The quality of existing lakes, ponds, and streams on or near the site needs to be examined carefully for algae, bacteria, weed growth, nitrates, and causes of swimmer's itch, all of which are problems for campers. Shoreline types, bottoms, and distance from camping areas are important to note. Flood plains should be carefully studied, as they can be used for some recreational purposes but rarely for permanent development.

Vegetation/Ecology

Trees and shrubs should be carefully surveyed to note the character and location of the general types. Considerations are for those that offer quality camping and that includes morning sun, afternoon shade, and the ability to withstand high use levels. Young hardwoods are the best for these characteristics. Species that are rare or unique should also be identified for protection.

Cultural Features

Existing roads, buildings, and utilities should be examined for possible use in the campground. Property boundaries, easements, and other encumbrances should be noted, as they affect planning. Adjacent land uses, potential locations of facilities, and necessary buffer zones are important influences on the quality of camping.

Environmental Factors

Very useful in planning are such things as direction and intensity of prevailing winds, seasonal storm patterns, rainfall rates, distracting odors, noises, views, pollution sources, natural barriers, and hazards.

The more information available for analysis, the better the analysis will be. Early in the process, consideration must be given to the level of development and the operational, marketing, and management objectives of the business enterprise, because these decisions affect the type and quality of facilities developed.

Your Campground Design

Several design concepts should be created so they can be analyzed and compared. Usually the final design plan will be a combination of various alternative design plans. The final design takes into consideration details that will contribute to the ultimate success of the campground.

Plan the entire area, and plan for the highest volume you think is realistically possible. Even though only a portion of the campground will be developed initially, it is necessary to plan for the future. This is known as phased or staged development. In order to minimize debt service costs, the first phase should include the amenities and service facilities but only about a third of the developed campsites. It usually takes several years for a business to build to the point of needing all of the campsites, and this allows minimal development costs when cash flow is lowest.

Locate essential features and facilities first. Examples of facilities layouts are shown in Figures 4.1 and 4.2. Some important points to recognize in these layouts are:

- Front office should be adjacent to front entrance/exit.
- Ample parking for RVs is needed adjacent to the check-in/check-out.
- Children's recreation activities are grouped on one side, accompanied by a snack bar (profit center).
- Adult recreation activities are grouped on the other side, accompanied by lounge and restaurant profit centers.
- Swimming pool is placed in the center of the recreation area, observable from the store.
- Make the water attraction easily accessible to campers. Avoid placing a primary road adjacent to such attractions.
- Plan for the least number of roads to save on initial development costs and maintenance later on.
- Plan narrow loops to conserve land area.
- Locate seasonal and monthly sites in loops apart from other campers.
- Name the loops rather than numbering or lettering them.

Figure 4.1

Campground Facilities Layout

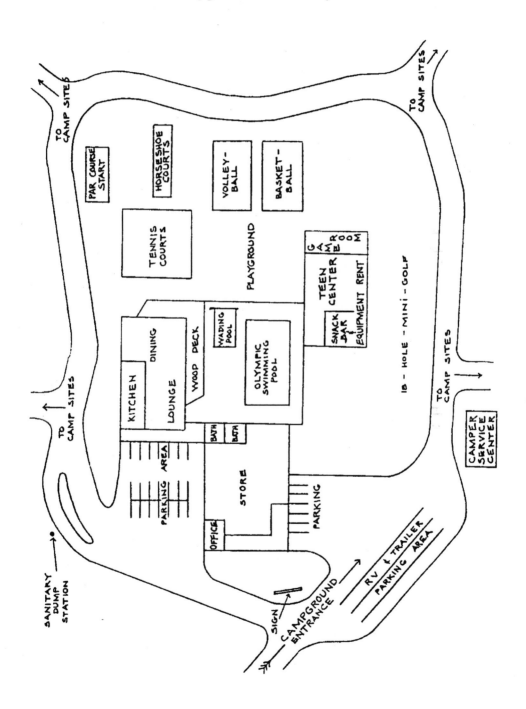

Figure 4.2

Campground Facilities Layout

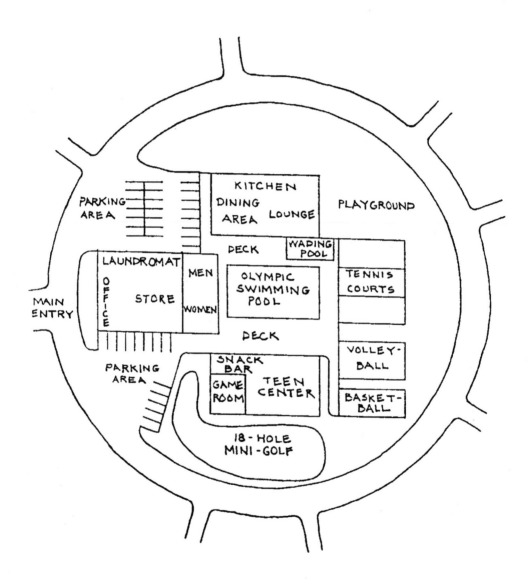

User-Friendly Design

Critically important to a successful campground is that it be user-friendly. This is especially emphasized in the customer relations chapter. It is also important in the design of a campground. Easy access to the water and other attractions and absence of coin-operated showers are examples. Always try to look at various aspects of the design from the point of view of the camper.

Security and Convenience

For security purposes, locate the front office in clear view of the entrance drive so that everyone entering and leaving the campground can be seen from the front office. It doesn't have to be adjacent to the public road leading to the front entrance, but it should be located somewhere on the entrance drive, in front of the developed portion of the campground. Ideally, it should be right at the front of the developed portion so that at times when the campground isn't busy, the person running the front desk can also operate the store and supervise other areas.

Plan adequate parking at the front office so that there is a minimum of traffic lined up during busy check-in times. Plan the front entrance so that campers don't queue up on the public road leading to the campground. Incorporate one-way traffic patterns to lessen costs of wider roads that would be required with large rigs meeting on roads.

Have only one entrance/exit for security purposes. An alternative emergency exit is a good idea, but it should normally be kept closed. Locate the office, store, game room, and any other activity centers that require supervision in close proximity so that one person can operate the campground during slow periods.

Locate the children's playground near the toilet facilities and some of the campsites to accommodate parents with young children. Make multiple use of as many areas as possible. Place sports areas in sections large enough to permit full-sized fields and buffer or safety zones.

Orient sports fields to the sun, such as having ball diamonds 45 degrees on either side of the northline. Use trees as windbreaks and as shade for children's play areas. Place walkways where people would naturally walk that are easily accessible. Screen out objectionable sights, hazardous roads and railroads, and industrial sites. Take advantage of drainage conditions or natural barriers to separate areas and enhance natural beauty.

Basic Loop Design

Campground sites are usually laid out along roads that make up loops. In staging development, one or more loops are built in a given phase. Sometimes one road loop is built with site development including hookups, while only the road is built for the next stage. That road can then be used for campers who prefer to be away from the rest and for overflow on busy weekends.

Loops should be laid out in a narrow configuration like the shape of a peanut or hot dog. This conserves land area.

Campsite Size/Density

Campsite size should be related to the primary type of camper your campground will attract. Destination campers prefer larger sites than transient, or overnight, campers, for example. Campers with large RVs need larger sites than tent or pickup campers. Campsites should therefore vary in size. A 25-by 35-foot living space is a good size. The parking spur is additional space.

Campsite density varies with campsite size, topography, and type of camper (overnight versus destination). National Park Service campsites are 12 to 15 sites per acre. Private campgrounds have a wide range of density, although 15 to 20 sites per acre appears to be representative. Wisconsin regulations stipulate a maximum of 20 sites per acre.

Landscaping

Take out the diseased, very old, and undesirable varieties of trees such as shallow rooted. It is much easier to do this before the campground is developed. Vegetation between sites is very important for several reasons. Such growth provides a visual and sound barrier between sites. Vegetation gives the campers a feeling that they are further away from the next campsite. Campers who want to be close to nature prefer such sites. A mistake made by developers is to "brush" the camping area of all vegetative growth less than two inches in diameter. A better method is to cut only for the roads, and then brush only the areas for the individual campsites.

Vegetative Barriers/Screening

Like so many other aspects of camping, there is a considerable range of preferences regarding screening, meaning the vegetative growth between camp sites. Therefore, it is a good idea to provide a range of different degrees of screening.

Privately owned campgrounds tend to have too little screening. However, the reverse can be true. One example is screening that blocks the view of the lake or river attraction.

Meandering roads are more aesthetically pleasing in the campground than straight roads laid out in a grid system like city streets. These roads also allow for saving trees or other objects that offer appeal.

Signs within the campground should reflect the overall image of the campground. For example, if the campground is to have a rustic image, the signs should also be of a rustic design; alternatively, the signs could follow some type of theme for the campground. Signs should be easy to see, easy to read, and easy to understand. The messages should be user-friendly; rules should be stated positively.

Find out what the local and state regulations are for construction of buildings, roads, sites, swimming pools, and so on. If you violate some aspect of the administrative code, you'll probably have to correct it before your license will be issued.

Design at least one building as a storm shelter where campers can go in case of a severe storm, such as a tornado. Such a structure will increase development costs but may save many lives.

Plant hardy native trees and shrubs to lower maintenance and replacement costs. Group trees and shrubs together to lower maintenance time (mowing, pruning, and watering). You can save money through design, plant selection, and horticulture. Tips on how to do so follow:

- Select the right plants for the climate and the site.
- Find out how large the plants will grow, and choose plants and locations accordingly.
- Mass plants by planting them in groups.
- Design to make mowing easy. Make curved rather than square corners.
- Do not enrich the dirt put back in the hole when planting, because the roots will tend to stay in that richer soil area.
- Mulch! Cover the soil surface with any shredded material, such as bark or wood chips. Apply it at about three inches depth. This practice con serves moisture.
- Prune properly. Never leave a stub because it will only decay. Don't top a tree. Take out old growth in shrubs near the ground. Do this in late winter or early spring.
- Keep lawn area to a minimum where possible, but not at the expense of aesthetic beauty.
- Keep annual flower planting to a minimum to save labor, but not at the expense of aesthetic attractiveness, especially around the front entrance and office/check-in.
- Avoid using "problem" or high-maintenance plants, such as roses.
- Do not rely on fertilizer to solve plant problems.
- Compost yard waste. Leave grass clippings on the lawn if not too heavy.
- Buy at wholesale prices if possible.
- Negotiate quantity discounts when buying many plants. Negotiate a lower price by foregoing the guarantee.
- Buy bare root nursery stock when possible.
- Order bare root nursery stock through the mail.
- Investigate the Department of Natural Resources (Conservation) for large quantity purchases (500 or more).
- Find out if the county land conservationist has a tree program. Check out nursery and garden store plant sales in the fall.
- Buy smaller plants. They cost less and adapt more quickly. Piggyback on local parks department plant orders.
- Seek advice from the local horticulture specialist in selecting plant types.

Bathroom Facilities

The bathroom facilities are the most important facilities in the campground. More complaints are registered about toilet and shower facilities than any other part of the campground. These facilities are not good places to cut costs. Given that they need to be cleaned several times a day during busy camping periods, using high-quality construction materials that are easy to clean is a must. The layout shown in Figure 4.3 for a service building is commonly used in campgrounds.

The service hallway through the center of the building is especially efficient, because the plumbing can be accessed from this hallway. This means that most plumbing repairs can be performed without closing the facility for extended periods of time. Larger proportions of toilet stools, urinals, showers, and sinks to sites may be installed to add to camper convenience. Also, shorter maximum distances to sites than required may be desired to improve the quality of the camping experience. Often, the laundromat is located across the end of the toilet/shower facility. This affords efficiency in being close to the plumbing of the bathroom facilities and allows easy access for campers.

Another bathroom design concept that works well in some campgrounds is unisex facilities. Each facility has its own private entrance, usually to the outside. Also common is for the showers to be separate from the toilets and sinks. This works well when there is another major recreation activity that requires such facilities in conjunction with the campground. Some states do not permit unisex toilet facilities, so be sure to check the regulations in your state.

Adequate drains are necessary in the bathroom floors. Floors should slope to accommodate water coming from wet clothes, splashing from sinks, cleanup, and so on. Plenty of shelf space, hooks, and seats will make it much more convenient for campers to change clothes, hang up towels when not using them, and place toilet kits over the sinks or on a shelf when not being used.

All of the above facilities should be as attractive as possible. Campers would like for campground bathroom facilities to be just as good as at home. A pleasant camping experience can be created or lost with the toilet/shower building.

Moisture buildup in bathroom facilities is a common problem, and adequate ventilation is necessary to prevent this from becoming unpleasant. Al Daniels, owner of the Normandy Farm Family Campground, in Foxboro, Massachusetts, has installed skylights in the roof, which can be opened when necessary. If covers for such openings allow light to pass through, sunlight can contribute to the drying process as well as light the facility. An egg carton ceiling will also allow moist air to escape.

Insects are always attracted to a building in which the lights are left on at night, and good screening on windows and doors is necessary.

Nondistracting methods of insect control should be seriously considered. Another restroom/shower facility consideration is to plan easy access for people with disabilities. Check your state regulations and the Americans with Disabilities Act.

Site Layout

There are many considerations in choosing the final site layout. One is the proportion of sites with various electric, water, and sewer hookups. The proportion of water and electric versus tent sites (no hookups) should be based on the proportions of campers who prefer each.

Some campers prefer to camp in groups. A recent study showed that 43 percent of respondents prefer space for large groups. The campground owner must decide on a policy for offering camping to large groups. It is a sizeable segment of your potential market, so not catering to group campers may negatively affect your sales potential. However, large camping groups do require special management procedures. If large groups can be placed in separate, isolated camping areas, they are less likely to disturb other campers.

Small group camping—two or three camper parties desiring adjacent sites—is also preferred by many campers. These campers can often be assigned sites at a comer or near the end of a road so that they can be somewhat isolated from other campers.

Depending on the camper and the type of camping equipment used, campers will probably prefer a back-in or drive-through system for their sites. The majority of older campers prefer the pull-through campsites. Back-in campsites work well for tents, small motor homes, and pickup campers.

The hookups are on the left side (driver's side) and near the rear of the vehicle, so the water, electric, and sewer outlets should be on the left side of the parking spur. The outlets should be placed back from the edge of the spur to avoid damage from parking errors and slide-outs of RVs.

Another type of site is the pull-off site, good for places where there is not enough space for a back-in or pull-through site. Still another type of campsite is the "buddy" campsite. In the interest of making the design user-friendly, the buddy campsite is desirable for campers who come and bring extended family and/or friends. These campers like at least two sites close together. Buddy sites meet this need.

Some campers need extra parking space. As an example, mom and the kids will come during the week and dad will come on Friday night for the weekend. Therefore some of the sites should have space for more than one vehicle.

The living area and the parking spur should be level. Try to locate the sites so that a minimum amount of cutting and filling of soil is necessary to level the site.

Hultsman, Cottrell and Hultsman (1998) recommend that if more than a three percent grade is required to get from the road to the spur, the ramping section should be paved.

They also recommend defining the site with six by eight hardwood cross-ties. Lay the cross-ties with the 6-inch side up and down. Fasten them together with 6-inch pole barn nails and hold in place by driving 3-foot, 5/8-inch rebars through them and into the ground. Make 1/2-inch holes in them through which to drive the rebar. Make sure the rebar is recessed in the cross-tie. Then depending on soil conditions, fill the living area with 6 inches of road gravel, tamp, and then fill with 2 inches of fine gravel and tamp.

Dump Station

Dump stations are usually located near the entrance to the park but on the exit road. These should be in clear view of the office if dumping fees are charged. They should be near sewer lines servicing other campground facilities. Check your sanitary regulations concerning the construction of the dump station. Dump stations are usually required if RVs with holding tanks are permitted in the park.

Should You Hire a Professional Designer?

First-time campground owners and developers are often reluctant to spend any of their limited budgets on design consultants. They assume that, from their own previous camping experience, they know how to design a campground. Hiring a design service may be expensive. However, high-quality design plans can pay for themselves many times over during the construction phase, to say nothing of the reduced operating and maintenance costs later on. Actually, the consultant's fees are a relatively small portion of the total development costs, land values, and operating costs over years of operation. However, make sure you hire a good, well-qualified designer.

Note: Much of the information in this chapter came from the publication, *Site Planning in Park Areas*, Robert D. Espeseth, University of Illinois at Urbana-Champaign, North Central Regional Extension Publication 290. Other information came from the book *Planning Parks for People* (1998), John Hultsman, Richard R. Cottrell, and Wendy Z. Hultsman, Venture Publishing, Inc., 1999 Cato Ave., State College, PA 16801, (814) 234-4561, Fax (814) 234-1651. A third source was a 1990 workshop handout by Michael Schneider of Kenosha, Wisconsin.

Figure 4.3

Campground Facilities Layout

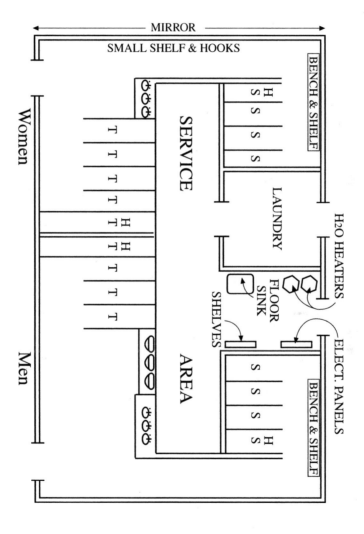

Chapter

5

BUSINESS ORGANIZATION OPTIONS, CONCEPTS, AND AGREEMENTS

What is the best form of business organization for you? One of the first steps in starting your campground or in taking over an existing campground is deciding which legal form of business is best for you. Changing tax laws and fluctuating availability of capital are two reasons you need to seriously consider the best form of business organization. It is possible to change from one form of business organization to another. Going from sole proprietorship to partnership, for example, could result in shared expertise and financial resources. Switching from a partnership to a corporation could enhance management continuity. This chapter briefly summarizes the major forms of business organization from the standpoint of federal law. You should review your state laws as they apply specifically to your situation.

The Sole Proprietorship

Small businesses often start out as sole proprietorships, because this form is quite simple and satisfies many needs of new businesses. It is the least regulated form and is taxed as part of the owner's individual income.

Advantages

The advantages of the sole proprietorship follow.

Ease of formation. To establish a sole proprietorship, all you need to do is get the necessary licenses and begin operating. The name of your organization doesn't need to be registered, but you may decide to protect it by registering it. There are no further regulations that apply to you as an individual.

No profit sharing. You don't have to share the profits with anyone. (You don't have to with a corporation either, if you own all the stock.)

Little government regulation. There are fewer reports, meeting requirements, and legal fees than with other forms.

Vested control in single owner. There are no partners or boards of directors to consult or to report to regarding decisions. You alone make the decisions. However, most campgrounds are family-run operations, and generally, all family members affected by decisions should be involved.

Flexibility. Because there is so little structure, you can meet day-to-day business needs by responding quickly.

Disadvantages

Disadvantages of the sole proprietorship follow.

Unlimited liability. As a sole proprietor, you are responsible for all the debts of your business, which may exceed your investment in the business. This liability extends to your other assets (including your house and car), except for your protection under the bankruptcy law. Of course, you may purchase insurance for protection from physical loss or personal injury liability.

Unstable business life. Your enterprise may be terminated by your death or incapacitation.

Limited capital. Usually there is less access to capital with this form of organization than with the other business forms. One person has less net worth with which to guarantee loans than if there were several partners.

Limited management capabilities. You are limited to your own and your family's management capabilities. Other forms have several owners participating in the decision making. Of course, this assumes your business is too small to afford to hire other expertise.

Note: Much of the information in this section was taken from Antonio M. Olmi, *Selecting the Legal Structure of Your Firm,* Management Aids Number 6.004, Small Business Administration, Albuquerque, New Mexico.

The General Partnership

"An association of two or more persons to carry on as co-owners of a business for profit," defines the partnership in the Uniform Partnership Act, a federal law that has been adopted in many states. Distinguishing the partnership is the co-ownership of assets, the liability of at least one partner for the debts of the others, and the sharing of management skills and profits. Losses can be applied against personal income from other sources.

Advantages

The advantages of the general partnership follow.

Easy formation. No government forms need to be filed. A written agreement is not required but is advised.

Combined capital. The general partnership allows two or more individuals to combine their capital, which allows the acquisition of possibly many times the amount of capital obtainable in a sole proprietorship. The amount of capital that potentially can be pooled depends on the number of individuals who are interested, plus the volume of assets that each partner has to contribute to the business.

Skills sharing. This is another big advantage of the partnership. A complete range of physical skills, knowledge, and managerial capabilities can be brought together under one business enterprise.

Partner selection. With the capability to pool capital, skills, and knowledge/experience goes the right to select the ones preferred.

Direct rewards. Profits accrue directly to the partners according to their agreed-upon proportions. Thus, they are motivated to apply their abilities by sharing the profits.

Flexibility. As in the case of the sole proprietorship, management decisions are still relatively easy, usually decided by majority rule. This depends on the number of partners involved, and prior agreements relative to decision making.

Freedom from governmental control and special taxation. This business form is free from much of the control and special taxation, as are corporations.

Disadvantages

The disadvantages of the general partnership follow.

Unlimited liability. The big disadvantage of this form of business organization is the unlimited liability. Not only are you liable for your own debts, but you are also liable for the debts of your partners. Further, your debts and your partners' debts can be attached to your personal assets, as in the sole proprietorship.

Difficult decision making. All the partners participate in the decisions, so the larger the number of partners, the more difficult the decisions may be. Further, your influence on decisions will depend on your ability to convince your partners of your point of view.

Limited business term. Here, as in the sole proprietorship, the enterprise will cease to exist upon the death of one of the partners, unless the partnership agreement provides for transition of ownership and continuity of the business organization.

Profit sharing. When capital, skills, and other resources are shared, profits are also shared. With two or more persons sharing profits, there is always the possibility of one contributing less than the share agreed upon. Unless specifically accounted for in an agreement, that person will share in the profits regardless of such contributions.

Taxes levied as personal income. This can be a considerable disadvantage. However, if there are losses, they can be applied against other personal income for that purpose.

The Limited Partnership

The limited partnership has characteristics of the general partnership and the corporation. It differs in permitting investor participation with liability limited to the amount of the investment, or as otherwise agreed upon in the partnership agreement. Thus, the limited partnership is able to attract more capital, which is the main reason for its formation.

The limited partnership must include at least one general partner who is liable for the debts of the limited partnership. The limited partnership is taxed as a partnership. Both general and limited partners are taxed at their personal income tax rate on their share of taxable income from the enterprise. The limited partnership itself is not taxed.

A summary of the written agreement (discussed in detail in the next section), with the business name, must be filed with the Secretary of State's office in most states. That office, in turn, will forward a copy of the business agreement to the appropriate county recorder's office. The limited partners must be individuals, whereas the general partner may be a corporation.

Advantages

The advantages of the limited partnership follow.

Required written agreement. A written agreement is required. This avoids costly misunderstandings.

Partnership control. The general partner maintains control of the business.

Investment ability. The limited partner can invest, with liability limited to the extent of the limited partner's investment, provided he or she does not participate in the day-to-day management of the business.

Capital opportunities. It is easier to attract capital in this partnership than it is in the general partnership because of the above limitation on liability of the limited partner.

Viability. The business is not terminated with the death of a limited partner.

Tax advantage. Partners pay individual taxes on their respective shares of profits, and if there are losses, they can be applied against other personal income to lower such tax liability. The business itself is not directly taxed.

Disadvantages

Disadvantages of the limited partnership follow.

Organizational complexity. It's a more complex organization. The organization agreement has to be filed with the Secretary of State or a similar office.

Control limitation. The limited partner has no control over the business or his/her investment and cannot actively participate.

Termination possibilities. The business is usually terminated with the death of the general partner.

Responsibility. The general partner is personally responsible for all the business.

Taxed income. Profits are shared and taxed as personal income.

Partnership Agreements

A written agreement, prepared by an attorney, is advised for persons entering into a partnership. It usually outlines the contributions of the partners, rights, responsibilities, management, continuity arrangements, profit distribution, and any special conditions. A checklist of possible "articles" included in a partnership agreement follows:

- name, purpose, location;
- duration of the agreement;
- Character of the partnership (general or limited, active, or silent);
- contributions of the partners, at start up, and later on
- handling of business expenses;
- a description of who has the authority in typical management decisions;
- separate debts;
- books, records, and method of accounting
- division of profits and losses;
- distribution of draws and salaries;
- rights of a continuing partner;
- death of a partner—what to do upon dissolution;
- employee management—whose responsibility it is;
- release of debts;
- sale of partnership interest;
- arbitration;
- arranging additions, alterations, or modification of the partnership agreement;
- settlement of disputes;
- required and prohibited acts; and
- absence and disability.

The Corporation

The corporation is a separate legal entity. This means it can enter into contracts, is liable for debts, pays taxes, and in effect, is a legal person. Capital is acquired by the sale of stock in the corporation or by trading stock for assets. Such stockholders are the owners of the corporation. Stockholders are generally not liable beyond the current value of their shares of stock. Separate legal identity gives the corporation continued existence. A corporation never ceases to exist unless the decision is made to terminate it.

Double Taxation

There is a separate tax schedule for corporations. After-tax stock dividends distributed to shareholders are taxed again as personal income, except for the personal dividend exclusion.

This is not a problem for most small campground businesses, because most of the corporate taxable profit can be paid to the owner/operator as salary. It is then deductible as a business expense to the corporation and becomes taxable personal income to the owners, the same as any other income. For larger income-producing corporations, the land can be held personally. The corporation can then pay rent to the owners for the use of it, thus transforming double-taxed profit into a deductible expense. All of these arrangements must be reasonable, such as the amounts of rent and salaries paid, or they won't hold up under audit.

To incorporate, the owners must go to their Secretaries of State offices, fill out an application, and usually pay an incorporation fee. The exchange of stock is governed by state law to facilitate such exchange and to protect the stock-buying public. Special registration is usually required for sale of stock to the general public—check with your appropriate state agency regarding this.

The articles of incorporation have to be drawn up and filed in the appropriate Secretary of State's office, and/or the county office in which the corporation is located. After approval, the state will issue a certificate of incorporation, allowing the corporation to commence with business activities. The corporation name must be filed, which reserves the name and avoids duplication. Again, you should check with your state agency on filing your corporation's name. Articles of incorporation should be written with the assistance of an attorney and a certified public accountant. At the minimum, an annual meeting for your corporation must be held, and an annual report must be filed.

Many sole proprietors think they should incorporate to limit their business liability. Such limited liability is advantageous, but unless the assets are substantial, as the business owner you may still be required to sign for the loans along with the corporation. You can also be sued as the manager of the business, so you need liability insurance for protection in the event of such suits. Further, in the event of suspected fraud, you and all key personnel will be charged along with the corporation.

Advantages

The advantages of incorporating follow.

Required agreement. A written agreement is required, which ensures understanding of agreements.

Shared financial resources. For large operations it may be easier to attract capital, but just as in a debt form of capital acquisition, you must convince a potential stockholder of the ability of the business to earn money and of your ability to manage it successfully.

Shared personal resources. As in a partnership, you can bring in other people with skills, knowledge, and experience.

Perpetual life. Because it is a legal entity, it can theoretically continue forever.

Easy ownership transfer. With the sale or trade of stock, the transfer of ownership is easy.

Limited personal liability. Limited personal liability, also called the corporate shield (veil), means that unless you have to sign personally for loans, you are limited in liability to the extent of the current value of your owned capital stock, plus any personal loans you've made to the corporation.

Tax advantages. There is the possibility of being in a lower tax bracket. There are advantages for estate planning/transfer to heirs. Fringe benefit plans are available, as are pension and profit-sharing plans.

Disadvantages

The disadvantages of the corporation follow.

Possible double taxation. Your corporation pays taxes on its income, and then you pay personal income on the stock dividends you receive. There is no way for losses in the corporation to offset other outside personal income.

Organizational and managerial complexity. The corporation is more complex than the partnership, and certainly more so than the sole proprietorship. The owners elect a board of directors, which in turn hires the management.

Increased regulation. Annual meetings and reports, plus two sets of tax forms, the corporate forms, and your personal forms must be held, filed, and accurately completed.

Social Security/Self-Employment Tax

The Social Security and self-employment tax implications are considerations in selecting the form of business organization. Self-employment tax for sole proprietorships is about the same as social security tax for an employer. That is, you have to pay 15.3 percent as a sole proprietor and can deduct 7.65 percent on your taxes (a net of 7.65 percent). As an employer (corporation), you have to pay 7.65 percent on employees' wages, and you withhold 7.65 percent of employees' paychecks. This changes periodically, so check on the current tax regulations when you consider the form of business organization that's best for you.

There is also the possibility of deducting certain fringe benefit programs as a corporate employer, such as health insurance and retirement programs.

The Sub Chapter "S" Corporation

The sub chapter "S" corporation is exactly the same as the corporation, except that it has the advantage of special tax treatment. It is taxed as a partnership —the "S" corporation itself is not taxed. Instead it must file an informational return. Income is allocated to the shareholders and is taxable to them, regardless of whether or not it is distributed to them. Losses are treated the same as in a partnership. Procedures for creating an "S" corporation are the same as those for establishing a corporation. The "S" corporation should be considered when the following conditions are present:

- owners expect operating losses;
- large dividends are expected; and
- owners' individual tax rates are lower than corporate rates.

To be eligible, the following conditions must be met:

- there are fewer than 35 stockholders;
- each stockholder must make the proper election;
- stockholders must be individuals or estates;
- the corporation has only one class of stock; and
- it is a domestic corporation.

Lawyers and tax accountants can provide more specific information. It is especially important to follow the most recent changes in the tax laws. It is also advisable to get an IRS ruling regarding the income of your business before electing this option.

The Statutory Close Corporation

In some states, small businesses are allowed to avoid the formality problems of corporate structure by electing to be a "close" corporation. For example, the law in many states allows the corporation to choose not to have a board of directors, and not to hold annual meetings. It also allows that failure to follow the formalities of the law will not cause the corporation to lose its limited liability status.

Check with your attorney to find out if your state has a close corporation law. If so, it may be the most advantageous form of business organization for your campground.

The " 1244" Corporation

Section 1244 of the Internal Revenue Code provides tax advantages for individual shareholders in certain small business corporations. It may be beneficial for you to look into the feasibility of forming a Section 1244 corporation. The tax advantages accruing to individuals owning stock may ease the problems of raising capital to start the business. The rules allow special treatment for losses. Contact your attorney for more specifics on Section 1244 status.

Attorneys and certified public accountants (CPAs) can assist in making decisions to determine which of the forms of business organization is best for you. They can also inform you of other forms of business organization that are useful in unique situations. If you have special problems, it's a good idea to check with your attorney and CPA. Sit down with both of them when you are in the process of deciding the type of business organization to use.

Chapter

6

CAMPGROUND OWNERSHIP CONCEPTS AND AGREEMENTS

It is important for all concerned with campground development—consumers, developers, and operators—to establish a terminology that refers to concepts unique to the industry. The American Land Development Association has taken a lead in this regard. Their *RV Park and Camp Resort Fact Sheet* is an excellent source of information about the camp resort industry, and is the primary source of information for this chapter. *Note:* Much of the information that follows was obtained from the unpublished paper, *Ownership/Membership Forms of Campground Development—History/Issues,* by Brian Whitemarsh, Recreation Resources Center, University of Wisconsin-Extension, May, 1985.

Contract Terminology

Two major types of campground contractual agreements are *camp resort ownership* and *camp resort membership*. The term "camp resort" is used in the industry to describe those types of agreements that include a number of arrangements through which the consumer can purchase an interest in a park or system of parks from campgrounds, which are rental operations. Many campgrounds use the term "resort" in their names, which probably is not indicative of the above type of agreements.

The *traditional rental campground* has been a fixture in American camping and is the agreement concept most often associated with camping. Most of this book is concerned with this type of camping and campground management. These operations are open to the public on a rental fee basis. The length of stay varies from nightly to weekend, week, or season.

The two most important elements of the camp resort, either membership or ownership, are the sites and the common facilities. These are also important to the traditional rental campground, as will be discussed later. In most camp resort programs, there is an annual maintenance fee for the up-keep of the common facilities, similar to the fee and maintenance arrangement for a condominium organization. There may also be a daily use fee for various amenities. The common facilities can be owned and operated either by a developer or by a separate entity known as a property owners association (POA). In this situation, the POA holds the title to the common areas, and governs and sets fees as warranted.

Camp Resort Agreements

The two basic camp resort programs or agreements are ownership and membership; there are variations on these basic concepts.

Camp Resort Ownership Programs

In ownership programs, the camper-purchaser actually owns a portion of the camp resort. In the common programs used today, the purchaser receives a deed or a share:

- in a specific campsite, known as a divided interest;
- in the general camp resort, and not in a specific site, known as an undivided interest; and
- in the corporation, which in turn owns the camp resort, known as the cooperative approach.

In ownership programs, the buyer is actually a part owner of a particular site or of the entire camp resort. It is important to note that there are many possible variations in the ownership arrangement. Some of these variations are described below.

Deeded divided interest—full-time exclusive availability. The buyer actually owns an individual site, and receives a deed. The buyer may use the site anytime, rent it out, or let others use it, subject to the rules of the camp resort.

Deeded undivided interest—full-time availability. The purchaser receives a deed entitling him or her to use a site at any time. The site that is actually assigned is based on availability.

Deeded undivided interest—part-time availability. The buyer receives a deed entitling him or her to use a site on a space available basis. Reservations are often required in this situation.

Cooperatives. Each purchaser receives stock in the corporation. In turn, the purchaser is given a proprietary lease entitling him or her to use a site.

Camp resort ownership programs were started in the early 1970s, fostered by the factors discussed earlier, but also aided by the energy crisis of 1973. Because of the higher cost and shortage of gasoline, many people wanted to vacation closer to home. This placed demand on facilities within two hours of their homes, mainly in metropolitan areas. The ownership program increased in attractiveness to cost-conscious buyers.

Ownership programs flourished through 1977 and then began to slow in annual sales as development costs increased. Lots that once sold for $3,900, rose in price to between $10,000 and $15,000. The greater cost of these sites had the obvious effect of screening out a large segment of potential buyers for ownership campground sites.

Camp Resort Membership Programs

Because of the increasing costs of ownership sites and because campers don't use their sites all the time, a new concept emerged: *the camp resort membership program*. In 1984, 74 percent of the camp resort programs were membership types, where 23 percent were ownerships.

In membership programs, which are currently the most used types of agreements or programs, the purchaser pays for a membership in the particular camp resort or system of resorts offered by the developer. Title remains with the developer, for both the sites and the common facilities. When a camping party becomes a member, it does not own any interest in the campground nor in its facilities and amenities. The party owns only the right to use certain camping resorts and facilities. Campers are not buying shelter, real estate, or an investment, in the traditional sense of the term. Rather, they are buying the "right to use" for a specified period of time. Members are given the right to use a site on a space-available basis. Advance reservations are generally advised or required. There is usually a minimal fee required to camp, such as one dollar per night.

Membership camp resort developers are able to sell more than one membership per site, since most campers do not use their sites all the time. The ratio of memberships sold to sites available depends on use–demand factors unique to the given camp resort. These ratios typically range between 7:1 and 15:1. The profit potential of these ratios of sales to sites is what makes this type of development attractive. Contract language and rules of the camp resort indicate the precise rights of the membership.

Some programs incorporate both campground rental sites and deeded-divided interest sites. This is attractive to campground developers desiring the immediate cash flow, which can be realized by the sale of a portion of the campground sites.

The camp resort ownership and membership programs differ from time-sharing approaches. A time-sharing approach is popular in the recreation industry in cases of sales of partial interests in improved structures. This approach hasn't been used extensively in the camp resort industry.

Membership Sales Regulation

Traditional land use controls are not sufficient in scope to regulate the membership sales industry. After problems arose, state governments enacted separate laws to regulate this portion of the industry. Traditional land use controls are more applicable in the regulation of ownership camp resorts where local

71

zoning and condominium ordinances apply. The Federal Department of Housing and Urban Development (HUD) has authority to regulate these sales as well.

Usually, existing rental campgrounds are converted to membership camp resorts, so these uses are considered "grandfathered" in normal practice. Under most existing zoning ordinances, there is no provision for the regulation of such uses that address the common problem areas.

Most of the problem areas involve the marketing practices of the developer. Complaints have arisen concerning discrepancies in sales inducements offered, failure to fully disclose facts regarding the sale, and unfulfilled promises made by high-pressure and overzealous salespeople.

Campground Conversion

Most ownership/membership camp resorts have been converted over from existing rental campgrounds. Generally, a successful camp resort should be two hours or less from a major metropolitan area or should be located in a well-known tourism destination area. Further, the campground must have the combination of natural features and services to make it a viable prospect for conversion. Because of the high profit potential of these camp resorts, many owners of existing rental parks see this as an option either to get out of the business, or to stay in the business and make larger profits. Because of this, some rental campground owners have been hurt by unscrupulous marketing companies and developers out to make quick profits.

To avoid being taken advantage of, the rental campground owner should thoroughly study the industry before making a commitment to the camp resort business. The American Land Development Association is a good starting point. This organization will provide you with statistical and educational information necessary for making an informed decision. It is also good to talk to people who have been through the conversion process.

Contact an expert to analyze your campground to provide you with advice on conversion. Someone experienced in buying campgrounds or who is familiar with this type of program can give you advice. You should also seek legal advice. After all the information and advice have been obtained, decide which concept best fits your individual situation—ownership or membership.

Consider your long-term goals when making this decision. For example, do you want to leave the business completely, or do you want to retain ownership and management of the business? If you wish to leave the business, consider either selling to a development company or pursuing the camp resort ownership concept.

If you sell an undivided interest on a fee-simple basis, you can structure the business so that you can leave it by turning it over to a property owners association (POA) once your project is fully sold out. The POA will manage the facilities and collect the dues.

The Development Process

If you own an existing rental campground, there are several considerations to remember when selling to a camp resort developer, or when working with a camp resort developer or marketing firm. When approached by someone intending to buy your campground to develop it into a camp resort, ask as many questions as you feel are necessary. Insist on information and proof about his or her financial background. Many times he or she will ask to buy your campground with the provision that you provide some degree of seller financing, such as a land contract, contract for deed, or installment sales contract. This is an acceptable method of sale, and most of the time it's the only way to complete a sale. The key is to get a sufficient down payment to protect yourself.

It is easy to be influenced by an outstanding purchase offer, but without a substantial down payment on the part of the developer or buyer, it is easy for him or her to walk away from the deal, leaving you with property that is now encumbered by campers who have paid substantial sums for the right to camp there.

The same advice applies to the ownership concept. In a deeded campsite program, you need to make sure the buyer doesn't come in, sell the best lots at the outset, and then walk away from the deal. You can see the need to get good legal advice, a substantial down payment, and contract structuring.

Most camp resort developers are honest, legitimate business people. But, as in any industry, there is the possibility of abuse. Many camp resort companies will request the campground owner to thoroughly check their company before negotiations even begin. It is important to meet the key people in the company and check on past projects they've developed. Have they been successful in doing what they said they would do? Ask them where they bank, and do a follow-up check. Screen these companies by asking for references from people they've bought campgrounds from, as well as from their banks.

The same advice applies to choosing marketing companies. If you decide to develop the camp resort yourself and you're looking for a marketing company, closely check their track record, financial capability, and references. Can they do what they say they can do at the price they quote? Ask them to prove it. You should have a comprehensive contract that protects both parties; again, legal advice is imperative. The need for the expertise of an experienced consultant throughout this process is invaluable.

Cash Requirements

The cash requirements of starting a membership or ownership park resort are great, even if the campground is owned free and clear. Such costs are high, mainly because of the level of services provided and the costs of the marketing program. It is necessary to have strong financial backing, either through personal means or from your bank

Campers investing $5,000 to join a camp resort expect service and amenities from the outset. This begins with the first membership sold. The nature of membership sales creates a negative cash flow in the first years of operation, until the sales volume increases to a point that receivables generate a profit. You must be prepared to withstand these costs. The magnitude of such costs depends on the number of memberships you are trying to sell each year. Thus, if you don't have such financial resources, you're probably better off to find a marketing company willing to finance the cost of sales, or to cooperate with a camp resort development company.

In membership and ownership sales, the campground owner typically provides financing. Typical contract terms include a down payment of 20 percent, with the balance paid over five to eight years at a 12 to 15 percent interest rate.

For an example of negative cash flow, assume a membership sells for $5,000, and you receive a 20 percent down payment at closing, or $1,000. Assume also that the marketing cost of generating that sale is 45 percent, or $2,250. The result is a negative cash flow of $1,250 for the sale ($2,250–$1,000 = $1,250). If you sell 20 memberships, it will take $25,000 just to stay in business. Though there is profit potential in the business, this profit comes from the volume of sales. You can see the importance of realizing the cash requirements of going into this type of development. One of the common ways to stretch out cash resources from a developer's standpoint, is to purchase the campground on a land contract at a modest interest rate. This helps to conserve cash by keeping interest costs down.

Raising cash by borrowing against receivables has become the most popular way to raise working capital. The financing of these receivables in the membership industry is getting more common and therefore easier to obtain. There has been some difficulty with banks that are unfamiliar with receivables contracts. They do not know how to treat these contracts or how secure they are. There is no real estate contract standing behind them, because the title does not pass to the buyer. In lending against these contracts, lenders must consider the possibility of forfeiture and delinquency.

Most forfeitures occur before the first payment is made, so lenders who do lend against these contracts require a certain number of payments to be made prior to accepting receivables as collateral. In order to get this type of financing, a track record must already be established. Lending institutions are becoming more experienced with these contracts.

There is great potential for profit in this industry, as witnessed by those who are prospering in it. At the same time, some people have had difficulties, either with the product itself, financing, or a poor marketing program. If you are considering the camp resort business, take the time to learn all you can about the industry, talk to people with experience in it, and look at your own capabilities and potential. Then weigh the risks and benefits before making a decision.

Resorts and the Industry

The advent of these camp resort concepts in the campground industry has caused concern, particularly on the part of the rental campground owners. Their concerns are mainly in the areas of market share and image. There is concern that the large membership companies, with their high membership sales-to-sites ratios, are absorbing large shares of the traditional rental market segment. Membership companies claim that a large share of their members are buyers who did not previously camp. Whether these concerns are valid is still unclear. The characteristics of those buying the membership product seem to indicate that because of the cost of the product and its fixed location requirements, only a limited portion of rental campers would buy such a product.

Chapter

7

RECORD KEEPING

Only with the best possible information can the best management decisions be made. Therefore, record keeping and accounting are among the most important functions performed in a campground business operation. This subject will be divided into two chapters—this chapter will deal with record keeping, and Chapter 8 will discuss accounting. Where does record keeping or bookkeeping end and accounting begin?

Bookkeeping or record keeping involves "the making of records of transactions in the business." It is leaving clear tracks regarding the business operation. The purpose of this chapter is to show how to transfer current records into commonly used financial statements, and to explain such statements and their relationships. It does not have the depth of an accounting course and will not make the reader a professional in this field. However, this chapter covers how to keep accurate records and why it is so important to do so.

Why Keep Accurate, Current Records?

Good record keeping and accounting can cost time, money, frustration, and anxiety. It can also lead to a feeling of satisfaction, of feeling in control of your business operation. Why put forth the effort to do it? Perhaps the question should be, how can you afford not to do it?

Satisfying state and federal requirements for taxes and other payments to the government is one reason for the effort. When records are not properly kept, penalties can be severe, as can be the mental anguish involved in an IRS audit.

Investors—including stockholders and silent partners—need to know financial information. So do creditors, banks, and other lenders who know that a business must be operated successfully for their money to be paid back.

You will probably want to sell your campground business eventually. Potential buyers determine the worth of your campground on the basis of how profitably you have operated it for the last few years. They learn this by studying your financial statements. These statements are a good indication of how much profit they can expect to earn from your campground if they decide to purchase it. If your records are in some way deficient and they must estimate rather than see hard financial data, they may offer to pay less for your campground than if they have access to accurate, hard data.

If a campground owner hires a manager to operate the campground, financial statements are an excellent measuring stick for evaluating the effectiveness, efficiency, and overall success of the manager. Accurate records are also a means of safeguarding the assets of the business.

Finally, and most importantly, good records are critical tools for running your campground. Good records enable you to see where you've been so you can decide how to get where you want to be in the future.

Have you ever been traveling in an unfamiliar place, gotten lost, and looked at your road map but were unable to identify your location? When you don't know where you are, the road map becomes almost useless as an aid in knowing where to go.

The same is true in managing your campground business. You need to know where you stand financially. Are you making a profit? If so, how much? Further, it's critical to know where in your business you're making or losing money.

Only with this financial information is it possible to intelligently plan for next year's business operation. For example, how can you determine what site rates to charge if you can't compute a break-even rate—one that will cover only your business expenses? How can you tell if you're making a satisfactory return on your investment unless you have good records?

Records and Record Keeping

Accounting records usually begin with cash receipts (cash in) and expenditures (cash out). Cash (currency) doesn't leave tracks, so you must keep records. Otherwise, you can't prove you paid those bills, and you'll find yourself paying income taxes on income equal to such expenditures.

Daily Cash Recap

This is the first record to keep. Keep track of each day's cash intake and outflow. It is the record of the original transaction and includes information from cash register tapes, handwritten receipts, admission ticket counts, cash counts, sign-up books for equipment rentals, and so on.

The daily cash recap should include everything in cash that came in and went out of your campground business on any given day. It should have a place for the day's date, cash on hand at the start of the day, sales broken down as much as you desire, bank deposits, and other cash outflows. There should be a means of reconciling the intake and the overflow with the amount of cash left at the end of the day.

Seldom will the amount of cash left at the end of the day be exactly equal to the amount of cash on hand at the beginning of the day, plus sales, and less expenditures and deposits, as it should be. Operators say the amount of cash over and cash under usually balances out over time. If you're constantly short of cash, your employees may be stealing cash from you. An example of a daily cash recap form is shown in Appendix A at the end of this chapter.

Which Accounts Should You Maintain?

In other words, what sources of income intake or expense outflow do you want to keep separate from the rest? In deciding this, keep in mind that these accounts form the basis of your financial statements, your operating or profit and loss (P&L) statement, and your balance sheet. In doing so, you should keep things separate by groupings that assist you in making management decisions. Usually this is done by what is called profit center or income center analysis.

This means the income generated in a given profit center is matched with the expenses associated with it. If done accurately, it will tell you how much you made or lost in that profit center. Thus, separate accounts should be kept for income and expenses associated with each profit center you're operating. Examples of common income and expense accounts for campgrounds are shown in Appendix B at the end of this chapter.

Whichever accounts you decide to keep should be maintained yearly and changed only if absolutely necessary. These accounts will show in your daily recap sheet, if there is a daily intake or outflow of cash. They will also become the basis of your operating statement.

A few accounts are necessary from a legal point of view. For example, if you have a store operation and a state sales tax, you'll have to keep one account for the taxable items sold and another account for nontaxable items. If you sell fishing licenses, you are no doubt required to keep such money received in a separate account, or at least keep the cash in a separate envelope or box.

There may be exceptions to the guidelines just mentioned regarding separate accounts by profit centers. Short-cut methods may allow the same information to be obtained more easily. An example is the ice and slush machine. To get the same sales information, just keep track of the bags or paper cups used. Multiply the number sold by the price charged to get the gross sales from that profit center. This assumes, of course, that none were given away. The sign-up book for sports equipment rentals will give the same gross sales information on such rentals and likewise for billiards, if the shooter ball is signed out to users.

Remember that separate accounts cost you time and money, so if you don't need separate accounts, don't keep them.

Daily Cash Expenditures

The accounting profession highly recommends that cash (currency) expenditures be kept to a minimum or zero, if possible. The recommendation is to write checks whenever possible and thereby run all, or as many expenditures as possible, through a checking account. The checkbook is then a complete, or almost complete, record of all expenditures—or an expense record. Again, the main reason is to make tracks so that you can prove you did incur such expenses and, therefore, won't have to pay income taxes on an equivalent amount of income. Of course, it also allows you to more accurately determine the profitability of your profit centers and your business overall.

In some cases, you can't avoid paying cash or currency for expenses. Therefore, many operators have a petty cash fund that should be maintained at a minimal level, such as at $25 or $50. Every time a small outflow of cash occurs, it is taken out of the petty cash fund, and a paid-out slip is placed in the petty cash fund container. The paid-out slip should include the date and a brief explanation of the payment. An example is shown in Appendix A.

When the petty cash fund gets low, write a check to your campground petty cash fund, and place cash from the cash box or cash register into the petty cash fund container. In this manner, these cash expenditures are accounted for in your checkbook.

Never allow a large amount of cash to accumulate. Even if you have what you think is a safe keeping place, you're courting danger. Make frequent trips to the bank during busy times when cash is coming in rapidly.

Further, don't allow your checking account balance to get larger than you need for paying bills and taking advantage of cash discounts. As soon as you get an extra thousand or two in your checking account, transfer the funds to some liquid, interest-earning account. Interest-bearing checking accounts are also an available option.

Be aware that the more liquid or readily available the funds from an account are, the lower the interest rate will be, all other things being equal. More information on this topic is discussed in the section on cash management in Chapter 9, Financial Management.

Record Keeping Systems and Forms

This discussion covers the more common types of small business record keeping systems, starting with the family-style checkbook system and proceeding to the more sophisticated systems.

Family Checkbook/Account Book Systems

When starting out from scratch with a small campground, it is acceptable to use the same kind of checkbook used by individuals or families. Either the check stub or the check register style can be used. The check register is perhaps handier because it is easier to read than check stubs. It's also easier to write in and store. In fact, the check stub system has given way to the check register system as a personal checking account. Receipts are usually kept in a large envelope or box, as quantity dictates.

With this system, a small business account book is commonly used. Information on each check is copied into the account book in a section entitled "Operating Expenses." An example in Appendix B at the end of this chapter shows 31 rows, one for each day of the month, and numerous columns, each designed to handle a separate account. Account titles should be written in the blank spaces at the tops of the columns. Expenditure items are entered by date in the respective account columns to which such expenditure items are intended to be charged. At the end of each month, the columns are totaled, and the totals are transferred to the yearly summary on the line designated for the particular month.

The same is done for receipts (income). A section of the account book, titled "Site Rentals and Other Sources of Income," provides a place for the totals of each daily recap sheet (see Appendix B). A row for each day of the month, and columns for breaking down the income by source, or profit center, are provided. Again, a yearly summary is provided to aggregate the data by month.

Another section, entitled "Merchandise Purchases," is for items purchased for resale. If you have a small store operation, it's important to keep such merchandise purchases separate by profit center account so that a "Cost of Goods Sold" can be determined easily and routinely, along with the resulting *gross profit on sales* for the store (see the example in Appendix B). Gross profit will be discussed in the next chapter.

The same record keeping should be done for other profit centers at which merchandise is purchased for resale. Such purchases should be kept in separate accounts also.

A *wages record* is also included for the recording of wages paid to employees. Ideally, wages should be separated by profit center. An employee record of earnings must legally be kept for each employee. It includes information on hourly rate of pay, date employed, date terminated, withholding amounts, and net pay. An example of these kinds of records is shown at the end of this chapter in Appendix B.

An *inventory* or *depreciation schedule* for capital goods is included for such accounting procedures. Near the end of the account book a monthly profit and loss summary is included (see Appendix B), along with an annual profit and loss statement and balance sheet. The latter are explained in the accounting chapter.

One-Write Bookkeeping System

The *one-write* or *pegboard bookkeeping system* is the next step up the ladder of sophistication for record-keeping systems. It has a hard cover folder (folding poster) that holds checks, journal pages, and other records firmly in place by a row of pegs about a fourth of an inch long and down the left hand side, hence the name pegboard. The checks and journal pages contain rows of holes down the left-hand margin. In this manner, all records on what is to be written are held securely in place so that they line up, one on top of the other. You should ask your local office supply store operator to show you a one-write, or pegboard, bookkeeping system.

It's called the one-write system because one writing will make up to five imprints on the various record forms. This offers the advantages of accuracy and efficiency. There is no possibility of transposing numbers or making other mistakes, as there is in copying numbers into another account book.

To explain how the one-write system works, the following illustration is shown in Appendix C. On the bottom are the journal pages, the original and a copy. The left-hand portion of the journal page is the checkbook register. Shingled checks are placed on the page so that the bottom check has the payee line directly over the line you want it recorded on in the check register.

Let's suppose you want to pay a bill from a supplier. Simply write out the check just as you'd write any other check, across the center line of the check. The date, payee, gross amount, and discount are all written. All of the information you wrote transfers through the carbon to the checkbook journal. Remove the check from the pegs, sign it, write in the payee's address, place it in the window envelope, and mail it. In one step you've written the check, made the appropriate entry in your checkbook journal, and addressed the envelope.

Next, deduct the amount of the check from the checkbook balance, and write the new balance at the right of the check amount, on the checkbook portion of the journal page. By doing that, you have completed the checkbook portion of the check writing task. Then *immediately* transfer the amount of the check to the column representing the account or accounts to which you wish to charge it. At this point you have completed the bookkeeping function for that expenditure.

When writing payroll checks, a similar procedure is followed, with minor modifications. One style of check and record keeping system is the *combination system* (payroll and disbursements), in which case the payroll information is written across the center of the check, and a small employee's copy is inserted under the check along with your employee's earnings record. This is called a "center-write" check, as compared to the "top-write" payroll check in which the information is written across the top of the check.

An *employee's earnings record* form is inserted under the check so that a copy of the information written on the check will be transferred to the appropriate line on the employee's earnings record. In addition, an employee's receipt is inserted to give to the employee.

A separate *payroll system* can also be used, in which case the payroll information is written across the top ("top-write") of the check on a removable stub, which becomes the employee's record of earnings. A carbon sheet transfers the same information onto the employee's record and your checkbook.

Finally, the net amount of earnings is transferred to the appropriate account on the bookkeeping portion of the journal page to which you want to charge the labor, and for which you wrote the check.

The payroll check writing has the advantages of efficiency and accuracy, and it prods you to do the bookkeeping function at the same time you write the checks. This system is always accurate and easy to check. Add all of the columns down, add the rows across horizontally, and then add the totals across the bottom and down the left column. If the two totals are equal in the lower right hand corner, you can rest assured your numbers are accurate.

The combination system is recommended for up to 25 employees. For 25 to 50 employees, a separate payroll system is recommended. For campgrounds with over 50 employees, it is recommended that a computerized data processing system be used. Whichever system is best is up to you to decide. The combination system can probably be purchased for about $150 to $200. This includes the folding poster and journal binder, plus personalized checks, journal pages, employee's earnings records, and window envelopes. After the first order, only checks, earnings records, and journal pages need to be reordered.

Duplicate Check System

Another low-cost system is available that allows you to have someone else do the bookkeeping for you. This is the duplicate check system. The checks come in pairs, and the check on the bottom is the duplicate, as the name suggests. As a check is written, a carbon copy is automatically made. You need to indicate on the check an assigned expense account to whom it will be charged, by name or code number. Then send or take your duplicate checks to your accounting firm periodically for computerized data processing.

The accounting firm then runs your checks through a data processing system and gives you a computer printout listing any of your expenditures, as well as a summary of your general journal by account. This is your bookkeeping system.

Another advantage of duplicate checks is being able to file the duplicate check with the invoice as payment is made. This saves copying the information from the check onto the invoice. Duplicate checks are a little more expensive than regular checks, but many operators feel the savings in time justifies the additional cost.

Data Processing System

In data processing, you can have either your own computer or your accounting firm's system write all of your checks, do all of your record keeping, and prepare all of your financial records by use of a computer. Computers are becoming more user-friendly and less expensive as a component of campground management systems. As they become more popular, they will probably be more cost effective for use in such data processing systems. The 1998

National Operations Survey of the RV Park and Campground Industry shows that 74 percent of the campgrounds reporting used computerized systems, while 46 percent used manual record-keeping systems and 24 percent used outside bookkeeping services. Some campgrounds use more than one system, thus the percentages exceed 100 percent.

Choosing the Most Appropriate System

The cost of the system varies according to how much of the bookkeeping you do yourself and how much you have done for you. The more your accountant does for you, the more it will cost.

Regardless of the type you consider using, it is good practice to shop around and get competitive bids from at least three different suppliers of accounting services and computers. When deciding on a system to use, be sure to place a value on your own time, if you're considering doing the bookkeeping yourself. Even though your time is not an out-of-pocket expense, it means you can't do anything else during that time.

When you work with records, you get very familiar with the numbers that are important in making financial decisions concerning your campground. Performing the bookkeeping function will make you very familiar with these important numbers.

A Few Bookkeeping Tips

Following are a few pointers on how to get the most out of the system you select.

Write everything down. This appears obvious, and yet it's perhaps the most difficult thing to do. A good suggestion is to carry a small notepad around at all times. If something is purchased, it can be noted on the pad and later transferred to the account book.

If the one-write system is used, it's harder to carry the system around because of its bulky size. If this discourages the writing of checks on impulse, and you encourage the hardware store to keep a charge account for you, so much the better. If, on the other hand, checks are taken out of the folding poster and written in the absence of the rest of the one-write system, several purposes of the system are defeated—accuracy, saving time, and keeping the books up-to-date.

Keep separate accounts. Keep a separate checking account for your campground business. Don't combine it with your family checking account or another business checking account.

Always get signed receipts. Write the number of the check on the receipt, or attach a duplicate check to the receipt along with the invoice. In case of a tax audit, you need a signed receipt and a canceled check to prove payment.

Keep a routine. Set aside a routine time each week and/or month to pay checks and do the bookkeeping. Plan this so you'll not be interrupted, and stick to the schedule.

Take advantage of discounts. Not taking advantage of a 2/10, net 30 cash discount is the same as paying annual simple interest at the rate of 36 percent! (30 minus 10 equals 20 days. 365 days in a year divided by 20 is approximately 18. Two percent times 18 is equivalent to 36 percent simple annual interest.) A 2/10, net 30 discount means you can deduct 2 percent of the bill if you pay it within 10 days; otherwise, the entire amount is due at the end of 30 days.

Pay by check. Pay all but the smallest bills by check. This is so you establish a set of tracks via your checkbook. Pay the rest via a petty cash system.

Handle cash properly. Deposit cash in the bank at your earliest convenience. Keep duplicate deposit slips on file. Enter all deposits on the check record. Maintain your checkbook balance at all times. Use a petty cash system, and keep it to a minimum size.

Appendix A

Sample Daily Cash Recap Forms

Daily Summary of Sales and Cash Receipts

Cash sales (from cash register tapes)
(Record in monthly sales and cash receipts
journal)

Camp fees	_____
Store sales	_____
nontaxable	_____
-taxable	_____
Games	_____
Activities (bike, archery)	_____
Mini-golf	_____
Honey wagon fees	_____
Laundromat	_____
RV service	_____
Marina	_____
Advance deposits	_____
Total cash sales	_____

Miscellaneous receipts (detail on reverse)	_____
Collections on seasonal fees	_____
Total receipts to be accounted for	_____

Cash on hand (end of day)	
Cash in register	_____
Bills	_____
Checks	_____
Credit cards	_____
Total in register	_____

Less change and petty cash fund	
Petty cash slips	_____
Coins and bills	_____
Total change and Petty cash	
fund (fixed amount)	_____
Total cash deposit	_____
Cash over or short	_____

(Record for each cash register; if more than one, do a summary sheet for all.)

Paid-Out Slip

No. _____

Date _____

Received of Petty Cash

Amount $ _____

For _____

Charge to _____

Received by _____

Approved by _____

Miscellaneous Receipts

Slip Number	Who from	What for	Amount
			$

Appendix B

Income and Expense Accounts Sample

Income Accounts

Site Rental
- Overnight
- Seasonal
- Cottage/cabin rental
- RV/tent rental
- Day use receipts

Store
- Groceries
    nontaxable
    taxable
- Vending machines
- Souvenirs/gifts
- Bottled gas
- Wood/ice
- Beer/wine
- Camper supplies
- Gasoline

Recreation Income
- Bike/moped rental
- Game room
- Mini-golf
- Watercraft rentals
- Bait sales
- Fishing tackle
- Guide services

Other Services Income
- Laundromat
- Honey wagon/dump station fees
- Coin-operated showers
- Snack bar/restaurant
- Bar/lounge
- RV storage
- RV repair
- RV sales

Other Income
- Income on bank accounts

Expense Accounts

Cost of sales

- Groceries
- Camper supplies
- Vending machines
- Wood/ice
- Souvenirs/gifts
- Beer/wine
- Bait/fishing tackle
- Bottled gas
- Gasoline
- Snack bar/restaurant
- Bar/lounge
- RV repair
- RV sales
- Other

Labor

- Wages
- Payroll taxes and benefits

Operating and cleaning supplies
Recreation equipment repairs and maintenance
Repairs and maintenance
Swimming pool maintenance
Machine hire
Licenses and permits
Dues and subscriptions

Taxes

- Real estate
- Personal property

Gas (natural, bottled)
Electric
Fuel
Telephone
Advertising and promotions

Insurance

- Liability
- Fire, wind, theft, and so on

Professional services

- Accounting and legal

Office supplies
Garbage disposal
Interest (short term)
Rent
Entertainment
Travel
Vehicle expense
Miscellaneous

Operating Expenses or Site Rentals and Other Sources of Income

Month					Year			
Date	$	$	$	$	$	$	$	$
1								
2								
3								
4								
5								
6								
7								
8								
9								
10								
11								
12								
13								
14								
15								
16								
17								
18								
19								
20								
21								
22								
23								
24								
25								
26								
27								
28								
29								
30								
31								
Total								

This form may be used for either Operating Expenses or Site Rentals and other Sources of Income.

Employee's Earnings Record

Employee's name _____

Social security no. _____ - _____ - _____

No. withholding exemptions _____

Address _____

Phone number (_____) _____

Started Work _____ Pay _____

Wage Period Ending	Cash Wages	Other Remuner- ations	Total Pay	Social Security F.I.C.A.	Federal Income Tax Withheld	State Income Tax Withheld	Total Deductions	Net Pay	Paid by Check Number
	$	$	$	$	$	$	$	$	$

Merchandise Purchased for Resale

Account/Profit Center:

Date	To Whom Paid	Check Amount	Check Number
		$	

Use one page for each account or profit center.

Monthly Cash Profit and Loss Summary

Year _____

Month	Total Cash Revenue for Month	Less: Cost of Goods Sold	Gross profit (or Loss)	Less: Cash Expenses for Month	Net Profit (or Loss)
January	$	$	$	$	$
February					
March					
April					
May					
June					
July					
August					
September					
October					
November					
December					
Total					

Capital Goods, Assets, and Depreciation

Description of Property (Kind) and Quantity	Date Acquired	Cost or Other Basis	Salvage Value	Depreciable Balance	Est. Life (Yrs.)	Deprn. Method Used	Deprn. Allowed Prior Yrs.	Remaining Cost	Deprn. Expense This Year	End of Year Value

One-Write Bookkeeping System

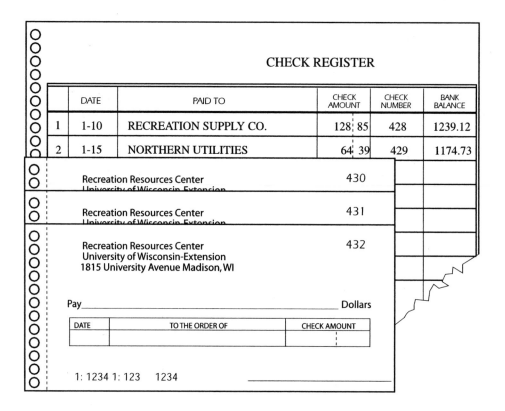

CHECK REGISTER

	DATE	PAID TO	CHECK AMOUNT		CHECK NUMBER	BANK BALANCE
1	1-10	RECREATION SUPPLY CO.	128	85	428	1239.12
2	1-15	NORTHERN UTILITIES	64	39	429	1174.73

Recreation Resources Center
University of Wisconsin-Extension   430

Recreation Resources Center
University of Wisconsin-Extension   431

Recreation Resources Center   432
University of Wisconsin-Extension
1815 University Avenue Madison, WI

Pay_____ Dollars

DATE	TO THE ORDER OF	CHECK AMOUNT

1: 1234 1: 123   1234

Chapter

8

ACCOUNTING

Accounting provides quantitative financial information on your business. It is historical in nature, with the exception of the budgeting segment of accounting. Accounting helps you to see where you've been in your business, and it puts you in a better position to decide how to guide your business. There are several types of accounting, which will be discussed in this chapter.

The Language of Business

Accounting is called the "language of business," and as a campground operator, you will need to know the meaning of the jargon that's used. For example:

Cost accounting is keeping track of costs so they can be controlled. It is usually used by companies involved in production of some type, as in manufacturing. *Budgeting* is the planning of business activities and related transactions before they occur. *Internal accounting* is the checking of records to make sure they are correct or accurate.

Assets equal *equity*. Assets are properties owned and are equal to equity, which is the rights or claims on that property. Equity can be divided into *liabilities* and *capital*, or *net worth*. However, it is customary in accounting language to notate it as:

Assets – Liabilities = Capital (Net Worth)

This is the fundamental accounting equation.

All business transactions can be stated in terms of their effect on assets, liabilities, or net worth. Assets are what you own, and liabilities are what you owe. Net worth includes your rights to those assets. *A balance sheet* is a statement of financial condition. It tells you what your net worth is at a particular point in time. The *profit and loss statement* (P&L) shows changes in your net worth that occurred during a certain period of time, usually a month or a year. It is also called the *operating statement, statement of operations*, or *income statement*. The balance sheet and the income statement are the two main accounting statements used in the financial management of a small business.

A 4-Year Accounting Example

The following example is presented to give you an understanding of the balance sheet and income statements, and how they are related.

Year 1

Al Operator/Manager is a young man, home for the summer, with no job. He likes camping, so he decides to try the campground business. His neighbor has a farm with a 50-acre woods adjoining a lake. It's on a main highway near a large city. Al has no money or any other assets.

Al rents the unused woods from his neighbor for $600, payable at the end of the summer. He cuts a hole in the fence, scrapes together some paint and plywood, and makes a sign reading: "Rustic Camping." Al also rents two portable toilets for the season for $200, payable at the end of the summer. During the summer, site rental income amounts to $4,750, with firewood sales of $250. The firewood expense was $200.

Let's look at Al's operating statement for the first year. Remember, the operating statement shows the change in net worth during a period of time.

Operating Statement: Year 1

Income	Year 1
Site rentals	$4,750
Firewood sales	250
Total cash receipts	5,000
Total gross income	**5,000**
Expenses	
Cost of sales	200
Rent—land	600
Rent—equipment	200
Total cash disbursements	1,000
Total expenses	**1,000**
Net Profit (net income)	**$4,000**

Now let's look at Al's balance sheet. The $4000 net profit from Al's operating statement is the change in Al's net worth during the year.

Balance Sheet: Year 1

Assets	Year 1
Cash	$4,000
Total assets	**4,000**
Liabilities	0
Total capital (beginning of year)	0
Profit	4,000
Total capital (end of year)	**4,000**
Total liabilities and capital (net worth)	**$4,000**

The Year 1 net profit goes into the balance sheet, and shows the change in net worth and total net worth at the end of the year. Cash equals total cash receipts less total cash disbursements. In this case, $5,000 less $1,000 equals $4,000. The assets of $4,000 are what Al owns. The liabilities of zero are what Al owes—nothing. The net worth is what equity Al has in his business—$4,000, or total liabilities and capital. It is not the market value.

Year 2

The second summer, Al Operator/Manager is home again, and again he has no job. He decides to go ahead with his campground enterprise because of the profits he made last year.

This year the land rent goes up to $800. He rents the portable toilets again for $200. Al joins the state campground owners association and buys an ad in the directory for a total cost of $500. He gets started a little earlier in the season, and he has some repeat business from the previous year. With the help of his advertising, the site rental income increases to $9,500. Firewood sales increase to $500, and cost him $400. Al buys a used pickup truck for hauling firewood, garbage, and to run errands. It costs him $1,500, and he depreciates it over three years on a straight line basis, so each year's depreciation expense is $500.

The operating statement for Year 2, including Year 1, is as follows. The figures in parentheses are minus figures, and are subtracted when tabulating column totals.

Operating Statement: Year 2

	Year 1	Year 2
Income		
Site rentals	$4,750	$9,500
Firewood sales	250	500
Total cash receipts	5,000	10,000
Total gross income	**5,000**	**10,000**
Expenses		
Cost of sales	200	400
Rent—land	600	800
Rent—equipment	200	200
Advertising	0	500
Fixed assets-truck	0	1,500
Total cash disbursements	1,000	3,400
Fixed assets—truck	0	(1,500)
Depreciation		500
Total expenses	**1000**	**2400**
Net profit	**$4,000**	**$7,600**

Balance Sheet: Year 2

	Year 1	Year 2
Assets		
Cash	$4,000	$10,600
Fixed assets—truck	0	1,000
Total assets	**4,000**	**11,600**
Liabilities	0	0
Capital		
Capital (beginning of year)	0	4,000
Profit	4,000	7,600
Total Capital (end of year)	**4,000**	**11,600**
Total liabilities and capital	**$4,000**	**$11,600**

The truck was entered in the income statement because it was a cash expense. Later, after cash disbursements, it was removed from the income statement and entered into the balance sheet, because it is an asset.

The depreciation of $500 is not a cash disbursement but rather an expense of doing business in Year 2. The truck shows in the balance sheet with a value of $1,000, rather than the $1,500 that was paid for it, because it was depreciated by $500 during the first year. A net profit of $7,600 was realized— $10,000 of total income, less $2,400 of total expense.

In the balance sheet for Year 2, cash is equal to the cash from Year One, plus total cash receipts from Year 2, less total cash disbursements from Year 2 ($4,000 plus $10,000, less $3,400 equals $10,600). The capital for Year 2 is the capital for Year 1 (at the beginning of Year 2), plus the net profit from Year 2 ($4,000 plus $7,600 equals $11,600). The net profit reflects the change in net worth, which is what the balance sheet shows, as stated earlier. The total assets less the total liabilities equal the net worth, or capital.

Year 3

Because he had such a good experience in Year 2, Al Operator/Manager is very enthusiastic about operating his campground enterprise again in Year Three. Site rental income increases to $13,000; people are telling others what a nice place it is to camp and are coming back themselves. Also, Al is a very personable fellow and really treats his campers as though he wants them to have a good time.

He rebuilds his front entrance sign and purchases a membership and ad in the state association directory, for a total cost of $600. Firewood sales increase to $1,000, and the cost of sales is $800. He hires an accountant to do his tax and accounting work for $100. Rent goes up to $1,000.

Al agrees to let two camper families rent their sites for the entire summer. However, they never get around to paying their seasonal fees of $1,000 ($500 each), and Al is so busy running his campground that he doesn't get around to collecting them. This introduces us to a new term: *receivables*, which will show in the income statement. Receivables represent income that is earned, but not yet received. If your accounting system factors in receivables, it is called an *accrual basis* system. In this system, your operating statement reflects what is actually earned and spent during the accounting period rather than what is received or paid out in cash. If the system accounts only for what is received or paid out in cash, it is called the *cash basis* system of accounting.

Let's take a look at the operating statement for Year 3.

Operating Statement: Year 3

	Year 2	Year 3
Income		
Site rentals	$9,500	$13,000
Firewood sales	500	1,000
Total cash receipts	10,000	14,000
Receivables	0	1,000
Total gross income	**10,000**	**15,000**
Expenses		
Cost of sales	400	800
Rent—land	800	1,000
Rent—equipment	200	200
Advertising	500	600
Accounting services	0	100
Fixed assets—truck	1,500	0
Total cash disbursements	3,400	2,700
Depreciation	500	500
Fixed assets—truck	(1,500)	0
Total expenses	**2,400**	**3,200**
Net profit	**$7,600**	**$11,800**

Balance Sheet: Year 3

	Year 2	Year 3
Assets		
Cash	$10,600	$21,900
Receivables	0	1,000
Fixed assets—truck	1,000	500
Total assets	**11,600**	**23,400**
Liabilities	0	0
Capital		
Capital (beginning of year)	4,000	11,600
Profit	7,600	11,800
Total capital (end of year)	11,600	23,400
Total liabilities and capital	**$11,600**	**$23,400**

In the operating statement, total income equals total cash receipts plus receivables, or $15,000. Total disbursements equal $2,700. Again this year, depreciation is an expense, and reduces the value of fixed assets (the truck) in the balance sheet to $500. Net profit equals total income less total expense ($15,000 less $3,200 equals $11,800).

In the balance sheet, cash is equal to Year 2 cash plus Year 3 cash receipts, less cash disbursements, ($10,600 plus $14,000 less $2,700 equals $21,900). End-of-year capital equals beginning-of-year capital, plus net profit for the year ($11,600 plus $11,800 equals $23,400). Liabilities are again zero, so total assets less total liabilities equal net worth. Stated another way, total assets equal total liabilities plus total capital.

Year 4

Al has a good business going now, so he proceeds again with the campground in Year 4. Site rental income amounts to $18,000, and firewood sales total $1,500. This year Al didn't get around to paying for firewood, which is an unpaid bill of $1,300.

Al received the payments from last year's seasonal campers that he forgot to collect. Also, he received an inheritance of $2,000 from a relative. His accounting bill increased to $200, and his advertising budget increased to $1,000. Further, Al had been living at home, free of charge all this time. His personal expenses had been provided from other sources. This year he withdrew $12,500 for his personal use. What does all of this do to his operating statement?

First, receivables from sales have to be deducted from income, because they were earned last year. The inheritance, although received in cash, has to be taken out of income, because it wasn't income of the campground business.

Cost of firewood, although not a cash disbursement, has to be an expense for the year, so it is shown as an expense in the form of payables. Depreciation is the third and last $500 expense on the truck, purchased earlier.

The personal draw needs to be shown as a cash withdrawal, so it is included in cash disbursements. But since it is not an expense of the business, it is deducted from expenses.

On the balance sheet, cash includes last year's cash balance of $21,900, plus this year's cash receipts of $21,500, less this year's disbursements of $14,900, for a total of $28,500.

Payables are a liability—namely, the firewood bill of $1,300, which Al owes.

Al Operator/ Manager's capital is the sum of last year's total capital (end of year), plus net profit and capital contributions (Al's inheritance). Al's withdrawal is a reduction in his capital, since he took it out of his business for personal use ($23,400 plus $14,300 plus $2,000 minus $12,500 equals $27,200).

Again, assets of $28,500 equal the total of liabilities of $1,300 and end-of-year capital of $27,200.

Operating Statement: Year 4

	Year 3	Year 4
Income		
Site Rentals	$13,000	$18,000
Firewood sales	1,000	1,500
Inheritance	0	2,000
Total cash receipt	14,000	21,500
Receivables from sales	1,000	(1,000)
Inheritance (end of year)		(2,000)
Total gross income	**15,000**	**18,500**
Expenses		
Cost of sales	800	0
Rent-land	1,000	1,000
Rent-equipment	200	200
Advertising	600	1,000
Accounting services	100	200
Personal draw	0	12,500
Total cash disbursements	2,700	14,900
Payables (end of year)	0	1,300
Depreciation	500	500
Personal draw	0	(12,500)
Total expenses	**3,200**	**4,200**
Net profit	**$11,800**	**$14,300**

Balance Sheet: Year 4

	Year 3	Year 4
Assets		
Cash	$21,900	$28,500
Receivables	1,000	0
Fixed assets	500	0
Total assets	**23,400**	**28,500**
Liabilities		
Payables	0	1,300
Capital		
Capital (beginning of year)	11,600	23,400
Profit	11,800	14,300
Withdrawals (personal)	0	(12,500)
Capital contributed	0	2,000
Total Capital (end of year)	23,400	27,200
Total liabilities and capital	23,400	28,500

Source: Albrecht, Fred, CPA. Unpublished handout used at Campground Owners' Short Course.

The diagram on this page shows how your cash income and expense records are traced through your financial record system.

A Picture of Your Financial Records

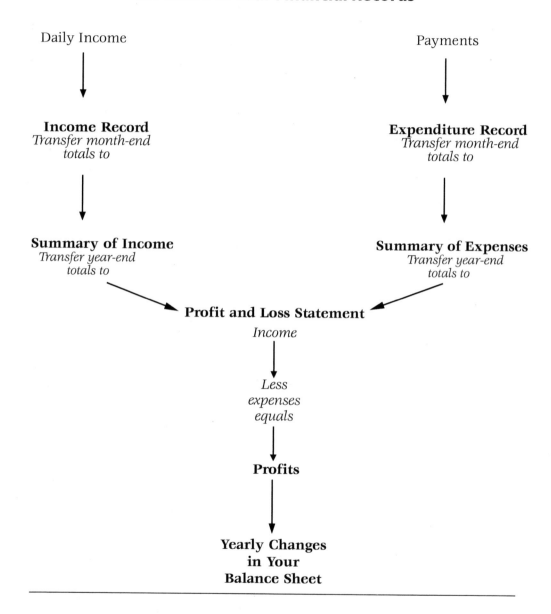

Daily Income

Payments

Income Record
*Transfer month-end
totals to*

Expenditure Record
*Transfer month-end
totals to*

Summary of Income
*Transfer year-end
totals to*

Summary of Expenses
*Transfer year-end
totals to*

Profit and Loss Statement
Income

*Less
expenses
equals*

Profits

**Yearly Changes
in Your
Balance Sheet**

What Can Accountants Do for You?

Should you do your bookkeeping and accounting yourself, or should a professional accountant do them for you? Every campground operator has asked this question at one time or another. The factors of cost, preference, availability of time, and having the necessary skills should be considered.

Cost, Need, and Trust

Accountants usually charge according to the amount and kinds of services they perform. The bookkeeping tasks can usually be performed by paraprofessionals. The charge for this level of skill is approximately $50 per hour. These people become very proficient in processing your financial data, so don't assume it will take them the same amount of time it takes you to process your numbers by hand. On the other hand, remember that you may find it difficult knowing how much time they actually spend processing your data, so it is important to trust the accounting firm you select.

For the accounting tasks, or preparation of your financial statements, a paraprofessional with a computer software program can do an effective job. Accountants may charge from $75 to $150 or more per hour for their services. Be sure to find out if they start charging you for their time the minute you walk into their office so you know whether or not you pay for the small talk and negotiating that takes place before you get down to business. Such time should not be counted as billable time. Again, you have to trust them with much billable time they spend on your business records. How much accounting services cost depends on the type and amount of work accountants do for you.

The main advantage of going to an accountant for preparation of your financial statements and tax forms is the use of her or his expertise. If you wouldn't feel comfortable having your accountant manage your campground, maybe you should also not feel comfortable preparing your own financial statements and tax forms, unless you happen to know a lot about accounting. Your accountant knowing just one tax advantage that you don't know could save you your entire accountant's fee for a year, or much more. Maybe you should ask yourself if you can afford not to hire an accountant.

Another consideration is whether or not you like to do the bookkeeping. If you like to do it, you'll probably do it in a timely manner and not let it build up until tax time. If you keep your own records, you'll become familiar with your financial condition, and will be in a better position to make financial management decisions than if you don't do your own bookkeeping.

However, if you don't care to do the bookkeeping, you may end up putting it off until the end of the season or until tax time. Then you've lost the opportunity to make corrective management decisions that would have been possible during the season, had you been familiar with your financial records. This is not good financial management.

Wanting to do your own bookkeeping is also related to the availability of time for doing it. There is much work to be done around the campground, especially during the camping season. In most cases, there is too much for one person or couple to do. Certain tasks must therefore be done by hired labor or be contracted out to others. What you choose to do yourself should depend (at least in part) on your skills. If one or more of your management team previously worked as a bookkeeper, this person or these people should probably do your records. If no one has the skill or desire to do them, there's no problem deciding to have someone else do them.

It's good management practice to become familiar with bookkeeping and accounting practices so that you understand enough to be able to use your financial records in making sound management decisions. Also, you should be able to tell whether you're getting good services from your bookkeeper and accountant.

An important service an accountant can provide you with is advice on how to make more money in your business. He or she can help you through better tax planning and by identifying profit centers that are not making the profit that they should.

Working with Your Accountant

It is of utmost importance to hire a *good* accountant. A good accountant is one who knows the campground business, usually by virtue of having worked with several successful campgrounds over the years. Experience working with other types of recreation tourism businesses is also beneficial to find in your accountant. Try to avoid contracting with an accounting firm that has never worked with the campground industry. You may be paying for the time they spend learning about the financial aspects of your industry, and you may not get good advice.

Choose an accountant in whom you have confidence, because it is important to be able to share confidential information. If you can't trust your accountant to keep your financial information confidential, don't hire her or him. To get the best advice possible from an accountant, you must provide all the information you can about your business. You can't afford to treat your accountant like an IRS auditor.

Tell your accountant what you expect. For example, let your accountant know that you are interested in knowing the profitability of each profit center. Tell her or him that you need help in allocating overhead expenses for the profit centers.

Don't be afraid to terminate the services of a particular accounting firm if you feel you're not getting good service and advice. Accountants make mistakes the same as everyone else, only some make less than others.

The accounting profession has a certification system. People who meet certain professional standards are called certified public accountants (CPAs). Each state provides a testing program that accountants must pass in order to be certified. This assures a minimum level of knowledge among CPAs. Accountants can practice without being CPAs. You should be aware of this when selecting an accountant.

Do Your Own Computer Analysis

You may want to do your own analysis of your financial records, especially if you do your own computerized data processing. Accounting systems are available and are used by most campgrounds, according to the *National Operations Survey of the RV Park and Recreation Industry, 1998.* Such systems include a data input system, an accounting package and a management spreadsheet package.

You can use the management spreadsheet package to make income projections and occupancy projections. For example, you can insert various site rates and determine the effect on income. Or you can change the occupancy and determine the impact on other profit centers and, of course, those that do not profit. Many other management options can be analyzed with the use of spreadsheet analysis. Suppliers of computer software systems can be found in the January issue (*Buyer's Guide*) of *Woodall's Campground Management*, 13975 West Polo Trail Drive, P. O. Box 5000, Lake Forest, IL 60045-5000.

Chapter

9

FINANCIAL MANAGEMENT

This chapter explains how to use your financial records in making decisions. It explains business ratios and ratio analysis, and how to use these in managing and controlling your business. It gives you tips on how to manage your cash. Sections on making investment decisions and how to get a loan are included in the next chapter.

Why Are You in Business?

Financial management is useful only when you know what you want to achieve. Your goals and objectives don't have to be only financially related, however.

Goals and Objectives

The goals and objectives that you set for your business provide you with direction. Long-range goals might describe what you want to accomplish in 10 years. Intermediate goals might be targets that you want to reach in three to five years. Each year, you should state several specific objectives that you want to achieve. These should be revised periodically to reflect the changes that have occurred since they were developed. Your short-range goals should be much more specific than your long-range goals.

Objectives are the yardsticks that can measure your progress. After a year is over, you can evaluate your success in terms of how well you achieved your objectives. Objectives are formed at the start of your business plan. Annual objectives should be specified in at least three general areas.

Facility related. You need to make regular improvements in your physical facilities. Otherwise your campground will eventually need a major renovation project to bring it back into good condition. It is necessary, then, to plan for improving your facilities. During this year, for example, you may plan to improve the toilet/shower facilities, paint the front entrance sign, improve 10 sites, and paint the inside of the game room.

Next year, you may want to redesign and repaint the store, put in a new mini-golf course, build 10 new seasonal sites, redo the landscaping in your front entrance up to your front office, and replace the entrance gate. These improvements need to be done on a regular basis, and must be planned over a period of time.

Financial related. The financial objectives relate to the level of profits you want to achieve. They can be stated in relation to percentage changes from past profit performance and/or in absolute dollars. They may also be defined in terms of return on investment. Such objectives, if specific, will be easy to measure after you prepare your operating statement for the year.

Marketing/sales related. In order to achieve your financial or profit-related goals, you need clear objectives for levels of sales volume. The more specific they are, the more useful they will be. For example, you might want to define your sales objectives in terms of a certain dollar or percentage increase in overnight site rental income, seasonal rental income, or a specific profit center income increase. With such objectives, it's easier to develop specific goals and strategies to achieve them. These financial goals are a critical element in the budgeting process, which is discussed later in this chapter.

Marketing objectives should involve specific results of your marketing efforts. Examples might be 10 new seasonal campers, a 5-percent increase in mid-week peak season business, and/or a 10 percent increase in off-season site rentals. All of the above result in much easier management decisions as you operate through the year.

Good Records

As stated in the last two chapters, management decisions are only as good as the quality of the financial records. Records must be accurate and specific enough to provide the information necessary to make decisions. Being more specific than is necessary only makes analysis of the records more difficult, and is also too time-consuming. The usual income tax statement often isn't quite detailed enough to be useful in making management decisions, especially if there are several profit centers that should be kept separate for control purposes.

The Operating Statement

Now let's look at some of these figures from the standpoint of determinants of financial success. Table 9.1 presents the financial data from a hypothetical 100-site campground. Other figures from a national economic survey are shown in Table 9.2. They include gross income, total expenses, and net profit by size of campground.

Table 9.1

Hypothetical Operating Statement for a 100-Site Campground

Revenues	Total Dollars	% of Gross Income	Dollars per site
Site rental	$130,000	65.0%	$1,300
Overnight	80,000	40.0	800
Seasonal	50,000	25.0	500
Day guest receipts	4,000	2.0	40
Groceries	16,000	8.0	160
Beer/Wine	10,000	5.0	100
Vending machines	4,000	2.0	40
Souvenirs	10,000	5.0	100
Mini-golf	6,000	3.0	60
Equipment rentals	4,000	2.0	40
Game room	8,000	4.0	80
Wood and ice	6,000	3.0	60
Laundry	2,000	1.0	20
Total gross income	200,000	100.0	2,000
Cost of sales	40,000	20.0	400
Gross profit	$160,000	80.0%	$1,600
Operating Expenses			
Salaries/wages	$26,000	13.0%	$260
Payroll taxes/benefits	3,000	1.5	30
Operating supplies	10,000	5.0	100
Vehicles expense	5,000	2.5	50
Maintenance	12,000	6.0	120
Utilities	10,000	5.0	100
Telephone	2,400	1.2	24
Advertising & promotions	10,000	5.0	100
Dues/subscriptions	1,000	0.5	10
Licenses & permits	1,000	0.5	10
Legal /accounting/computer	2,600	1.3	26
Office expense	3,000	1.5	30
Property taxes	10,000	5.0	100
Insurance	10,000	5.0	100
Miscellaneous	4,000	2.0	40
Total expenses	$110,000	55.0%	$1,100
Net profit	$50,000	25.0%	$500
(before income taxes, debt service, and depreciation)			

Table 9.2

1997 Median Gross Income, Expenses, and Gross Profit Ratios by Size of Park

Number of Campsites	99 or Fewer	100–249	250 or More
Median Gross Income	$143,955	$211,105	$914,500
Median Total Expenses	$119,907	$166,000	$769,239
Median Net Profit	$21,141	$44,561	$300,000
Median Profit/Income %	14.7%	20.4%	32.8%
Median Income/Site	$2,215	$1,487	$2,583
Median Profit/Site	$313	$275	$547

Source: National Operations Survey of the RV Park and Campground Industry, 1998.

The first item of note is that the income exceeds the expenses, so there is a net profit before income taxes, debt service, and depreciation. Notice also that much of the income comes from profit centers other than site rentals. This other income is an excellent way to build gross income and contributes substantially to net income.

On examination of the expenses, you'll notice that some of them are fixed—they tend to remain the same regardless of changes in camping volume. Insurance, property taxes, dues/subscriptions, licenses and permits, and legal/accounting costs are examples. Notice further that many of the other variable expenses (expenses that fluctuate with the volume of camper business) don't fluctuate very much. These are semi-variable costs. Examples are: vehicle operating expenses, maintenance, telephone, office expenses, and miscellaneous expenses. The variable costs that fluctuate considerably are: salaries/wages, operating supplies, utilities, and advertising and promotions.

The point of this discussion is that some minimum level of sales volume must be generated in order to make the campground operate in the black. Thus, income other than site rental income may be critical to the financial success of the business, because it contributes to gross and net income, with a given camper volume.

Gross sales must be considered in relation to the level of investment. For example, $150,000 in gross sales may look very good for a campground valued at $200,000. However, it wouldn't look so good for a $2,000,000 investment. You need to decide what you want to achieve in terms of return on investment and build it into your objectives in the form of net profits and related gross sales.

Cost of sales (cost of goods sold) is the cost of the goods purchased for resale. It is calculated as shown in the following example:

Beginning inventory	$3,000
Plus purchases	+35,000
Equals cost of goods available for sale	= 38,000
Less ending inventory	– 4,000
Equals cost of goods sold (cost of sales)	= 34,000

Subtracting the cost of goods sold from the total gross income gives us the gross profit. The gross profit percentage is a measure of the markup on the various profit centers. This subject is discussed in a later chapter. The cost of sales percentage must be kept separately by profit center to be a useful management tool, however.

Using Operating Ratios to Make Decisions

Now we're going to take the financial statement one step further and develop operating ratios. An operating ratio is computed by dividing each item in the operating statement by the gross income. The result is a percentage, which shows the mathematical relationship between each item and the gross income. These operating ratios, or standards, were shown in the previous table in the percentage column.

Notice first that the revenues or gross income total is $200,000, and the percent for that is 100 percent ($200,000 divided by $200,000). Notice next that overnight site rental income is 40 percent, which added to the seasonal income of 25 percent amounts to 65 percent. This leaves other profit center income 35 percent of total gross sales. Some campgrounds bring the income other than site rentals up to as high as 50 percent of total gross income. The potential for producing income in profit centers other than site rentals is, of course, constrained by the volume of campers; others who can be attracted to the campground; and the number of profit centers and how well they are operated. Such profit centers do provide the potential for increasing income and profits, given the above constraints.

Controlling Expenses

Ratio analysis is very helpful in monitoring your expenses. You always try to save as much as possible when you purchase various items needed in operating your campground, but how do you gauge the success of your efforts? The answer is in the use of operating ratios.

Comparing and Contrasting Operating Ratios

Operating ratios are useful in comparing and contrasting your operating ratios from last year, and/or your projections (budget) for the current year. Your operating ratios can also be compared with others' ratios that are similar to yours. Where do you find this information? One way is to join a "20 group." This is a group of business operators, such as campground operators, about 20 in number (as the name suggests), who get together periodically and compare their financial statements through ratio analysis or other methods. They discuss such analyses and any other problems that concern them. In this way, they become familiar with the operations with which they are comparing their own. There are 20 groups within the National Association of RV Parks and Campgrounds (ARVC).

Another way to discover information on operating ratios is through the use of economic research reports. No up-to-date economic studies of this type are known. However, Table 9.1 is based on previous economic studies and is believed to represent campgrounds with about 100 sites.

Divide each income and expense account in your operating statement by your gross income. The results are the percentages, or operating ratios, for your campground. Compare your operating ratios with those in Table 9.1, if your campground is around 100 sites in size. If you have a large campground, refer to the group 20 figures in the Appendix to this chapter.

A Payroll Problem

Now that you've analyzed your operating statement using operating ratio analyses, what can you do if some of your expense items are out of line? Suppose that your labor cost is more than the average for the industry. What can you do to reduce it, other than lay off employees? Assume further that extra personnel are necessary to get jobs done. First, you might try to do a little better *planning*. Keep track of how much labor you hired the past season so that you know when you're going to need more help. Then, hire people with *flexible* schedules, with the understanding that their work day will be over if there is nothing for them to do. Remember, though, that the more regular work schedules you can offer your staff, the higher will be the quality of the workers you can attract. *Forecasting* the amount of business on given days or weeks will also assist in scheduling employees. Using previous years' records, this can be done fairly accurately.

With proper *scheduling* of work, there is a chance of saving on the amount of work that has to be done. Always try to increase the *efficiency* of the tasks to be accomplished. Do some tasks really need to be done, or can they be done at another, slower time when a staff person is present anyway? For instance, someone working the front desk may have time to do office work. This person might tabulate camper registration forms to determine the market origins of your campers in his or her spare time. Locating the profit centers near each other so they can be operated by one person during slack times is another example of labor efficiency.

Another use of the labor ratio is in planning. Suppose you have a labor target of 15 percent of gross sales; and less if you contribute family labor without charging for it. This means that in order to justify another $100 in labor, you need to generate $1,500 in additional sales.

For another example, suppose your insurance ratio is above the percent shown in the national economic survey. What are your alternatives? You must have insurance. Decide exactly the type and amount of insurance coverage you need. Then ask for itemized bids from several insurance agencies for the coverage you want. If you let them know that you are getting several bids, you may have a better chance of getting your desired insurance coverage at a lower cost than you previously paid. Increasing the deductible will also lower premiums. Insurance and risk management will be more thoroughly discussed later.

Analyzing By Site

Many campground operators like to analyze their financial statements on a per-site basis. To compute your per site figures, divide each number in your operating statement by the number of sites in your campground. Compare your key income accounts, cost of goods sold, gross profit, key expenses, and net income with your previous year's performance and with industry averages, if available and comparable. Table 9.1 shows per site figures for gross income, total expenses, and net profit.

Analyzing Your Business with Other Ratios

This section will cover a number of other types of analyses and show how they can be used in planning.

Occupancy

Occupancy rate is defined as the ratio (percentage) of sites rented to the number of sites available for rent. It's stated as a percentage and is a very useful management tool. It can be calculated as shown in the following example:

Assume the following:　　　　100 sites

15 seasonal rentals

Operating season: May 15 to Oct. 15

4,300 site nights rented

- The number of sites available for rent is 85 (do not include seasonals).
- The operating season is 16 days in May, 30 days in June, 31 days in July, 31 days in August, 30 days in September, 15 days in October, for a total of 153 days.
- Site nights available for rental are: 153 days x by 85 sites = 13,005.
- Occupancy rate = 4,300 divided by 13,005 = .331. Move the decimal two places to the right (multiply by 100) to convert it to a percentage (33.1 percent).

The occupancy rate is useful in evaluating the performance of your campground during the year. It reflects the ability of your campground to attract guests; it reflects your success in the marketing program you chose, hosting and hospitality, quality and quantity of activities offered in the campground and in the area, and the quality of the service facilities. You should definitely compare your occupancy from the current year to last year's and the year before that and compare with industry averages.

It is useful to check occupancies for several months—by weekdays and weekends—because it will provide you with direction for allocating your marketing dollars. The occupancy rate also measures the efficiency of operation at your current capacity. This is useful in helping to decide when to expand, which will be looked at later in a discussion of making investment decisions. The 1998 National Operations Survey reports a median occupancy of 51 percent, with a high of 100 percent and a low of 5 percent.

Average Site Rate

This can be calculated by dividing the total overnight site rental income by the total site nights rented (do not include seasonal sites). This ratio gives you the actual or effective average dollar amount received per site rented. It will be something less than your actual site rate because of discounts, free camping promotions, and so on. It shows you what such promotional activities cost you. Because of this, it is useful in determining your rates and analyzing your profits. When analyzing your occupancy, site rates, and operating expenses, ask yourself the following questions:

- Is my occupancy low enough to justify additional marketing efforts?
- In what times of the week and months of the year are the most sites not rented?
- If I raise my site rates, what will be the effect on occupancy and on gross income?
- If I lower my site rates, what effect will it have on occupancy, on gross income, on profits?
- Is my occupancy high enough to justify adding more sites?

Answers to these questions can be very revealing, as well as useful in management decision making.

Current Ratio

The current ratio equals current assets divided by current liabilities. This indicates your ability to pay off your debts, even if business is poor. Current assets consist of cash and other assets that can be quickly converted into cash. Current liabilities are those obligations that need to be paid relatively soon out of current assets or by the creation of other short-term liabilities, such as a short-term note payable.

This ratio should be 1.0 or a little over. At this level, you can pay off all your short-term debts at any point in time. If it is much higher than one, you should consider converting some of it into higher-yielding securities. If much lower than one, you should ask yourself how long you can go without paying those bills. If you can pay them with the peak season just around the corner, you're probably all right. If not, you should consider taking out a bank loan to pay them off. If you don't, your creditors may suggest it. Bankers like to have a current ratio of .85, which gives them a margin of safety.

Debt-Equity Ratio (Leverage)

Long-term debt compared to the owner's equity gives the debt-equity ratio, which is also referred to as leverage. It indicates how much you, the owner, are supported by outsiders. It is usually expressed in numbers, as 2:1, 5:1, or 8:1.

You can use the ratio to see how it varies in your business from year to year. Does it increase over the years, and if so, is it because your assets (equity) are valued at cost and have not been adjusted for changing market values? If so, you ought to adjust your balance sheet accordingly. If it is high, such as 8:1, will one bad year wipe you out?

Today lending institutions don't like to lend if your debt equity ratio is more than about 2.33:1. This amounts to an owner having about 30 percent equity in the business.

Return on Equity

Return on owner's equity is the ratio of net profit (after taxes) to owner's equity. This ratio indicates what rate your investment is earning for you. This ratio should be compared to previous years' ratios. Be aware that as your equity increases in size, the rate of return will decrease, other things being equal. In this analysis, ask yourself the following:

- Has performance improved?
- Could I sell my campground, take my equity, invest it elsewhere, and earn a higher return? Would I have to work less? Would my investment be more secure?
- Is my equity apt to appreciate considerably in the long run?
- Is the rate of return low now but capable of great potential improvement in the future?

When you answer these questions, a reasonable salary for your time must be considered, in the event you did not charge it as an expense. Also, be clear as to whether your equity is valued at book value (face value of corporate stock) or market value.

Budgeting

Budgeting is another tool you can use to manage your business. It is defined as the planning of business activities and related transactions before they occur. It goes hand in hand with the setting of objectives, discussed earlier in this chapter.

A practical approach is to start with last year's operating statement. Then review your objectives and translate them into estimated revenues and expenses for the coming year. Adjust the figures from last year's statement accordingly. Then adjust them again, considering other factors such as price increases and any other management changes you plan to make in the coming year. The result will give you a projected operating statement for the coming year.

Then do the same with your balance sheet, as many of your physical improvements will be reflected as capital expenditures. Improvements, therefore, show as assets, and the payments show as liabilities. During the operating season, events may occur that make necessary changes in your plans and related budget items necessary. Adjusting accordingly when the need arises is sound business management.

Cash Flow Management

Cash flow management involves managing so you have enough cash available to pay your bills each month while preventing unneeded cash build up. There are many ways to even out your expenses so you don't have to borrow so much money to make it through the slow season. For example, review the monthly cash flow from Table 9.3. This table shows the hypothetical monthly cash flow for a small campground in the snow belt.

Table 9.3

Monthly Cash Flow

	Percent Total Sales/Month	Sales	Cost of Goods	Gross Profit	Expenses	Cash Flow
January	-	-	-	-	14,465	(14,465)
February	-	-	-	-	2,520	(2,520)
March	-	-	2,000	(2,000)	3,565	(5,565)
April	3	2,400	950	1,450	4,065	(2,615)
May	6	4,800	4,000	800	4,405	(3,605)
June	21	16,800	2,400	14,400	5,435	8,965
July	33	26,400	2,550	23,850	6,740	17,110
August	25	20,000	3,000	17,000	6,430	10,570
September	8	6,400	750	5,650	3,030	2,620
October	4	3,200	350	2,850	1,610	1,240
November-	-	-	-	-	1,655	(1,655)
December	-	-	-	-	2,080	(2,080)
Total	100	80,000	16,000	64,000	56,000	8,000

Notice that the net cash flows in parentheses are negative for January through May, then positive from June through October, and negative again in November and December. The annual summary is shown in the far right column.

The purpose of cash flow management, as stated earlier, is to minimize the negative balances and excessive overages. How can you do this? To answer, lets take a closer look at the monthly expenses shown in Table 9.4.

Table 9.4

Monthly Expenses

	J	F	M	A	M	J	J	A	S	O	N	D	Total
Payroll	-	-	-	500	750	1750	2750	2700	550	200	-	9200	
Office expenses	300	-	-	300	-	200	-	200	-	-	200	-	1200
Supplies	-	-	800	950	850	500	565	170	100	65	-	-	40000
Insurance	4800	-	-	-	-	-	-	-	-	-	-	-	4800
Maintenance, supplies, & repairs	1700	700	600	-	200	350	750	500	-	-	-	-	4800
Telephone	60	65	75	90	100	110	110	80	70	70	60	70	960
Utilities	400	415	340	300	450	660	850	775	325	275	300	350	5440
Property tax	4000	-	-	-	-	-	-	-	-	-	-	-	4000
Advertising	500	200	300	500	400	400	300	600	-	-	-	400	600
Dues & subscriptions	200	-	-	50	-	-	-	-	400	-	-	150	800
Legal/ accounting	700	-	-	-	250	-	-	-	250	-	-	-	1200
Licenses	250	-	150	-	-	-	-	-	-	-	-	-	400
Vehicle Operating expenses	500	-	-	250	250	250	250	250	250	-	-	-	2000
Debt service	1000	1000	1000	1000	1000	1000	1000	1000	1000	1000	1000	1000	12000
Miscelaneous	55	140	300	125	155	215	165	155	85	-	95	110	1600
Total	14965	2520	3565	4065	4405	5435	6740	6430	3030	1610	1655	2080	56000

The following are suggestions on how to manage the cash flow in the previous example:

Borrow money in the off-season. You may need to borrow money to get through the off-season until you start collecting cash receipts.

Split the property tax payment. In most states you can pay half your property tax in January and the remainder in July. Check to see if this is possible in your state.

Pay insurance during your peak season. Your insurance company will work with you to arrange your payments in late August, near the end of your peak summer season, or when your peak season occurs.

Split your accountant's bill. Your accountant may let you postpone some of your accounting fees until you have more cash coming in. It may cost you a little more, but it's certainly worth investigating and negotiating.

Make your principal and interest (debt service) payments during your peak season months. Your lender should work with you to time your payments to your convenience.

Level your utility payments. Utility companies usually have a plan in which you can pay a uniform amount every month of the year. Thus, at the time of the year when your utility payments are high and it is not your peak season, you won't be overwhelmed with high utility bills.

Have your seasonals pay in January, March, and May (prior to your peak season). One of the advantages of renting to seasonal campers is that you can have them pay before the peak season gets underway, when you really need the cash.

Make major repairs right after your peak season is over. You should have more cash available at this time, rather than just before your season starts.

Cash Management and Security

As your business begins to build, you'll find yourself and your staff handling large amounts of cash. There are some things you can do to earn interest on it, as well as to minimize the chance of losing cash. A good plan for cash security keeps everyone aware that you always know how many dollars should be deposited each day. Following these tips can help you keep your operation secure.

Record and deposit receipts regularly. Doing this daily during your busy season is recommended. Use night deposit facilities on weekends. Take the large bills out of the cash register regularly, and do not let large amounts of cash build up in your possession. Go to the bank at a different time each day—don't make it easy for someone to rob you. If security becomes a problem, consider buying a safe with a slot in the top of it for employees to drop in the receipts.

Provide a cash tray for each employee starting a shift. Each tray should be checked back to you at the end of the shift so you can ring out the cash register. Each person is then responsible for his or her own shift and cash register. Any shortages can be traced to a particular shift and person.

Use a petty cash account. This is explained in the record keeping chapter. If you pay for items out of your pocket and then pay yourself out of the till, your record keeping system, as well as your security, will be at risk. If you can walk over to the cash register and remove cash, why can't your employees do the same? The problem is that you may not be around when they do it.

Some cash registers now have a "Pay Out" key that takes the place of a petty cash fund. If using such a cash register, be sure to get receipts because the IRS requires them. This type of cash register provides the documentation that the petty cash system provides.

Compare the cost of sales to gross income (operating ratio) regularly. For example, if you have a markup on food of 25 percent, you should have a cost of sales to gross sales ratio of 75 percent. In other words, you should have a dollar in the cash register for every 75 cents paid for food. If you don't have this ratio, you either aren't charging enough, the portions are too large, someone is taking food without paying for it, an employee may be taking money, or there are too many mistakes being made. Chapter 17, Campground Store Operations, covers this in further detail.

Keep your records up-to-date. If you don't, you lose the tools you have available to assist you in controlling your operations. Consider depositing your receipts in an interest-bearing account. Then transfer them into your checking account as you write your checks. In this way, your money is earning interest for as long as possible. Paying your bills when due establishes a good credit rating, but don't pay them before they come due. Most invoices request payment within 30 days. Take advantage of that time to keep your money earning interest for you.

Have a check cashing policy. Most campgrounds accept personal checks and have few losses. If you have a problem with bad checks, consider buying check cashing insurance. You must make a toll-free call to get authorization every time you cash a check. If the check is bad, the insurance company pays you for it. If you use this system, monitor it closely to make sure that it doesn't cost you more than the bad check losses you suffered prior to using the system.

Appendix

Revenue, Expense, Net Income and Operating Ratio for a Composite of 20 Groups, 1997.

	$ Amount	% of Total Revenue
REVENUE		
Site sales	$593,483	64.9%
Site service sales	130,127	14.2%
Retail sales before returns and allowances counted	190,553	20.9%
Retail sales net	190,185	20.8%
Total revenue	$913,795	100%
EXPENSES		
Retail sales costs	$122,607	13.4%
Site service costs	23,368	2.6%
Total cost of sales	$145,975	16.0%
Utilities	$91,035	10.0%
Professional services	11,398	1.2%
Insurance	18,975	2.1%
Office/licenses/dues	24,143	2.6%
Taxes	19,688	2.2%
Leases	15,100	1.7%
Education/travel/promotion	11,128	1.2%
Franchise	8,406	0.9%
Repairs/maintenance	75,620	8.3%
Total operating costs	$275,492	30.1%
Advertising	$14,595	1.6%
Promotion	12,197	1.3%
Publicity	1,192	0.1%
Total marketing costs	$27,984	3.1%
Payroll	$189,884	20.8%
Benefits	24,506	2.7%
Payroll taxes	19,570	2.1%
Total compensation	$233,959	25.6%
Total interest	$42,512	4.7%
Total expenses	$725,922	79.4%
Net income before depreciation and owners' salary	$187,873	20.6%
Owner'/investors' salary	49,453	5.4%
Net income after owners' salary	122,508	15.1%

Source: National Operations Survey of the RV Park and Campground Industry, 1998, Conducted for the National Foundation for RVing and Camping, Vienna, VA.

Chapter

10

EXPANSION AND FINANCING

How do you make the decision to add a profit center? How do you get a loan to do it? Successful campgrounds have substantial income from profit centers, aside from site rental income. In fact, adding a profit center is a way to increase profits in view of being able to attract only so many campers. Thus, it's good to add these centers, but only if they'll earn a profit or provide an attraction that brings more campers. Let's take a logical approach to this question. We'll start with a snack bar example.

Addition of a Snack Bar

First, estimate the investment that a snack bar will require. Get prices and estimates on construction, furnishings, and kitchen equipment. Next, estimate the sales volume you can expect to earn from it. How do you make such an estimate? Check with comparable campgrounds that have snack bars. Determine the distance from other snack bar types of food service, and talk with campers about their preferences. Ask a campground consultant.

For large (250 +) campgrounds, snack bar gross revenue would be about 2.5% of gross sales, whereas for a 100-site campground, gross revenue would be about 4 to 5 percent of gross sales. Thus, for a 100-site campground with gross sales of $200,000, snack bar revenue could be $8,000 to $10,000.

The next step is to estimate the associated expenses. Calculate the cost of sales from the markup you plan for the food. Markup is explained in the chapter on store operations. Then estimate the labor costs and other expenses for supplies, and so on. that you anticipate. Last, subtract the estimated expenses from your estimated gross sales to get an estimated net profit. The procedure is summarized in Table 10.1.

Table 10.1

Worksheet Summary for Making the Decision to Add a Snack Bar

	Estimate
Investment	
Construction	$ _____
Furnishings	_____
Kitchen equipment	_____
Total investment	_____
Gross Income (food sales)	_____
Cost of Goods	_____
Gross Profit (gross income less cost of goods)	_____
Expenses	
Labor	_____
Utilities	_____
Maintenance	_____
Supplies	_____
Insurance	_____
Etc.	_____
Total expenses	_____
Net profit (gross profit less expenses)	_____
Return on investment (net profit/investment)	_____ %
Years to pay off investment	_____ yrs.
(total investment/net profit)	

Source: Schink, 1999

Divide the net profit by the total investment to determine the return on investment. The final step is to divide the net profit into the total investment, then determine how long it will take to pay off the investment. Then ask yourself if it's worth it. Are there possibilities to build the sales volume over a few years?

The Addition of a Swimming Pool

Many campground operators wrestle with the decision to add a swimming pool because they are very expensive, yet present such an attraction to campers. Increases in campground income may arise from charging higher rates, because of the swimming activity offered and increased occupancy because of the attractiveness of the pool. A logical approach to this decision is shown in Table 10.2.

Table 10.2

Worksheet Summary for Deciding to Add a Swimming Pool

Cost of a swimming pool _____
Increased income from increased rates
   rate increase × ***# of sites*** × ***days open*** × ***occupancy*** _____
Increased income: from increased occupancy
  rate × ***# of sites*** × ***days open***
  × ***increase in occupancy*** _____
Total increased income _____

Increased expenditures
Pool maintenance _____
Added operating costs
  due to increased occupancy _____
Total increased expenditures _____

Added profits from swimming pool _____
Return on investment
  (Profits/investment) _____ %
Years to pay off investment
(Investment/net profit) _____ Yrs.

Source: Schink, 1999

Look over your figures and decide if the increased income merits going ahead with the swimming pool investment.

The Addition of Sites

Simply being full on a few weekends does not usually justify a campsite expansion. There is a logical procedure to follow to arrive at this decision. Its purpose is to determine the difference in net profit from adding more sites versus not adding more sites. This process is outlined in Table 10.3.

First, estimate the investment cost of adding the sites and any other facilities needed, such as a new or expanded toilet/ shower building.

Next, project the additional site rentals and resulting site rental income, along with other campground gross income. Use past occupancy and overflow records for this decision. If you aren't keeping track of your overflow campers—or turn-aways—it's a good idea to start doing so.

Last, project the additional expenses you'll incur if you make the expansion. Include the debt service on the new investment, or the return you expect on the money you invest in it. Consider any other factors that may weigh in making the decision. Finally, compute the net income, return on investment, and years needed to pay off the investment. Then decide whether or not to proceed.

Table 10.3

Worksheet for Deciding to Add More Sites

Estimated investment

Roads/site construction	$ _____
Plumbing (water)	_____
Plumbing (sewer, if sewer sites)	_____
Electric	_____
Picnic tables	_____
Toilet/shower facility (new or expanded)	$ _____
Signs	_____
Landscaping	_____
Other	_____
Total estimated investment	_____

Projected Income

Occupancy Trend, Last Three Years

	Number of Sites Rented	**Occupancy Percent**	**Number of Parties in Overflow Area**	**Number of Turn Aways**
Last year	_____	_____	_____	_____
Year before last	_____	_____	_____	_____
Year before that	_____	_____	_____	_____

126

Projected Income, Next Three Years

	YR 1	YR 2	YR 3
Sites rented without expansion	_____	_____	_____
Sites rented with expansion	_____	_____	_____
Increased site rentals with expansion	_____	_____	_____
Average site rate	_____	_____	_____
Increased income from site rental	$_____	$_____	$_____
Increased gross profit, other profit centers	$_____	$_____	$_____
Total increase in gross income	$_____	$_____	$_____

Projected increase in expenses	$_____		

Increased operating expenses	$_____
Debt service on new investment	_____
Total increased expenses	_____
Projected increase in net profit	_____
(Increased gross income – increased expenses)	
Projected return on investment	_____ %
(Projected net profit/projected investment)	
Projected years to pay off investment	_____ yrs.
(Projected investment/projected net profit)	

Balancing the Addition of Profit Centers with Improvement
Often you face the decision of adding a profit center or some improvement such as infrastructure changes or ones to improve the appearance or image of your campground. Capital is usually limited, either through profits or borrowing capacity.

One approach is to add a profit center and use the profits from it to help pay for the other improvement. Sometimes the infracture, such as the septic system, has to be upgraded. Also, improvements in the image (appearance) are necessary because they influence business volume, especially in severe situations. Thus, decisions on these expansions and improvements are difficult; they influence the financial makeup and the long-run success of your business.

Expansion Financing

Campgrounds often find the need to obtain additional capital to finance expansion, revitalization, or a campground purchase. There are many sources of capital for campgrounds, and the ability to raise such capital may spell the difference between expansion and success or failure.

There are two types of financing: debt financing and equity financing. Debt financing is the borrowing of money that must be paid back sometime in the future, usually along with interest, and subject to some other terms. Equity is a permanent contribution by the owner(s), which doesn't have to be paid back. Holders of equity own a share of the campground.

Sources of Equity Capital

The campground operator is the most convenient source of equity, assuming the operator has the cash. Friends, relatives, and other private individuals are potential sources of equity. They may be partners, limited partners, or stockholders in the corporation. If your business is unsuccessful, however, it might ruin a personal relationship.

Venture capital companies provide venture capital to small businesses. This is the most sophisticated of the many sources of capital. These companies often purchase minority equity positions, although they sometimes buy controlling positions. They expect a very high rate of return. You run a fairly high risk of losing control of your business to them. These companies are mainly interested in small businesses with promise for substantial growth in size and profitability in 5 to 10 years. Lists of such companies can be found in *Venture* magazine.

Sources of Debt Financing

Debt financing is usually easier to obtain than equity financing. It is obtained from some of the same sources as equity financing (capital). A lender wants to be shown how a campground operator plans to earn the money to pay back the loan. They also want the operator to share some of the risk. This is done by making the operator put up some cash or collateral, so that failure is a risk for the operator as well as the lender.

Banks are the most important source of loans for small businesses. However, the owner/operator/manager is the easiest to convince to make a loan to the business. In many campgrounds, the sole proprietor regularly contributes capital from another source, such as an outside job or other business. Friends, relatives, and sometimes employees are also sources. A "rich aunt" or some other "angel" may be a source.

Commercial banks, credit unions, and savings and loan associations are major sources of mortgage loans. They prefer to have their loans fully secured with personal guarantees. They are not very interested in start-up loans, although they do make them to campgrounds. After an operator has established a good credit rating, the banker may make signature-only loans. This is still true in small communities, where the banker knows the operator personally.

Usually major loans are secured as real estate mortgage loans, where you mortgage a home, the campground, or some other real estate to secure the loan. In some cases, the chattel mortgage for a short-term loan is used; you offer some other kind of property other than real estate to secure the loan.

Lending institutions are now making loans in conjunction with government agencies, and sometimes loans are available directly from such public agencies. The major purpose of these programs is to stimulate economic development, especially the creation of new jobs. Programs keep changing within these agencies.

You may be able to obtain loan guarantees from the Small Business Administration (SBA). Minority small business investment companies in the larger cites make equity loans. The Community Block Grant Program makes development loans, based to a large extent on the number of potential jobs created. Check with the regional office nearest you. Individual states also have loan programs. Some have programs for disabled persons. There are also economic assistance loans available for veterans from World War II, Korea, Vietnam, and Desert Storm. Check with your local Veterans Office for details.

Suppliers are sometimes a source of financing, mainly to the extent of their sale to you. Some encourage buying by offering interest-free delayed payments, especially if they own merchandise stock and know you need it before your season starts but will have difficulty making payments until after your season gets underway. Also, your accountant or lawyer may accept delayed payments to coincide with your cash flow situation. It may cost you a little more to compensate for interest incurred.

Loan Application

Most campground operators find it necessary to get loans to finance capital improvements and expansions. Many disappointing situations can be avoided if you do your homework ahead of time and go to your lender prepared. When you start getting serious about borrowing money, you need to consider several issues before going ahead. Ask yourself the following questions.

Why do I need the money? Is it for expansion in sites, adding a profit center, additional working capital, or making it through the off-season?

How much do I need? Carefully determine this number so you don't end up borrowing too much or too little.

How and when will I repay the loan? Usually profits from the business are used to repay business loans. Businesses don't usually take out a two-year loan for the current year's working capital needs or to tide the family through the off-season. If a new expansion is planned that will generate income over a number of years, the loan repayment should be spread over a number of years also.

Can I afford it? This is a major decision, which should be answered in your loan application. As a matter of practicality, you don't want to borrow the money, nor does anyone want to lend it to you, unless you have the ability to pay it back.

Lenders need to see how you plan to earn the money to pay the loan back over the established period of time. To do this, they look at the potential of the business to earn the money, and they look at the operator's personal credit history and ability to operate the business profitably.

In order to demonstrate an ability to earn enough money to pay back the loan, the following materials are needed before you go to your lender:

Description of Your Business

- the type of business, in terms of an RV park, family campground, or condo campground;
- pictures of your campground that highlight its best features;
- location, with respect to cities, counties, and towns; and
- your objectives, detailed as they apply to the reason for your loan request.

Market Potential

Need for expansion. What is the market justification for the expansion? Why will this project succeed? How many more sites will be rented? How much more income will be generated, and what will be the added cash flow? Occupancy and turn-away records for the past three years will serve as documentation of the need for expansion.

A customer profile. Describe the market targeted for expansion. Give a brief description of the average camper customers by origin, preferred style of camping, occupational category, and so on.

The marketing program. Describe the marketing plan to attract the customers who are going to contribute the gross income that will make your project successful.

Financial Analysis

Investment costs. List investment costs and bids from contractors to show what it will cost to build the project.

Operating statements for the past three years. Demonstrate a track record of successful campground operation to prove that you can assume this expanded operation and manage it successfully.

Projected operating statements for three years. Project operating statements for three years, incorporating the new project into the operation, showing how the operation will increase in value as a result of your investment.

Property appraisal. The main purpose is to show the value of what is owned, in order to show how much can be pledged as collateral for the loan. Also provide a projected appraisal of the completed project.

Current operating statement. Produce a current operating statement to show how the business is doing right now.

Personal Information

Background. Provide a personal biography or resume. Describe your educational background and your work experience, with emphasis on those experiences that qualify you as a successful campground operator.

Personal balance sheet. Describe your personal finances, including other sources of income, debts, and assets.

Management capabilities. Describe anything that will document your ability to manage a campground successfully. A Certified Park Operators (CPO) certificate from ARVC or your state campground owners association is impressive. So are adult education seminars and workshop certificates.

If you do these things and the results look positive, you have a very good chance of getting a loan.

A Loan Request Presentation

When you go before your lender to present your loan application, you are in a personal selling situation. You need to sell the lender on making you the loan. To do this you must be a good communicator:

- Know exactly what you want to say.
- Rehearse your presentation several times before you go.
- Have your materials ready.
- Make your presentation simple and to the point.
- Speak clearly, be confident, and be enthusiastic.
- Dress well but conservatively for your banker.

If you get turned down, find out exactly why. Don't take it personally, or think that your campground is not good enough. There may be many reasons other than you, your proposal, or your presentation that your loan was turned down. It may be that they just aren't making loans at this time. Find out the bank's lending limits. They may not be able to make a loan, and often they won't tell you. If your personal credit rating was the reason for the rejection, find out why. There may have been mistakes made in the records.

The Valuation of Your Campground

How much is your campground worth? You've no doubt raised this question or been asked it on several occasions. Appraisals for tax purposes and transfer of ownership, fire insurance needs, and loan applications are the major reasons. This section explains how professional appraisers arrive at a value for a business enterprise, and how you can use the system to make decisions.

Three approaches are used in most business enterprise evaluations:
- income capitalization approach;
- market comparison approach; and
- replacement cost approach.

Income Capitalization Approach

Income capitalization appraisal is the process by which a present value is placed on the future returns of an investment. Such logic has made the income capitalization approach the main way to determine the value of real estate investment held primarily for the purpose of generating income.

The basic mathematical equation for determining the present value of a future income flow is:

Value = Income/Capitalization Rate

In this formula:

- Value (V) is the present value of the business.
- Income (I) is the net profit before debt service and depreciation.
- Capitalization Rate (R) is a rate of interest, expressed as a percentage, which is the combination of the value you place on your equity and the value the lender (bank) places on its money.

Once two of the values in the equation are known, the third can be calculated. For example, if Income (1) = $20,000, and the Capitalization Rate (R) = 10 percent, then Value (V) = $200,000 ($20,000 / .1 = $200,000).

In addition, the formula can be used to determine the income or cash flow. For example, if a campground is for sale for $400,000 and you want to earn a rate of 10 percent on your investment, you can determine what you should be able to earn, as follows:

V = I/R is the same as I = V × R, and

I = $400,000 × .10 = $40,000

In this case you would need to earn $40,000 cash flow. When considering the purchase of a campground, check on previous operating statements, which should be provided by the seller, and see how the net cash flow compares with $40,000.

The cash flow net income to use in the formula is the net income before deducting debt service and depreciation. To adjust your financial statement, you may need to add back in the depreciation that was deducted. This is because depreciation is an accounting entry used to decrease the amount of taxable income.

How is the capitalization rate determined? Suppose you have to take out a mortgage loan on your business, and you will be contributing some of your own equity into the campground. The capitalization rate can be computed by weighting the contributions of the lender and yourself. The following example shows how:

Financing source	Percent of total × interest rate = yield
Mortgage	.70 × .12 = .084
Your equity	.30 × .18 = .054

Capitalization rate = .138

Thus, the capitalization rate is .138 or 13.8 percent.

Market Comparison Approach

The market comparison approach is also known as the comparable sales and market data approach. It rationalizes that previous actions of buyers and sellers in the market is a good indication of value. It assumes that people will pay no more to buy or rent property than what it costs to buy or rent comparable or substitute property.

Three or more comparable (recent similar sales) need to be used. The sale price of each needs to be adjusted to account for differences in the campgrounds, as compared to the campground being appraised, since no two campgrounds are exactly alike. Examples of such differences include size and campground quality.

Replacement Cost

This method is used in determining value for fire insurance and property taxation purposes based on what it would cost to replace the facilities today, and then depreciating it for wear and obsolescence. It is based on the premise that one would pay no more than it would cost to replace it with a substitute.

An appraiser will use at least two of the three approaches and determine a value from each. Then, the appraiser using his or her best judgment, will adjust the average values up or down to arrive at an appraised value for the campground.

Highest and Best Use

An appraiser may place a value on a campground that is much higher than it would be considering the value determined as a campground. This is because there may be a more valuable use for the property. For example, the property may have a higher value (more appropriate) use as a residential condominium. Or the higher value use might be as a shopping center. Whatever the case, the appraiser should apply this principal to the appraisal process. At best, the appraisal process is a subjective process. It is a professional's best estimate of what the property will sell for on the market *today*.

The Problem of Skimming

A few words on skimming are in order at this point. Skimming is a practice in which a little of the cash received daily is not rung up in the cash register, so it does not get into the records and financial reports. Thus, the gross income is less by that amount, as is the net income, and consequently income and sales taxes do not have to be paid on it. This is usually why it is done. It is a felony, and it complicates making management decisions because it reduces income while expenses remain the same, thus throwing the operating ratios out of line.

Getting a loan is made more difficult because of skimming. The ability to get a business loan is based, to a large extent, on the ability of the business to show that it can pay the loan back through future earnings. The past financial track record has much to do with showing such capability. Therefore, to the extent that a business manager skims, the profitability will be that much less, and so will be the ability to borrow.

In addition, when a value is determined for selling purposes, one of the three bases for determining such value is the income approach just described. In this approach, the net income is capitalized at some capitalization rate. Suffice it to say here that the smaller the net income, the lower will be the value of the business. Thus, skimming is not only illegal, it makes management more difficult, reduces the ability of a business to get a loan, and lowers the value of the business enterprise.

Part

II

RUNNING YOUR CAMPGROUND

Some campers seem to be self-appointed experts in operating a campground. They seem able to give advice on any and all situations that may arise.

As stated in Chapter 1, Have You Got What It Takes? many skills and much knowledge are required in order to successfully operate a campground. The following section discusses major topics necessary to run a campground successfully.

Campground operations must focus on the camper guests and efforts to help them to have a meaningful and enjoyable camping experience. Paramount to this goal is the attitude demonstrated by the campground staff, commonly known as hospitality and service. "Moose" Speros, owner of Tiger Musky Resort and Campground, and secretary of the Wisconsin Department of Tourism, says, "There is one secret in this (tourism) business, and that's service!"

No small part of helping campers to have a good time is to provide recreational opportunities for them. This can range from the camping experience itself, all the way to a full-time recreation director and assistants offering a completely organized and supervised recreation program.

Recruiting, hiring, and training staff to exemplify the hosting or service attitude is another major segment of the campground operation. Making staff feel as though they are an important part of the overall campground operation is vital to a sense of satisfaction and self-worth as employees and leads to high levels of responsible productivity. Seasonal camping is a growing segment of the camping market, as many campgrounds have found profitable operations in marketing to and serving seasonal campers.

Offering a camping experience includes an exposure to risk and liability. Unfortunately, accidents do happen in campgrounds. Therefore, you need to know about liability and risk, how to reduce exposure to risk and accidents, and how to handle emergencies when they do occur.

Running the front desk, the central nervous system of the campground, requires organization, efficiency, and above all, a service attitude. Closely associated with the front desk is often a store operation. It needs to be run as efficiently as possible to serve your campers' needs and to be a contributing profit center for your campground. The above topics are discussed in detail in the following chapters.

Chapter

11

CUSTOMER RELATIONS

When campground guests leave your campground feeling happy and satisfied, they will often return and bring others with them. This increases gross income and net profits. Remember, 96 percent of unhappy customers do not complain. For every complaint, 26 others have problems, at least 6 of which are serious. Most importantly, 1 unhappy customer will tell 9 or 10 others, and 13 percent will tell more than 20 others! Why do many campground guests not complain? Some feel it is not worth the time and effort. Others feel it would not do any good, and a few do not know how or when to complain.

Those who complain give you a chance to keep their business. Fifty-four to 70 percent of complaining campground visitors can be won back by resolving the problem they have complained about. Up to 95 percent will become loyal customers if their complaints are handled well and quickly. *(Note:* Much of the above information came from Leisure Systems, Inc., for which the author is grateful. The numbers quoted came from surveys conducted by Technical Assistance Research Programs, Washington, D.C.)

Let's look at the positive by finding out what customers want, providing it for them, and avoiding the complaints and unhappy experiences.

What Do Campers Want?

Campers are people just like you when you are away from home, who like to enjoy a few hours, days, or weeks in your campground. These campers are probably no better or worse than your own neighbors visiting elsewhere. They arrive at your campground sometimes unfamiliar with the setting, often tired from a long drive, or frustrated by poor weather and traffic conditions. They are anxious to start their vacations. They may not respond well in unfamiliar circumstances because they already feel under pressure. Understanding this can make you and your staff more responsive to their behaviors and more able to anticipate their needs.

For example, when camper parties arrive, one or more may need to use restroom facilities right away. Perhaps the kids have been fighting and need to get away from each other. The same may be true for the parents. The family pet may need to run immediately also. The last thing they need is more stress at the registration desk.

Documented Camper Desires

Results of camper surveys conducted by the Recreation Resources Center, University of Wisconsin-Extension, indicate that the most important things campers look for in choosing a *campground* are:

1.	recreational activities;
2.	cleanliness;
3.	bathroom facilities; and
4.	good campsites—spacious, level, well-drained, and shaded.

Campers looking for a *campsite* gave similar responses:

1.	cleanliness;
2.	bathroom facilities;
3.	sites—spacious, level, well-drained, and shaded; and
4.	recreation activities.

Although there may have been confusion as to whether the questions related to choice of campground or campsite, the results are very clear about what is important to campers.

Surveys also suggest that these needs are not always met during campers' experiences. Leisure Systems, Inc., reports that the most common complaint of campers, next to dirty bathroom facilities, is the behavior of campground personnel. The message is pretty clear. Campers want to be treated well, as we all do. You do not want to be treated brusquely or impersonally. Neither do your campers.

Friendly Service Attitudes

A service philosophy shows up in a campground in many different ways, not just in the attitude and behavior of camp staff. Such things as overall campground appearance, design, signing, campground rules and policies, facilities, and, of course, the attitude and behavior of the staff can make a "user-friendly" campground.

Appearance

Imagine you're a camper in your campground. What does your campground look like? Is it attractive? Can you honestly say it looks like a nice place to go camping?

The front entrance should look generally neat, uncluttered, clean, and attractive. The front office should also look cheerful, clean, uncluttered, and welcoming. More specifically, it should look freshly decorated with warm colors. The front counter should be clear to allow space for camper registration and store checkout.

Outside, the trees and shrubs should be pruned, and of course, the grass should be kept neatly mowed. Flowers are attractive in front of the office, around the front entrance sign, and along the front entrance. The front entrance sign should look freshly painted with attractive colors. The entrance road, as well as others in the campground, should be graded and free of dust and potholes, and if hard surfaced, it should be kept in good repair. The entire front entrance should be well landscaped.

Lighting should be adequate, especially on walkways to service facilities. It should be warm, not bright and cold, especially in camping areas.

Clear, Friendly Signs

Your signs, both within and outside your campground, should look attractive and have friendly messages on them. They should be easy to see and easy to read and understand. There should not be more signs than are necessary.

The messages should be creative and state the campground rules and policies in a *positive* manner. For example, the message should state: *Please use walkways* instead of *Keep off the grass*. Another example is: *Please use waste containers* instead of *No littering*. A statement made at a recent campground convention describes basic human nature: *Tell them they can't, and they will.*

Proper grammar and correct spelling are also important. Many people don't care, and others won't know the difference. A few campers will notice, however, so make sure proper grammar and spelling are used in sign messages.

Positive Policies and Rules

The service philosophy—or perhaps more significantly, the lack thereof—is found in the campground rules and policies. It is especially evident in how they are stated. A campground rules statement is usually given to campers at registration. It is often attached to, or on the reverse side of, the campground map that shows campers how to find their assigned sites.

Campground rules, like most laws, arise out of efforts to solve problems or to prevent their recurrence. A sign in a restaurant revealed a typical problem. It stated: *Children not allowed to leave their seats.* Obviously, the restaurateur had a problem with parents letting their kids run around the dining room.

139

Wouldn't it be more effective to just politely talk to parents who allow their kids to run around? Parents for whom the rule is meant probably won't follow it, even if they do see it. A strong service philosophy helps to avoid such occurrences.

Just as you can become frustrated with all the rules, regulations, and laws you must live with, campers get frustrated with too many campground rules. Rules and policies are necessary for the safe and smooth operation of your campground. Your emergency procedures are absolutely essential. Rules relating to security, swimming, and payments are also essential. But creating a new rule as a knee-jerk reaction to a single problem situation may damage the friendly atmosphere of your campground more than it helps in the management of your campground.

Clean, Safe, Convenient Facilities

Campground facilities can be user-friendly or unfriendly. Consider for example, the toilet/shower facility. The entrance door should be easy to open and should close automatically, but not slam with a loud bang.

The lighting should be adequate, warm, and pleasant. There should be heat on chilly mornings and moisture control in humid conditions. The air should be clean, pleasant smelling, and insect free. Provisions for adequate privacy should be made. A private changing room in front of each shower stall should have raised mats to keep clothing dry when changing. Adequate toilet stalls with easy-to-use door locks and adequate visibility screening from the outside are important.

Sinks should be large enough and easy to use. Ample hooks and shelving around the sinks make it convenient to place towels, clothing, and toilet articles while cleaning, shaving, and so on. Adequate, working electrical outlets should be present for hair dryers, curling irons, and shavers.

Few camping experiences are less pleasant than getting ready to step into the shower and discovering that a coin is needed to turn it on, or misplacing your coin. Or perhaps worse is getting halfway through a shower and having the water shut off without the necessary coin to complete the shower.

At the very least, coin-operated showers should be easy to operate. There should be change machines nearby, and campers should be told at registration that there are coin-operated showers so that they can plan to have change ready. This information should be in the handout materials given to campers at check-in. As a camper, I believe coin-operated showers are user-unfriendly. Automatic push-type valves perform the same function. Any additional water heating cost should be added onto the site rate instead.

Such user-friendly facilities, or lack thereof, go a long way in telling the campers how much they're wanted at a particular campground.

Your Operational Critique

Carol Bialkowski, in a *1989 Club Industry* magazine article entitled, "Service—Going Beyond Amenities," states, "There is no easy way to attain high-end service. It is the natural result of a service-minded culture, which requires time and devotion to build. The logical first step is the mission statement, which needs to reflect senior management's service philosophy."

She goes on to quote the mission statement of Green Valley Athletic Club, in Henderson, Nevada:

We are committed to:

1. An obsession for cleanliness,
2. Enthusiastic (sincere) hospitality,
3. Honesty and integrity,
4. Flexibility (in handling member and guest requests), and
5. Enthusiasm for serving others.

The mission statement closes with, "Let there be no mistake about it: We are service professionals! Every action we take and every judgment we make is with the welfare of our members and guests first in mind."

Finally, she quotes management consultant Peter Burwash, noting that once the service philosophy is articulated, it needs to be instilled in employees: ". . . the real purpose of the boss is to serve the employee, and the purpose of the employee is to serve the customer . . . When that happens, the bottom line automatically takes care of itself."

Set the Example

Your family and staff may behave just as you behave. They'll also reflect the same attitude you reflect. Making jokes about your crazy campers privately with your staff may be fun at the time, but it may be costly in the long run if your staff develops a bad attitude toward campers. *Your* behavior at the front desk in registering campers, selling reservations over the phone, and dealing with camper complaints should set the example for your staff.

Hire Good-Natured People

Training staff to have a service philosophy is very difficult, especially if they aren't naturally good-natured and friendly. A few quotations from E. M. Statler (1917), founder of the famous Statler hotel chain, stress this point:

From this date you are instructed to employ only good-natured people; cheerful, pleasant, who smile easily and often. This ought to go for every job in the house, but at present I'll insist on it only for people who come in contact with guests.

You want to lessen complaints, don't you? You want your organization to be more efficient, don't you? Well, I've been studying the situation for months, and I'm convinced that it will help solve several problems we have—of complaints, of competition, of handicaps we've had in certain spots. Not immediately, perhaps; not tomorrow, or the middle of next week; but there will be noticeable improvements just as soon as it gets going.

It isn't enough to be courteous to 74 patrons and pert with the 75th. It won't do to be cheerful 58 minutes of the hour and disgruntled the other two. It isn't sufficient for 10 employees to give service, and the 11th to go slack on his job.

In another hotel another clerk may have sold the guest just as comfortable a room, another bellman may have handled his bag just as deftly, another waiter may have served his piping hot dinner just as promptly, but the thing that made the impression on the guest was that these latter employees seemed GLAD TO DO IT, they seemed interested in him personally.

Gracious service means more than "perfect" service. The guest will wait an extra minute for his chops if the waiter brings him a newspaper and explains the delay pleasantly.

Every hotel employee is a salesman. He must satisfy customers with the only thing he has to sell—service—and he must please them with the way he sells it. I believe that a majority of the complaints in a hotel are due more to the guest's state of mind than to the importance of the thing about which he complains.

Isn't the very same thing true in the campground industry today?

Train Your Staff

Hospitality/service training should be an important part of, if not the main part of, the training program for campground staff. It is advisable to begin here, because the service philosophy will have an impact on everything else in the training program. Publications that can help you to supplement your body of training information and materials appear in Appendix A at the end of this chapter.

Clean, neat clothing, which easily identifies staff members, good personal grooming, and an absence of smoking, chewing, and other offensive and distracting behaviors are characteristics of a professional staff.

Smiling is one of the most important behaviors and goes along with a friendly, cheerful, happy appearance and attitude. This attitude is contagious. The attitude of you and your staff really sets the stage for a happy camping experience. Remember to speak with a smile. Some telemarketing companies train their employees by sitting them in front of a mirror so they can see themselves smiling as they speak on the phone.

Calling customers by name whenever possible personalizes the conversation and indicates that you are interested in them. The importance of being polite and courteous cannot be overstated, and reflects your respect for the other person.

Being attentive and listening to the customer is very important but is difficult for many people. Try to make eye contact when campers talk to you, and stop whatever you're working on while campers are talking. These little things show that you are respectful and appreciate the camper choosing your campground.

Being talkative is not only good hospitality, it also helps in selling reservations over the phone and at the front desk. Use the time effectively to talk about your campground and its various unique qualities.

If you have more than one phone line, install a system that allows callers to be placed on hold. The following rules apply:

- Always identify your campground and yourself when receiving a call.
- Excuse yourself when placing someone on hold.
- Don't leave the person on hold more than 30 seconds without getting back to him or her with some information.
- Offer to call the person back if you have to put him or her on hold for an extended period.
- Thank the person for waiting.

Answering machines are becoming more common in household use. Consider using one if your phone is often unattended. By using an answering machine, you may generate some reservations that would have been lost otherwise.

The I-Love-New York Campaign

Several years ago the state of New York mounted a huge hospitality program that was very successful. Among the elements, of the program was a handbook of hospitality skills entitled, *How to Give Visitors a New York Welcome.* The key points of the program are summarized below, adapted to campground management where applicable.

Six Skills of Hospitality

1. Look enthusiastic.
2. Greet people.
3. Be diplomatic.
4. Be efficient.
5. Help solve problems.
6. Express pride in your region.

Look Enthusiastic

Hire people with zing. Smiles and friendliness will win happy, cooperative customers.

Greet people with a smile. Smiling takes little time or effort, and it tells customers that you care. It is the *most important* thing you can do.

Look right at people. If you don't look up, or if you're busy with other things, customers feel snubbed. When you're very busy, give at least a smiling nod to a new customer to show that you know they're there.

Be well-groomed. Your hairstyle and clothing can look sharp even when they're casual. Dress neatly and appropriately, never overdone or sloppy.

Stand and move with poise. Leaning, chewing gum, smoking, complaining, or yawning hurt your appearance.

Make a good first impression. Visitors are important to your campground, and you may be one of the first staff members they meet.

Greet People

You make your first impression with a friendly greeting. Every customer deserves your smiling hello.

Offer a friendly hello. *"Good morning"*, *"How are you?" "Good to see you!"* *"How's it going?"* There are dozens of ways to greet people. It's so much warmer than *"Your name, please,"* or *"May I help you?"* or *"How can I help you?"* (which usually gets a *"No, thank you; just looking"*).

Extend a pleasant compliment. Notice a customer's smile, clothing, child, hairstyle, tan, jewelry, sports gear, bright colors–anything about them that strikes you. Make a cheerful comment about a simple detail as you register people, take their orders, or give them directions. It must be sincere and natural and not forced. It's a routine breaker that sparks people's interest in you in return.

Ask an interested question. Ask campers how far they've driven, if it's their first trip, how long they've had that nice motor home, and so on. Such attention makes them feel welcome and shows that you care about them.

Remember names. People are pleasantly impressed when you remember their names after a long time, or even a short time. This is also true when their voice is remembered over the phone. Some people say they can't remember names. Such a skill can be learned by working at it. Work at associating the name with something in your memory. Say it back to the camper, and repeat it in your mind several times. Becoming good at this takes effort and is a challenge for many. But it does get easier, and eventually it becomes a habit.

Be Diplomatic

Diplomacy is your attitude of concern when you must disappoint people.

Use a gentle tone. Be polite and show concern with phrases like, "Would you be good enough to . . . " "We want to be fair to all of our campers, so would you please . . ." and "Because it's the state regulation, I have to ask you to please . . ."

End on an optimistic note. Never end a message with bad news. There should be some good news to go along with the bad. Offer a helpful suggestion, a likely alternative, or an offer to help and be reassuring.

Be Efficient

Efficiency contributes to your good mood and allows you more time with your guests. The lack of it contributes to your guests' bad moods when they have to wait for you to get something done. Fumbling, delays, mistakes, wrong directions, and a lack of information are signs of inefficiency.

Organize. Be sure people, supplies, furniture, and traffic patterns allow efficient movement. Establish an efficient routine at the front desk so that there is a minimum of delay when checking campers in at busy times.

Anticipate emergencies. Anticipate crowds, accidents, surprise weather, mechanical breakdowns, and shorthandedness. Having plans to deal with emergencies that may arise will minimize delays and discomfort.

Help Solve Problems

Campers come with high expectations yet often encounter hassles. Some are due to their own poor planning, whereas others are due to mistakes, poor planning, and so on, at the campground. Whatever the reason, use the problem-solving approach to restore their good spirits.

Listen. Let campers express their frustration without interruption. Don't be defensive, aggressive, or indifferent. Show concern as you listen.

Sympathize. Express understanding and concern for their upset, no matter who is at fault. Your caring will calm them.

Speak calmly. Speak conversationally and relax your body so they'll be more apt to relax. Be sure both of you understand the issue clearly. Ask questions, or state your campground policies if necessary.

Offer options. Avoid telling a person what to do. Suggest more than one course of action, even if one is clearly better or should happen first. In this way, you give people the opportunity of deciding on their own. Then they, not you, are responsible for their own decisions.

If you or your campground are at fault, offer something additional in camping or activities or campground store products. It's not enough just to substitute a right for a wrong. Offer a raincheck for future camping or another appropriate courtesy. If they want to leave, or you think it would be best for all concerned if they did leave, give them their money back and express an apology for their bad experience.

Express Pride in Your Region

Your campground's success depends in part on your area's ability to attract visitors. Help your campers learn about all there is to do and see in the area. Make enthusiastic recommendations to increase their enjoyment. Many campgrounds give slide presentations on attractions and activities in the area.

Visit your local attractions. Locals are often the last to discover their own local attractions. Take your employees to the local attractions in your area. Hold an open house, and invite the local community to your campground—it's an area attraction too!

Display visitor information. Create an attractive visitor information center or bulletin board at your front office. Even your regular campers will enjoy seeing local maps, events, calendars, photos, brochures, supper club menus, and guides on display.

Think like a hometown fan. Suggest what you think your campers would enjoy: scenic drives, good fishing, craft shops, antique shops, good restaurants, and factory outlet stores. *Help people while enjoying yourself!* That's the special fun of being in the tourism industry.

More Hospitality Tips

Motels and hotels have long provided amenities for the convenience of their guests. Such things as towels, washcloths, soaps, drinking cups, toilet and facial tissue, and so on are now taken for granted. In addition, shampoos, shower caps, body lotion, ice machines in the hallways, shoe shine cloths, sanitary napkin dispensing bags (a plumbing necessity), complimentary newspapers, and candies are becoming very common.

What can a campground owner do to make life more convenient for camper guests? Here are a few things you might want to provide:

- paper towels in restrooms;
- liquid soap dispensers over sinks and in showers;
- lists of and directions to local attractions;
- menus from local restaurants;
- garden rakes for cleaning sites;
- waste receptacles conveniently located around the campground;
- clean throw rugs in front of shower stalls; and
- a sign on the wall above the sinks reading, "If there is any toilet article that you need, please contact the front desk, and a complimentary product will be given to you, if not available in your store."

All these amenities have the effect of telling your campers you have concern for their comfort and convenience and making them feel wanted. It's that special touch that makes your guests return.

The use of the formal "How are we doing?" questionnaire in motels is a friendly gesture showing that the management wants to hear from motel guests. Why not try it in your campground?

I'm a Nice Camper ...

These words spoken by many nice campers may help you to stay on your toes!

> *You know me. I'm a nice camper. I never complain, no matter what kind of service I get.*
>
> *When I register at a campground, I'm thoughtful of the other person. If I get a snooty check-in person who gets cranky because I want to*

look at my campsite before making up my mind, I'm as polite as can be. I don't even believe rudeness in return is the answer. You might say I wasn't raised that way.

And it's seldom that I complain about the difficulty in finding my campsite, of the slope of the site which required more blocking than I had along with me to level my RV. And I didn't complain when the hot water turned cold on me when I was taking a shower, when I found the toilet paper had run out, and when my camper neighbors partied late the night before.

I'll go in the snack bar and sit and sit while the waitress gossips with her boyfriend and never bothers to see if my hamburger is ready. Sometimes someone who came in after I did gets my hamburger, but I don't say a word.

When I go in the campstore and get surly treatment and lack of sympathy with my browsing around, I don't make a fuss.

I never kick. I never nag. I never criticize. I wouldn't dream of making a scene, as I've seen other people do in public places.

I'm a nice camper! And I'll tell you what else I am—I'M THE CAMPER WHO NEVER COMES BACK!

That's my revenge for getting pushed around. That's why I take whatever they hand out . . . . I know I'm not coming back. It's true that this doesn't relieve my feelings at the moment, but in the long run, it's far more deadly revenge.

In fact, a nice camper like me, multiplied by others of my kind, can just about ruin a business. And there are a lot of "nice" campers in the world. When we get pushed far enough, we go down the road to another campground. We camp in campgrounds that are smart enough to hire staff who appreciate "nice" campers. Together, we cause the rude people to lose millions of dollars every year.

The one who laughs last, laughs loudest. I laugh when I see places frantically spending their money advertising just to get me back, when they could have held me in the first place with a few kind words and a smile. (Canadian Tourist Association)

Appendix A

Training Aids

1.   The National Association of RV Parks and Campgrounds (ARVC) has training videotapes and workbooks designed specifically to train camp ground employees in the hospitality area.

2.   *Courtesy Is Contagious: Guidelines for Improving Your Hospitality Skills.* Great Lakes Sea Grant Network.

3.   *Service Effectiveness Training.* An instructional handbook in cooperation with the National Recreation and Park Association and International Learning, Inc.

4.   *Customers: A Practical Guide to Profitable Customer Relations,* a bimonthly bulletin program by Dartnell, 4660 Ravenswood Avenue, Chicago, IL 60640-4595.

Many state tourism departments offer instructional materials on hospitality and customer relations. Check with your state tourism office.

Chapter

12

RECREATIONAL ACTIVITIES

Campgrounds offer a complete range of camping activities, from relaxation to aerobic activity. Camping, by its very nature, is a recreation activity. The basic elements of a campground—the campsite, the great outdoors, and the presence of other campers—provide the setting for recreation. Why offer recreation opportunities other than the campsite itself? There are many reasons, some of which are listed below:

- to make the campground unique, to set it apart from others;
- to make the campground more attractive to campers;
- to keep up with, or get ahead of, competition;
- to establish additional profit centers;
- to respond to the requests of campers;
- to create a greater sense of belonging on the part of the campers.
- to reduce vandalism—campers at play do not have as much time to get into trouble; and
- because of a belief in the values of recreation, including enrichment of family life, self-renewal, enhancement of social relationships, physical well-being, emotional stability, relief of tension, and a renewal of the human spirit. (Harrison, 1989)

Past camper surveys have asked campers, "What is most important when choosing a campground?" Most campers suggested campsites, bathrooms, cleanliness, recreation activities, general appearance, and location as their first and second choices.

Campground recreation can be planned or unplanned. If you only provide the opportunity for recreation, it's unplanned. The horseshoe pits, the swimming pool, and the volleyball court by themselves provide the opportunity. If you conduct a horseshoe tournament, a water olympics, or a volleyball tournament, the recreation is planned and involves leadership (Harrison, 1989).

How Much Recreation?

How do you decide which recreation facilities and activities to offer? The decision depends on a number of considerations, several of which are listed below.

- Number of attractions, events, and other activities in the area of your campground.
- Your occupancy level. Do you need to increase your business?
- Campers' length of stay. More activities need to be offered for those campers who stay for longer vacations than for those who just stay overnight, or for the weekend. In fact, your recreation program can be a tool for increasing the average length of stay.
- Opportunities for do-it-yourself recreation. Are there lakes and rivers that provide opportunities for fishing, boating, and sailing? Is there a public forest or park providing resources for hiking, hunting, nature study, and bird watching? If the answers to these questions are gener ally positive, you may not need to provide more recreation opportunities.

If the answers are negative, then you may want to consider providing your camp ers with at least a few recreational options. If you're not sure, you may want to survey your campers to find out what they want in recreation activities, or if they are happy with your current offerings.

Appropriate Activity Choices

You have two broad choices regarding the type of activities you have to offer. First, you can offer just what the campers request via suggestions, survey results, or even complaints. Or you can provide a shot of creativity and give them some activities they haven't experienced before. This adds some "spice" to the program. You or the recreation director needs imagination and the ability to sense the way your campers will react to new and innovative activities.

Your campers make a difference in the kinds of activities you should offer. If you have a family campground, you obviously will want to focus on family activities. In fact, if you have a family campground you have an obligation to society to provide all you can to enhance family togetherness: "The family that plays together stays together."

Which activities to offer also depends on the weather. Active programs are good in temperate climates, but more passive types of activities are appropriate on hot, humid days and during inclement weather. If you have natural surroundings, nature-oriented activities are always appropriate.

Campgrounds offer recreation activities ranging from simply the camping activity itself, to a complete program. For example, Donald Thorns, general manager of Point Sebago in Casco, Maine, says their staff offers 50 to 60 activities per day, with a recreation staff of 35 counselors. This staff also offers evening entertainment in the waterfront restaurant. On two weekends (in June and September) they offer "Pirates of Sebago," featuring buried treasure hunts and battles on the high seas with Bluebeard himself pilfering ships and villages. The activities and cast keep the entire family entertained.

Recreation Program Promotion

Don't leave out the important step of informing your campers about the activities you offer. Don't make your recreation program the best-kept secret in your campground. As campers register, it should be made obvious what activities they can participate in during their stay. Signs in your front desk area, bulletin boards located in the campground, and a handout sheet given out at check-in are good ways to spread the invitation.

Don't assume they'll read one handout or see a notice on the bulletin board and know all about your recreation program. They may be thinking about something else at the time or get distracted in some way. If you have a recreation director, he or she should be enthusiastic about the activities, should be constantly promoting them, and should be telling campers about them.

Low-Cost Activities

Following is a listing of low-cost recreation activities for you to consider offering, along with comments on how the activities might be organized. Appendix A lists two excellent publications on recreational activities. There are some descriptions of sports facilities at the end of this chapter, along with a contest/ tournament form. Keep in mind that the following are low-cost suggestions. More sophisticated and expensive variations can also be implemented, and sometimes this changes the game considerably.

Softball or baseball

Softball is a very popular sport. Do you have a fairly level piece of land that isn't being used? Then brush it if necessary, level it, pick up the rocks, and start mowing it. Softball and baseball field dimensions are shown later. A backstop isn't absolutely necessary, but it is better to have one. It can be built by setting 4-by-4 or utility poles in the ground and attaching some kind of wire mesh fencing to them (see Appendix C for field diagrams for softball and baseball).

Volleyball

Volleyball requires a space of approximately 30 feet by 80 feet. Set two posts in the ground to hold a net 8 feet high (see Appendix C for a court diagram). Volleyball can be played on grass, but often young people like to play the game barefoot in sand. An old garden hose makes a nice court boundary. Varying skill levels can be set up if campers get serious about playing competitively.

One interesting variation is to play it in water, perhaps a small distance from the shoreline on a gently sloping shore. Taller persons play in the deeper water, and shorter persons play nearer the shore.

Tetherball

A ball, quite similar to a volleyball, is attached to a tough string, the other end of which is tied to the top of a post about 6 feet high. The object of the game is to wrap the string around the post in your direction by hitting the ball with your hand. The other person tries to do the same in the opposite direction (see Appendix C for a diagram).

Basketball

Basketball can be played half court with one basket, or full court with two baskets. It requires a fairly level, hard, and smooth surface on which to run and dribble the ball. Make sure there are no obstructions sticking out of the ground. Encourage your seasonal campers to bring their own basketballs (see Appendix C for a court diagram).

Shuffleboard

Shuffleboard requires a very smooth and level concrete surface about 50 by 5 feet. Equipment consists of the court (dimensions shown at the end of this chapter), two sets of wood discs, and a cue (a long-handled stick slotted on one end) for each player. The equipment may need to be checked in and out to keep from getting lost. Play may need to be supervised in order to minimize damage to the equipment. Scoring equipment is also nice to have available (see Appendix C for dimensions and layout).

Horseshoes

Horseshoes is a good activity for people of any age. Horseshoe courts are easy to install. The court is approximately 50 feet in total, 40 feet between stakes for men, 30 feet for women and children. It's nice to have clay courts, but it is not required. The pits must be maintained, as holes tend to form in front of the stake and the stakes tend to lean toward the direction of the throw. A backboard about 4 feet behind each stake, and 6 to 12 inches high is nice for stopping rolling horseshoes and loose dirt. (Court dimensions are shown in Appendix C at the end of this chapter.)

Horseshoe tournaments are easy to organize. Simply have people sign up for a given time, and write their names on a single elimination form, shown at the end of this chapter in Appendix C. A low-cost prize makes it a little more interesting and fun. Depending on the age of players, suggest that the losers buy the winners a six-pack of soda or beer, which will increase your store sales.

Golf Tournament

If several of your campers play golf and you have a golf course nearby, golf tournaments might generate some interest. Have players sign up for a specific time to meet so that they can get to know each other and fill out a tournament form (single elimination). Here, as in horseshoes, players can compete as singles or as partners.

Badminton

Badminton requires only 20 by 40 feet of space with a grass surface. Nets, rackets, and birds are fairly inexpensive but also quite fragile. A small rope may do in place of a net. You can tear up an old sheet and tie narrow strips of the sheet to a rope to serve as a net. You may want to have a check-out system for the rackets and the birds, using a deposit system to ensure their return to the front desk. (A court diagram is shown in Appendix C at the end of this chapter.)

Ping-Pong and Table Tennis

This is an excellent evening or rainy day activity. Equipment consists of the table/court (5 by 9 feet), a net, at least four paddles, and ping-pong balls. The plywood or other material for the table (5/8-inch minimum thickness) can be purchased at a local building center, along with 2-by-4s for making the legs and support. It may require some supervision to minimize damage to the equipment. Tournaments may easily be organized, if there is interest. Avoid having slippery floors in order to reduce the risk of someone getting hurt.

Bingo

Almost everyone knows how to play bingo, and many enjoy playing it once in a while. You may have a camper who enjoys organizing the game, or calling the numbers. Be sure to check on your state's gambling laws concerning the collection of money and distribution of prizes. You should do this for any competitive activity.

Fishing Contests

Holding a fishing contest is always fun and adds excitement and interest if fishing is popular in your area. Winners are usually chosen by size and species of fish they catch. Variations include contests for different species on different weeks or weekends and offering panfish contests for kids. Pictures should be taken to further recognize the winners and to use in promoting your campground at your sport show booth, in your brochures, in ads, and in newsletters.

A good way to enhance fishing opportunities is to place fish attractors, made of brush piles, cribs or other materials in the water. These will attract small fish, panfish and predators that feed on the smaller fish. These can be marked with buoys so people can find them easily.

Hiking and Nature Walks

You can develop a very interesting hiking trail by simply brushing out, mowing, and designating a meandering trail through a wooded area, or an area allowed to grow wild. Signing trees, shrubs, flowers, and geologic formations by their common name will add interest. A fancier description might include the scientific name and information about where it is found, how it grows, and how large it is at maturity.

If you want a more sophisticated nature trail, make arrangements with a botany or naturalist student at a nearby college to identify and describe the plants for you. A free weekend of camping, plus a small fee will usually cover their needs.

To keep sign costs at a minimum, the sign need only contain the common name and an identification number. The rest of the information can be printed on a low-cost handout, copied, and given to the camper. You can also offer guided nature walks, directed by a naturalist on your staff.

Area Attractions

Some campgrounds make regular slide presentations of things to see and do in the area. Holding the slide show is itself an activity. If you are in an area where there are many things to see and places to go, this may take care of most of the recreation needs of your campers. You can provide a bulletin board or brochure rack with information about attractions and activities in your area. This rack can also include information and/or menus on nice restaurants and clubs in your area.

Movies and Videotapes

Videocassette recorders (VCRs) have replaced 16-mm movies, and are a common entertainment appliance in many American homes. You may want to enclose the TV and VCR in a finished plywood box for protection and place it in the recreation room. It could also be suspended from a wall or ceiling. These are excellent for rainy-day and nighttime activities.

Hayrides

Get a flatbed wagon and tow it with a small tractor to give people rides at scheduled times. You could also use horses for an authentic hayride. It is especially pleasant if you have someone to lead the group in singing along the way. Be sure to check your liability insurance, and the corresponding cost, for such an activity. This cost can be offset by selling rides to college or church groups.

Building a wagon box with 3-foot sides and seats built into the sides ensures that people won't sit facing the outside with their legs hanging over the edges of the flatbed. This helps campers to avoid being injured if the wagon passes too close to fixed objects. Portable or built-in stairs are helpful for people getting on and off the wagon.

Bicycle Trail Rides

If you're into bike riding, consider taking your campers on a bike hike in your area. You can be as sophisticated as you want to—including picnic lunches and even overnight camp-outs. You might extend this activity to other groups as well.

Horseback Trail Rides

If there is a riding stable in your area, you can easily organize a horseback trail ride for your campers. You may even include the operation within your campground as a profit center. Be sure to check on your liability insurance. Horseback riding is one of the largest liability exposures of all recreation activities.

Canoe and Tubing Trips

Campgrounds have found canoe and tubing trips to be successful recreation activities to organize. You can include a box lunch and transportation, depending on your situation. Realistic fees for such activities can be charged.

Religious Services

Sunday morning religious services are quite popular. Local clergy are often willing to come to a campground, as are seminary students. Offerings can be collected and given to the clergy person to use in a local or other outreach project.

Campers might also be attracted to a vesper service, a service usually including some camp songs or hymns, a scripture reading, and a prayer or two. It can be conducted by your local clergy, a member of your family, or a camper family member. It can be held around a campfire or on the waterfront overlooking the water at sunset.

Campfire Activities

Campfire activities require only a fire ring; campfire; logs, benches , or picinic tables for seats; long sticks; marshmallows; and someone who can lead the group in singing. These are good intergenerational activities for getting campers together to meet others and have fun.

Cards, Checkers, Chess, and Other Games

These are good games to have available for rainy-day activities. You may want to check these games out on a first-come, first-served basis.

Balloon Toss Games

The balloon toss is an outdoor, warm weather activity. Fill balloons about one-third full of water. Have people dressed in swim wear pair off and form two lines facing each other. Give the water-filled balloons to those in one line. Have them stand about a yard away from their partners. At a given signal, have all campers toss the balloons to their respective partners. Then tell each player to take one step backward, and at the signal, toss the balloons back to their partners. Keep repeating this process. When a balloon breaks, the pair is disqualified The pair with the last unbroken balloon is the winner. Ask the participants to pick up the broken balloons when the game is over to avoid a tedious clean up.

Trivia Contest

Develop a set of questions that are not too difficult to answer. The questions may include subjects such as sports, camping, and nature. Give players ample time to answer their questions. Award the winners a prize, such as your campground bumper sticker (a good promotional idea). It's a good rainy-day activity.

Scavenger Hunt

To hold a scavenger hunt, design a set of instructions that lead to a certain destination in your campground, with clues to successive locations en route to the final destination. Each team gets a separate set of directions. Place the prize at the final destination. You might award a watermelon, which can then be shared with all of the players. It's a fun activity for small teams.

Crazy Hat and Clown Contest

This kind of contest works better if you let the campers know you're going to hold such a contest before they come to your campground so that they can bring costume materials from home. Dressing up is fun for all ages!

Hide-a-Sweatshirt Game

Hide a campground sweatshirt or T-shirt somewhere in your campground. Leave clues in various places in your campground. The winner gets to keep the shirt.

Watermelon Toss

Grease a round watermelon with something like petroleum jelly. Then toss it in the water, and let players compete to bring it out of the water. The winner is the one who successfully retrieves the watermelon. Young teens love this game. Afterwards it can be cleaned off and eaten by the participants.

Treasure Hunt I

A treasure hunt for kids is a good way to get rid of store items that haven't sold well. Separate the kids into age groups: 4 to 7, 8 to 13, and 14 and above with adults. Teams can also be made up of families. Hide the objects in obvious places. Turn everyone loose at the same time to find the items.

Treasure Hunt II

Another version of a treasure hunt is to pile a large bag of wood chips or similar material on the beach, or some appropriate area, and mix with if a dozen rolls of pennies or wrapped candy. Use wood chips made from soft wood that will minimize slivers. This game will keep kids busy for hours.

Puzzles

Using a jigsaw, make a puzzle with large pieces. You might use a large map of your campground or of your state. Then hide the pieces around the campground. To protect your campers' privacy, don't hide the pieces in the camping area.

Yard Sales, Flea Markets, Auctions

These can be very popular, especially with your seasonal campers. You might hold one near the road and open it to the public. You might charge a small fee for a picnic table to defray promotional costs. If you open it to the public, keep it out of your camping area so the activity doesn't disturb your campers who aren't interested in participating. Keeping it separate from your camping area also provides security for your campers. Some campgrounds contract with an auction agency, which conducts the entire auction and brings the products to be sold.

Square Dances

Square dances are very popular in campgrounds. They can be held in your parking lot or on a dance floor. Amateur callers are sometimes adequate, but some groups may demand professional callers and high-quality dance floors. Some campgrounds are able to attract square dance clubs that bring their own callers and music.

Dance Bands

Big weekends and special celebrations are often good occasions for bringing in country/western, rock, or big band dance bands. Some campgrounds charge an admission or raise the site rental fee to offset the cost of the band.

Arts and Crafts

Many campers enjoy using their arts and crafts skills on camping trips. All that is necessary is an area in which to work, and shelf space for storing the craft materials and individual projects that are in process. Craft materials can be obtained at a very reasonable cost.

More sophisticated activities include an offering of classes by a skilled craft instructor, or at least a knowledgeable craft person in charge of the craft area, which includes getting out and putting away the craft materials.

The author knows of a resort that derives a major portion of its business from educational classes or workshops taught by nationally known painters, wood carvers, and photographers. Such workshops usually run for a week at a time. The attendee can bring his or her family to enjoy recreational activities while the workshops are being held.

Health and Fitness Activities

Health and fitness are important to most Americans, and some campgrounds have installed fitness centers as a camper activity. Depending on the equipment purchased, it is important to have an experienced person supervise the use of it.

Aerobics, both in and out of the water, are a popular activity. Classes can be offered on a regular schedule. A fee may need to be charged to cover the cost of the instructor. It is important to have an experienced or, if possible, a certified aerobic instructor to minimize liability for injury.

Pet Shows

This is a very exciting activity for kids as well as adults. Campers assemble with their cleaned and groomed family pets. A group of volunteer judges can perform the judging. Creative categories might include the happiest, friendliest, longest, shortest, biggest, smallest, longest or shortest ears, and so on. The object is to give every pet a prize. Pet shows, scheduled periodically, can be very enjoyable.

Doll Shows

Doll shows are run basically like pet shows, with different prize categories, of course. This works best when campers know in advance that a doll show will be held.

Ice Cream Social

Why not have an old-time ice cream social? Operators who find this successful, scoop the ice cream for their campers, and put the toppings out on a table for people to serve themselves and their children. A dollar or two charge per person will cover most of the costs.

Watermelon Seed Spitting Contest

On a hot summer afternoon, a watermelon seed spitting contest can be a crowd pleaser and doesn't take much effort to organize. Volunteer judges can identify the winners, and funny prizes will add to the fun. A variation includes eating watermelon in unusual positions.

Christmas in July

With a previous announcement, campers can decorate their campsites for a "Christmas in July" celebration. Prizes can be awarded in various categories.

A free camping weekend makes a good prize, as does 10 free games of mini-golf. Santa can arrive in any number of creative ways.

Children's Story Time

Gather your little campers together, and have someone read or tell children's stories. This provides mothers with a much-needed break and rests the kids as well.

Amish Bake and Craft Sale

Take advantage of your community resources. If you live among groups such as the Amish, encourage them to hold bake sales or craft sales in your campground. Just the horses and buggies and Amish dress alone are an attraction and are something for the campers to do and see. Discourage taking photos of them, as the Amish usually object.

Clean-Up Weekend

Repeat and seasonal campers enjoy coming to your campground in the early part of the season and may help you clean up your campground. They can be asked to bring rakes, paint brushes, and so on, or you can provide such equipment for them. It usually ends with a group meal. The campground furnishes the meat and beverages, and the campers each bring a dish to pass. This type of activity creates loyalty to your campground and can be lots of fun for everyone.

Graffiti Wall

Having a designated area for graffiti activity can keep other walls and surfaces clean. It also encourages campers to be creative, and it keeps them busy. Paint it once in awhile to let them start over.

Water Olympics

Water olympics can involve many of the games played at the waterfront. Examples include a tug-of-war in the water or on the beach, canoe races, tipping or swamping canoes, and seeing which team can get the most people in a canoe before swamping it. A lifeguard may be appropriate to manage the event.

Photo Clinic and Contest

Many campers are camera buffs. Lessons may be provided in photography. Contests can be arranged, categories established, and prizes awarded. Volunteer judges may pick the winners. This could be a source of pictures for your brochure or sport show photo album.

Stargazing

Stargazing can include a campfire presentation on star and constellation identification, calculating astronomical distances, and discussions about the galaxies. This can be followed by identification of stars and constellations. It needs to be done in an area that is completely dark. Some campgrounds have telescopes for better viewing, but they are not necessary.

Bocci Ball

Bocci (pronounced "bachie") ball is very popular in some areas. It is easy to learn, and can be played almost anywhere. The bocci balls are about the size of croquet balls. They are rolled underhanded, and the closest ball to the target scores the point each time the balls are rolled. The games are offered for sale where the sport is popular (in Minnesota, for example).

Mud Wrestling

Mud wrestling is a unique camping activity. All you need is a pit in the dirt filled with water and a garden hose to wash off participants after the wrestling is over. Winners may be awarded or have the privilege of purchasing a T-shirt with two mud handprints and an inscription.

Seasonals' Activities

Some campgrounds plan and coordinate special activities for seasonal campers, whereas others do nothing out of the ordinary for them. Some campgrounds help their seasonals plan their own activities. One campground schedules a "Treat Yourself" party at a nearby restaurant, complete with a band.

Guide Service

Campgrounds located in popular fishing and hunting areas may offer guide service to their campers. They may provide services themselves or make contacts with guides. Success is a large part of the fun of fishing and hunting, and guide services can improve campers' chances of success.

Creative Dramatics

Skit nights and puppet shows make excellent evening entertainment. These activities also give the participants a chance to be creative, and they keep them very busy.

Skill Activities

People enjoy learning to perform a new skill. Teaching people to swim, canoe, or cook outdoors are examples of skill instruction that are appreciated by campers.

Croquet

This game is played on a smooth lawn, about 50 feet by 100 feet. The court dimensions are shown at the end of this chapter (see Appendix C). It is fun for all ages to play. Playing can also be very sophisticated, with a groomed lawn playing surface and overhead lighting.

Giant Checkers

This game is played on an 8- or 16-foot concrete slab. The checkers can be made very inexpensively from sections sawed off the end of a log. (A diagram is shown in Appendix C at the end of this chapter.)

Tennis

A tennis court that offers reasonable or better quality of play is quite expensive. However, it could be provided on a level and hard dirt surface with two posts set in the ground to support the net. (Court dimensions are shown in Appendix C.)

The Best Activities for Your Campground

You want to entertain your camper guests and help them have a good time. Which planned and unplanned activities you offer depends how you personally feel about planning, coordinating, and leading the activities or getting others to lead the activities. If you don't feel comfortable leading the activities, they probably won't be very successful.

The kinds of activities you choose to offer also depends on your campground and the resources and facilities, on the activities available in the surrounding area, and on what your campers like to do.

Appendix A

Recreational Activity Publications

Woodall's Guide to Recreation Activities. 13975 West Polo Trail Drive, P. O. Box 5000, Lake Forest, IL 60045-5000, (800) 323-9076 or (847) 362-6700, FAX (847) 362-8776.

McEwen, Douglas, and Mitchell, Clare. *Fundamentals of Recreation Programming for Campgrounds and RV Parks.* Sagamore Publishing, 804 N. Neil St. Suite 100, Champaign, IL 61820.

Hultsman, John, Cottrell, Richard L., and Hultsman, Wendy Z., *Planning Parks for People*, Second Edition, Venture Publishing, Inc., 1999 Cato Avenue, State College, PA 16801, (814)234-4561, Fax (814)234-1651.

Appendix B

Tournament/Contest Form

Date _____   Game _____

_____

          _____

                    _____

_____

          _____

_____

                              _____

                              Winner

_____

          _____

_____

                    _____

_____

          _____

_____

Appendix C

Court and Table Diagrams

Source for all diagrams: National Recreation and Park Association

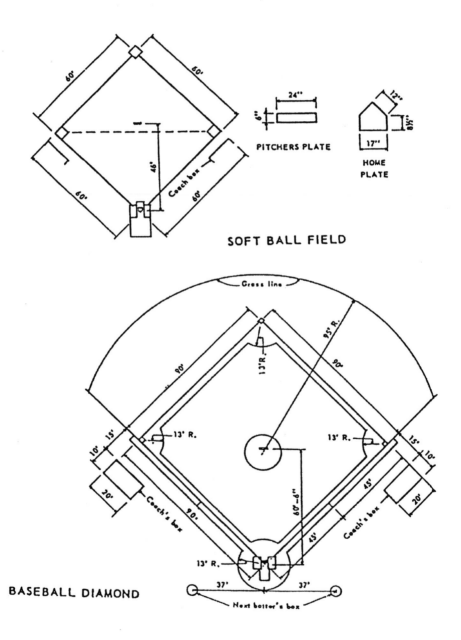

PITCHERS PLATE

HOME PLATE

SOFT BALL FIELD

BASEBALL DIAMOND

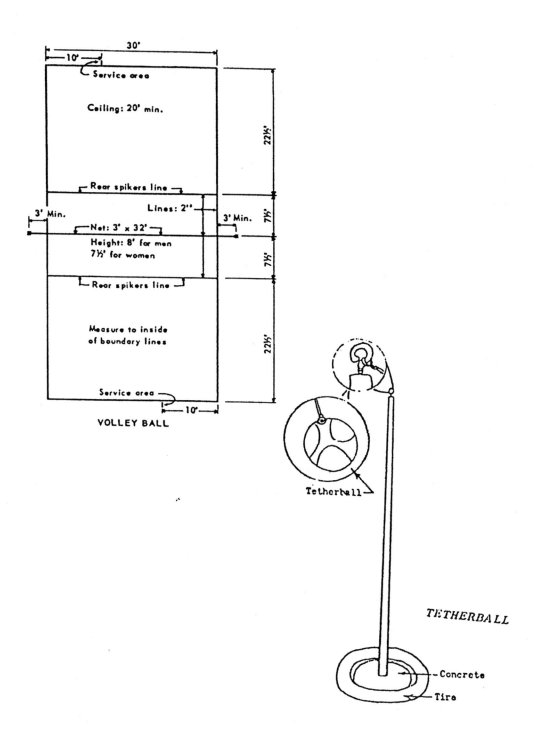

30'

10'

Service area

Ceiling: 20' min.

22½'

Rear spikers line

Lines: 2"

3' Min.

Net: 3' x 32'

Height: 8' for men
7½' for women

3' Min.

7½'

7½'

Rear spikers line

Measure to inside
of boundary lines

22½'

Service area

10'

VOLLEY BALL

Tetherball

TETHERBALL

Concrete

Tire

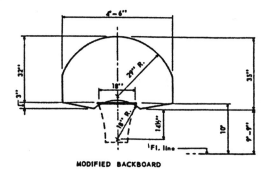

MODIFIED BACKBOARD

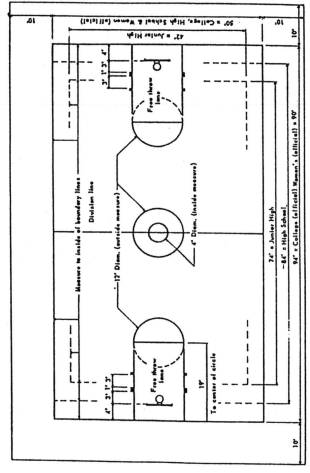

BASKETBALL COURT

166

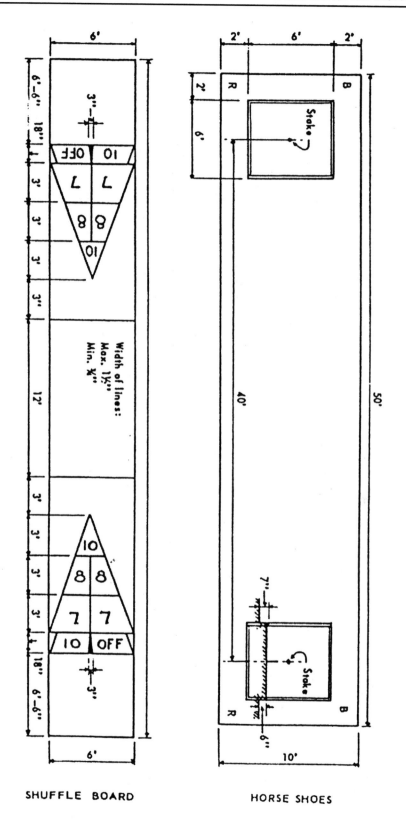

SHUFFLE BOARD

HORSE SHOES

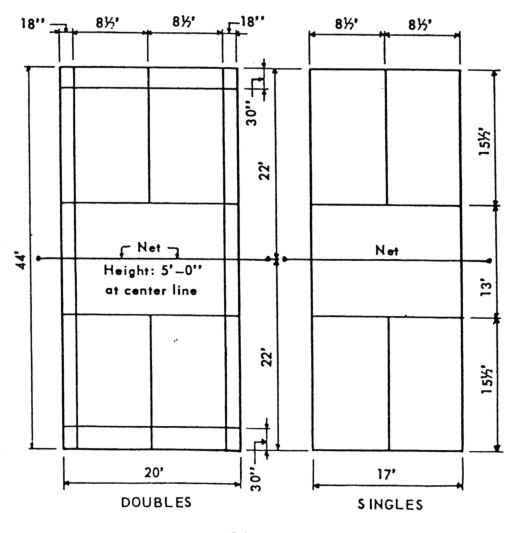

BADMINTON

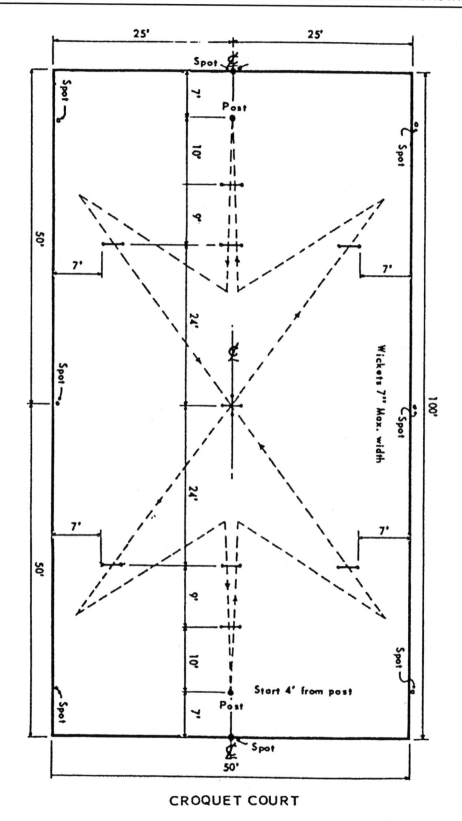

CROQUET COURT

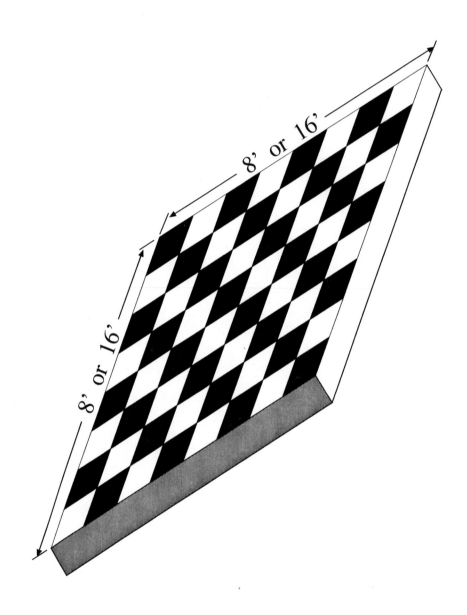

8' or 16'

8' or 16'

GIANT CHECKERS

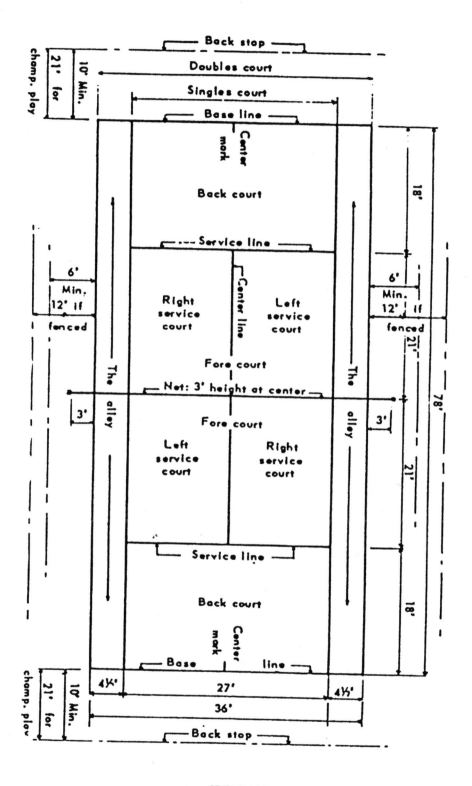

TENNIS

Chapter

13

STAFF MANAGEMENT

Personnel management has traditionally not been a high priority for campground operators, especially in small operations where there aren't many employees and where most of them work on a part-time basis, are seasonal employees, or are part of the family. However, the labor cost is a major operational cost, even in the small campground. Furthermore, your employees usually come in contact with your camper customers, and play a vital role in the service/hospitality function of your campground. They play key roles in hosting, creating a campground image, and providing customer satisfaction. It follows that the best possible effort should be made to get the most from these personnel salaries, and the best way to do that is through smart management of campground staff.

Why do you hire staff? *What* work needs to be done? *Who* is the best person to do it? *Why* is it being done? *How* is it to be completed? *Under what conditions* should it be done? These are basic questions you face as a personnel manager. This chapter deals with the principles of personnel management as they apply to the average campground operation.

Philosophies of Management

There are several attitudes toward labor in the typical campground business organization. Let's take a look at a couple of them.

Note: *Much of the following material was presented at the Wisconsin Campground Operators Short Course by A. Charles Wise, Area Business Agent, University of Wisconsin-Extension, West Bend, Wisconsin.*

Views Toward Workers

There are two different ways a manager can view employees. In one, managers assume that all employees dislike work. They think employees must be coerced and controlled into doing their jobs. This view holds that workers avoid responsibility, and won't volunteer to do anything extra. In the other view, managers assume that work is as natural as play. These managers believe that people will exercise self-direction, if given the opportunity. Other beliefs include: achievement is associated with commitment, people seek responsibility, creativity is shared, and human potential is only partially used.

Which View Do You Believe?

Many business organizations have a commitment to their employees that takes the form of a slogan, such as: *Our people make the difference,* or *People are our most important asset.* However, they sometimes go little beyond slogans. In terms of current strategic planning concepts, staff goals can be an integral part of the goals of the strategic management plan.

It is also important to treat employees the same way that they are expected to treat customers. Employees cannot be expected to treat customers with respect and consideration if they do not receive the same treatment from their employer.

Managerial Responsibilities

The campground operator/manager usually wears many hats. The following managerial functions must be performed:

Planning. The entire campground operation must be well-planned. The financial plan, the marketing plan, the long-range site plan, the daily operations, the maintenance plan, the emergency plan, the recreation program, the landscaping plan, the risk management plan, and the staffing plan are all the responsibility of the manager.

Organizing. The entire season's operations must be well-organized. The store, the front office, the recreation program, and the outdoor maintenance are a few notable responsibilities that should be organized.

Staffing. Deciding who does what job is the responsibility of the manager. Job descriptions, deciding how much can be done by one staff member, assigning duties to family members according to capabilities, hiring others according to capabilities needed, and decisions regarding volunteers all fall under the manager's area of responsibility.

Supervising. The campground staff must be supervised, some members more than others. Seldom will an operation run smoothly without such supervision.

Directing. The manager is the director and the leader of the campground operation. The manager has to direct the entire campground operation.

Controlling. Through overall observation of the day-to-day operations and regular evaluation of financial indicators in the financial statements, the manager controls the operation.

The Roles of Your Staff

Staff members fulfill at least these major roles:

- The staff is the spirit center of the campground. They set the tone and create the atmosphere for things to happen.
- The members of the staff reflect the values of the campground—the respect for people, the environment, the relationships.
- Staff members are communication agents of the campground. They reflect the campground objectives and attitudes in every action, deed, and word.
- The staff is the emotional barometer of the campground and can create a happy experience or a so-so experience.
- The staff can exercise a motivational influence on campers, as well as on the staff itself, through competency and creativity.

You can see that the campground staff is very important to the overall success of the campground operation, especially with respect to the marketing approach and the service image of the campground.

Staff Recruitment

Recruitment is identifying potential employees and getting them to apply for a job. Where do you find good employees? Some potential sources are listed and discussed below.

Current employees. You may try to rehire next year some of the people who are currently on your payroll.

Former employees. People who formerly worked for you may be good prospects later on, when they again become available.

Employee referrals. Current employees may refer people they know who could be potential new staff members.

Newspaper ads. An ad in the local newspaper is a good way to let prospective applicants know you are looking for new employees.

Schools and colleges. This is a good source for summer seasonal help. Schools may be especially useful for finding a recreation director or assistant manager if you contact colleges that have recreation, parks, and/or natural resource management programs. Such programs often have an internship program in conjunction with the curriculum or course program. This means a student may fulfill part or all of the internship requirement while working in your campground. Faculty in schools and colleges are also potential sources of good seasonal employees.

Campers. Many repeat or seasonal campers are potential employees for your campground. These campers may be student age or retirement age. Many campers are often interested in doing something to keep busy and are eager to help you.

Friends, relatives, and their children. Your own personal contacts are also sources of potential employees. You already know these people, so you can tell if they have the capabilities to be good employees. The disadvantage is that if they don't work out, it may be difficult to dismiss them.

Employment agencies. Both public and private employment agencies can be sources of potential employees.

The Hiring Process

How do you know if the person is right for the job? The knowledge and skills of the applicant should match the knowledge and skills required for the job. Before interviewing job applicants, a job description should be written, which contains the following information.

The Job Description

Job title. Titles should be short and descriptive of the job. They should be attractive to the person applying for the job. Examples might be "landscaper" for the outdoor helpers, and "receptionist" for front desk employees.

General responsibilities. A short narrative description of the job(s) to be performed tells the responsibilities. To whom is this position accountable? Who is the supervisor?

Knowledge/skills. What are the knowledge and skill requirements for the job? These can be included in any ads that are placed to serve as qualifiers for the job. In this way, you screen out applicants who should not have applied at all.

Specific tasks. What would you have the person in this job do on an average day of work?

Effect on end results. This section should briefly describe what the effect of this job is on the overall campground operation. What will be accepted when the job is done right?

Salary. It is good to state the salary or wage rate and employee benefits. In addition, some kind of bonus incentive is usually desirable. Some level above minimum wage will probably attract more qualified personnel.

The more accurate and specific the job description, the more helpful it will be in selecting the right people for the right jobs. An accurate job description will help to avoid misunderstandings between the supervisor and the employees.

Two personality characteristics are important to look for in anyone hired in a campground. One is friendliness. You are in the people business, and you should always try to hire friendly people. It is a characteristic that is very difficult—if not impossible—to teach to people.

The other characteristic is honesty. Knowing people ahead of time helps in identifying this characteristic. Hiring honest people will help to avoid many headaches and potential financial losses. *Always* ask for character references and *always* check them out.

The Job Application

For a few jobs, the job application form may not be necessary, but it can serve as a good screening device and thereby save needless interviewing time. It's especially important if you're hiring a manager or assistant manager for which you have advertised regionally or nationally.

The job application form should include the following: name, address, phone number, education, work experience, when the person is available for work, and references. Ask only questions related to the job. Be careful not to ask for information prohibited by the Equal Opportunities Act, such as age, religion, race, or marital status.

The Job Interview

The main purpose of the interview is to obtain more information to assist in the selection decision. However, it is also important to promote the job to the job applicant. Otherwise, the applicant may decide against the job when you offer it to him or her.

Be prepared before the interview. Assemble all your information ahead of time. Develop a set of questions that you plan to ask, and leave space on the page for comments you may want to note during or immediately after the interview. If you have an assistant manager or someone else who will be supervising the position, have him or her present at the interview to provide input into the decision.

Hold the interview in a setting that is comfortable, relaxed, and uninterrupted. Try to put the individual at ease by offering coffee or soda. Begin the interview with small talk. Discussing the task you just left to come to the interview might be interesting. You should briefly describe your campground, depending on what the applicant already knows about it. To get applicants started talking, ask them to describe their backgrounds as these relate to their qualifications for the job. You might also ask them why they applied for this job and how it fits into their lifetime career goals. Another frequently asked question is why they feel they are qualified for the job. The rest of your questions will depend on the particular job and will assist you in determining if you want to offer the applicant the job.

As stated earlier, in the course of the interview you should promote your campground and the job to the applicant. Tell him or her that your campground is a very enjoyable place in which to work because of the emphasis on good customer relations. This means everyone— guests and staff—are in a happy atmosphere, being friendly and courteous at all times.

Explain exactly what the applicant will be doing, if hired. Provide a copy of the job description. Go through it carefully to avoid later misunderstandings when the person comes to work. Give the applicant some idea of what to expect in the work schedule. Tell the applicant if you expect him or her to have a flexible work schedule—that is, if the work is completed early, the employee goes home early.

After completing the interviews, evaluate the individuals and rank the top two or three in the order that you would like to hire them. Guard against personal bias in your decision process. There are at least three dominant characteristics to look for: a willingness to learn, a willingness to work, and an ability to get along with others. In the campground, these are two more that should be at the top of the list, and they are friendliness and honesty.

Remember, even if the applicant does not want the job or you don't want to hire him or her, this person is still a potential camper customer.

Your Orientation and Training Programs

When your job offer is accepted, give all new employees a copy of your employee manual, tell them what day and time to come to work, and explain what type of dress you expect.

When employees report to work, orient them to the campground and their job. Set aside ample time, at least a half day. Choose a quiet, informal place, such as your family room if you live on the campground, or the campground lounge. Pick a time when the campground isn't busy, and when *you* aren't busy.

Introduce everyone, and provide name tags with first names that can be read across the room. Introduce your spouse, children, and family members and former employees who will be working in the campground this season. The reason for including them is that you no doubt have changed some policies and procedures since the last season.

Serve coffee, soda, juice, and snacks. Make everyone feel comfortable, relaxed, and generally at ease. Establish a caring relationship, and encourage new employees to ask questions. This is the beginning of your loyalty and team-building process. Employees are just like customers in that if you show them that you care for them, they will become loyal employees, work harder, cooperate more, sell your campground better, and do your recruiting for you. Most of all, they'll make your campers feel wanted and happy so your campers will become loyal repeat customers and seasonal campers.

It cannot be emphasized often enough that in dress, grooming, personality, and behavior, *you* are the example. You can't expect them to do it any differently than you do. Topics that should be covered in the orientation include, but are not limited to, the following considerations.

Objectives/Philosophy

First, you will want to share with all employees the objectives you have set for the campground for this year. Otherwise, they won't feel that they are part of a team with direction or goals to work toward. Whether it is a certain increase in camper volume, gross sales, or percent of occupancy, they've got to know what you're aiming for in order to help you attain it.

Closely related to objectives is the campground philosophy. The overall philosophy must be articulated to everyone. It helps everyone understand what you and your campground are all about. Much of this information may be found in your business plan. An example of a campground philosophy follows:

> *Our objectives are few. The most important of them is to make camping at Indian Trails the best camping experience our campers ever had. To do this we need to have a clean campground, friendly, courteous employees, and service. Always remember that the camper is the most important part of our business. (Employee Policy Manual of Indian Trails Campground)*

Types of Campers: Needs and Preferences

Your staff should be familiar with your marketing plan to the extent that they know the market segments toward which you are targeting your promotional efforts. They should know the anticipated needs of your campers. Perhaps a general description of your typical camper party would be informative. Your employees may then better understand your campground business, and will be better able to perform their job duties, including the anticipation of typical campers' needs.

Operating Procedures

The army calls it "standard operating procedure" (SOP). It's the way routine tasks are generally handled in your campground. You can even provide your own procedure manual.

Employee Benefits

The employee benefits that you provide should be explained, as they were in the job description or interview, along with pay periods, performance evaluation for pay increases, vacations, and so on.

Employee Obligations

Employees need to know what obligations they have regarding work schedules, advance notice expected for changes in work schedules, and advance notice expected if they decide to quit. This is a good time to tell them what they are expected to wear or that they are expected to be well-groomed, clean-shaven, and neat employees.

Safety/Emergency Procedures

This should be covered on the first day of work! Go through the emergency procedures to make sure everyone knows what to do if an emergency occurs.

Take everyone on a tour of your campground, and let each person look around and ask questions. Be sure to point out the fire extinguishers, and all other safety or emergency equipment and devices.

The above may give you ideas for an employee manual. A suggested outline for an employee manual is included in Appendix A at the end of this chapter. Your new employees will not remember everything you told them, so you'll have to tell them again. Have a written document available that they can refer to for guidance. You can refine it as you become more proficient in your campground operation. An example of what a typical orientation session might be like is included in Appendix A at the end of this chapter.

Training Aids

The Association of RV Parks and Campgrounds (ARVC) has a hospitality training program that includes a videotape, written trainer's guide, and a student "toolbook." It can be obtained by contacting the ARVC office at 113 Park Avenue, Falls Church, VA 22046-4308, phone: (703) 241-8801, fax: (703) 241-1004.

Staff Motivation

Supervision includes assuring that all the duties and tasks get completed. That may be the easy part. The hard part is motivating, disciplining, and training employees on the job. There is a theory that holds that employees motivate themselves. It is called the GRAPE theory and is based on the idea that all employees have a need for:

G rowth—some intellectual stretching;

R ecognition—of contributions and achievements;

A chievement—which offers a sense of personal satisfaction;

P articipation—in the work decisions that affect their jobs; and

E ffort—that contributes to the joy of accomplishment.

Another principle of supervision is that employee praise is done in public, and criticism is done in private. In fact, Jack Falvey of Intermark, a consulting company, says criticism is to be avoided at all costs. He says there is no such thing as constructive criticism, and all criticism is destructive.

"If you must correct someone," suggests Falvey, "never do it after the fact. Bite your tongue and hold off until he or she is about to do it again, and then challenge the person to make a more positive contribution."

If an employee is not performing as well as he or she might, it could be for these reasons:

- the person really doesn't have the ability;
- what is expected has not been made clear; or
- the employee has not been adequately trained.

Perhaps there is no better motivation than to recognize someone's good work. As Falvey says "the essence of good management is letting people know what you expect, inspecting what is done, and supporting those things that are done well." He provides the following example:

At Mary Kay Cosmetics, the budget for this year's legendary Dallas-based sales seminar was $2.5 million, and the attendees all paid their own expenses. If you are successful with Mary Kay you earn it, but when you do earn it everyone sure will know it when they see your pink Cadillac. Mary Ash has built a major corporation by recognizing the contributions of her employees. She doesn't solve problems, she just says thank you as often as she can, and in some of the most creative ways imaginable.

You don't have to spend much money to give recognition. Make it a point to tell every staff member what he or she has contributed each week, and how much you appreciate it. Set up informal visits with your staff. Listen and look to see what's going on. Find and reinforce strengths instead of problems. As a manager, your words and actions carry more weight than you realize. Just a little effort with these techniques will have an almost immediate effect. A concentrated, disciplined, and sustained thrust in these directions will produce incredible returns. Put positive notes on everything, and give them to everyone.

Many campgrounds hold special events for the staff. A party at the end of the season, a Christmas party, or a trip to a baseball game are all ways of showing your appreciation.

Legal Concerns

There is considerable legislation in place to protect employees. Be sure you are informed of it. The following points outline the areas about which to be concerned:

- pay for work performed;
- discrimination in pay, promotions, and working conditions on the basis of color, religion, or national origin;
- safe working conditions;
- social security, income tax, worker's compensation, and unemployment insurance contributions;
- federal, state, and local laws, including minimum wage, maximum allowances for board and lodging, and safety and health regulations; and
- the terms of the employment contract.

Appendix A

Employee Orientation Materials

Suggested Outline for an Employee Manual

1. **Introduction**
   - Welcome your campground staff.
   - State the philosophy of your campground, including your hospitality and service attitude.

2. **Describe a typical camper party**
   - Give a brief demographic profile, and explain what campers look for in services, facilities, and recreation activities.

3. **Describe your operating procedures**
   Include these points:

   - General areas of responsibilities; who's in charge of what
   - Work schedules, advance notice of change from regular shift
   - Hospitality and service attitude
   - Lost and found policy
   - Complaint handling procedure
   - Store clerk procedures

4. **Employee benefits**. List the things that you provide for your employees, including paydays, vacations, and any other employee benefits you offer.

5. **Employee obligations**
   These are a few personnel obligations:

   - Service attitude
   - Neat, personal grooming
   - Clean, presentable clothing (uniforms provided)
   - Regular, punctual attendance
   - Adherence to policies
   - Advance notice of resignation (two weeks)
   - Honesty

6. **Safety and emergency procedures**
   - Include a written emergency plan. (If you don't have one, write one). Spell out how you expect them to report any unsafe situations, such as loose or wiring, tripping hazards, missing lights, and so on. Detail what they should do when an emergency occurs. Such efforts may save someone's life.

7. **Shoplifting policy**

   - Spell out exactly how staff should act if they find someone shoplifting.

8. **Termination**

   - Describe under what conditions an employee will be terminated and how she or he will be warned prior to such an event.

Example of an Employee Orientation Meeting

The typical orientation meeting might proceed as follows:

The philosophy of this campground is that the camper is the most important person in this campground. This campground exists only because of the camper. Without campers we have no function.

We want to have a friendly, helpful attitude at all times. If a camper stops you in the campground and asks you a question, that question immediately becomes the most important part of your job.

We are all expected to be well-groomed, clean-shaven camp workers, who wear clean, neat clothing with the campground T-shirt when we come to work. The most important thing to wear is a smile! This is a place where people come to have fun, be happy, and build fond family memories that last a lifetime.

Why is all this important? It's important because it's the only way we're going to achieve our campground objectives. Last year we had an overall occupancy of 45 percent and 25 seasonal campers. This season we want to raise our occupancy to 50 percent and attract 10 new seasonal camper rentals. I think this is a reasonable objective to shoot for, but it's going to take everyone working hard and together as a team. We can do it. I know we can.

But to do this we need your help. You are our goodwill ambassadors. Whenever you are in the campground, regardless of the job you are doing, looks and behavior are extremely important. It doesn't matter if you are cutting the grass, cleaning bathrooms, or working at the front desk, your appearance and behavior are important. You may think no one is watching you, but if campers are around, chances are that someone is watching you. Act like you would if you were on stage.

This gives you an idea of how your session might proceed. For those who work the front desk and others when they talk to campers, the following instructions are helpful:

- Say hello cheerfully and with a smile.
- Call campers by name, if possible. Everyone likes to hear his or her own name.
- Be courteous and polite. Ask campers if you can be of assistance.
- Be attentive. Always listen to customers when they talk to you—kids included—as they may ask to come back or ask to go to another camp ground next time. Stop what you're doing when campers are talking. What seems like nothing to you may be very important to them.
- Make eye contact. Look campers in the eyes when talking and listen ing. This really makes an impression, because many people are not good at it.
- Be talkative. Ask questions. Talk about the answers to the questions they ask.
- Voice quality and clear speech are important, on and off the phone. Be happy, cheerful, and friendly. Vary your pitch; avoid a dull monotone. Speak clearly, and always avoid mumbling. People don't like to ask you to repeat, so many go away without getting the answers to their ques tions.

Chapter

14

SEASONAL CAMPING MANAGEMENT

A seasonal rental is a campsite that is rented for the entire camping season or year. The camper party usually has the exclusive use of their seasonal site. However, there are modifications in which the campground will store the seasonal camping vehicle off site and rent the site to others when the seasonal campers aren't using it. This usually results in a lower seasonal rate. Year-round storage may be included in the seasonal rate, meaning the rate is considered to be an annual rate.

Choice of the seasonal site rental is usually made after repeated stays at the campground. Thus the major market for seasonal campers is repeat camper parties. Often the attraction of the seasonal site is the community spirit or social bond developed with other seasonal campers and the campground operator and family.

Advantages and Disadvantages of Seasonals

For many campers the seasonal arrangement is, in effect, their second, or vacation home. Such a perspective shows the seasonal site rental to be a bargain. This is discussed in more detail in the seasonal rate determination section. Campground operators enjoy many benefits by renting seasonal sites. At the same time, seasonal campers present many challenges. These benefits and challenges, and the ways that campgrounds deal with them, are discussed below.

Income and Costs

First and foremost, the campground is able to rent sites that might not be rented on an overnight basis. In addition, more income from profit centers is enjoyed by the campground. There is an opportunity to generate income from seasonal campers' guests as well. However, seasonal campers generally do not spend as much in the campground store as overnight campers.

Sometimes the guests of seasonal campers don't pay, or the campground doesn't charge for them. Many campgrounds charge a visitor fee for guests of seasonal campers, just as they do guests of overnight campers. In addition, when friends camp in the absence of the seasonal campers, they are often charged regular overnight campsite rates.

Seasonal campers use more electricity than other campers. They usually have refrigerators, freezers, air conditioners, and generally more electrical appliances than the average RV camper. Further, they usually have more outside lighting, such as lighted flags, lanterns around their screened-in patios, and so on. Because of this, many operators individually meter the seasonal sites. Reports indicate that much less electricity is used with this method. Other operators simply raise the site fee to compensate for the extra energy cost.

Payment

An advantage to having seasonal campers is receiving the seasonal fees early in the year, when there is likely to be a cash flow problem. One method is to require three equal payments on January 1, March 1, and May 1. Another plan is to collect four equal payments due January 1, March 1, May 1, and July 1. Still another variation is to give a discount amounting to the next year's fee increase for payment before the end of the previous year.

On the negative side, some campgrounds may experience difficulty in collecting the seasonal fees. The above payment policies should eliminate such collection problems. These collection schedules also ensure that seasonal campers will rent for the coming season and an a good way to get an early commitment on a seasonal site.

Labor

Labor can be reduced by handling one or a few payments annually, compared to the day-to-day check-ins and collections from overnight campers. Seasonal campers will often help with the campground clean up. A Spring Fling or other type of spring promotion or cleanup weekend helps operators get work done at a relatively low cost. Schedule a potluck meal in the evening. The campground furnishes the meat and beverages, and seasonal campers can each bring a dish to pass. It's fun for the campers to renew friendships from the previous year and get their own site cleaned up.

Seasonal campers will often coordinate and lead recreation activities for you, such as Casino Night in the recreation hall. On the down side, you might have the added labor costs of cleaning up after these campers, chasing after them to collect fees, and providing a recreation director for their entertainment.

Security

Seasonal campers can be very helpful in watching the front desk for you, if you must run an errand. They can report suspicious-looking people in the campground. You know your seasonal campers and may trust them more than a number of new campers whom you've never seen before. You have a better chance of screening campers you want to have in your campground.

Sites

Seasonal campers may develop impressive sites with landscaping and attractive RV's. If your overnight business is slow, seasonal RVs make your campground look busy. If your campground looks empty, other campers may wonder what's wrong with your campground and drive on without stopping. This is especially true in the shoulder (other than peak) seasons.

They may also detract from the attractiveness of your campground by having messy-looking sites, old RV's, boats, and other recreation equipment at their sites. You need a policy regarding what seasonal campers can and cannot do with their sites. The seasonal lease discussion later in this chapter deals more with this area.

Ambassadors and Critics

Seasonal campers can be your welcoming committee to overnight campers in your recreation activity centers, or they can form cliques and shun overnight campers. They may share the games in the game room, or they may dominate the games and keep them among themselves. The same possibilities exist on the playground, in the laundry, and in the lounge areas.

These campers can also provide information to new campers about your campground, and attractions in the area. They can assist new campers who know little about camping. They can help them put up their camping equipment, teach them how to build a campfire, and how it cook on it. Seasonal campers can help sell other seasonal sites for you, or they may put down your campground to others.

You can obtain valuable feedback from seasonal campers to use in upgrading your campground, but guard against seasonals taking over your campground. "Our committee wants to meet with you concerning your rate increase for the coming year," is a red alert that seasonal campers may try to influence your policies in the campground.

Seasonal campers can be real assets to your campground or costly liabilities. The bottom line is that it is essential to understand seasonal campers to make them work to your advantage.

Marketing Seasonals

Note: *The material in this section was provided by Donald Schink, Chartwell Business Planning.*

The Right Product

Know what your potential seasonal campers desire in a seasonal camping experience. The typical seasonal camper will probably want the following benefits.

Resort atmosphere. Seasonal campers seem to be looking for a resort-type atmosphere in the campground. They want to meet people and establish friendships, even form a sense of community.

Attractiveness and cleanliness. Like all campers, seasonal campers prefer a clean and attractive campground. At least the seasonal campers you want should feel this way, or they won't be likely to keep their own sites clean.

Hospitality. There is no substitute for an excellent hospitality program and service attitude on the part of the campground staff for seasonal campers, as well as for other campers.

Activities. A complete recreation program is as desirable for seasonal campers as it is for overnight campers. They will probably prefer more adult activities, rather than family activities, due to their demographic profile (explained below).

Your Customer

It is important to know who your potential seasonal customers are. Seasonal campers tend to be in the 40 to 70 age range, empty nesters (no children at home), with above-average incomes, from occupations of skilled labor, such as foremen and managers. Often they are snowbirds. That is, they spend the winters in the south, and the summers in the north, sometimes in seasonal campgrounds in both areas.

Most seasonal campers are familiar with your campground before they rent a seasonal site. They have camped with you previously, have often been repeat campers, or have visited other seasonal campers at your campground on a regular basis.

Sell the Advantages

In your conversational selling and printed advertising, you should sell the advantages of being a seasonal at your campground. Sell sites conversationally and design ad copy in terms of how they will benefit from renting a seasonal site at your campground.

Second home concept. Compare a seasonal site at your campground with a second home they might choose to purchase.

Country club atmosphere: "Come join your seasonal friends!" This can be a real advantage for the camper over a second home.

Security. Your campground provides security not found in second home ownership. Second home owners often have to find someone to watch their property when they're not there. They may still get burglarized and vandalized. The safety of your campground is a good selling feature.

Convenient. Explain how easy it is to go camping, because they don't have to make a reservation every time they go camping. Everything is already set up for them. They don't need to tow their RV every time they want to camp.

Inexpensive. Your seasonal site is quite inexpensive compared to alternatives such as a second home or condo. Explain the advantages, such as lower costs for taxes, maintenance, debt service, and vandalism-caused repairs and theft.

Facilities/Activities. Highlight all the recreation activities and related facilities available.

Part of Your Total Marketing Program

If you want to build a strong base of seasonal campers, this should remain foremost in your mind when developing the marketing program. Include seasonal sales messages in local, area, and regional tourist publications in which you advertise. Your ads and listings in campground directories should also include the seasonal message. Include your message in direct mail programs to RV license holders, new RV purchasers, and repeat campers. Your media ads should mention it also.

Target Repeat Campers

Your own repeat campers are prime candidates for seasonal rentals. They're familiar with your campground, and have demonstrated that they like camping with you. Therefore, you should direct your promotional program toward them.

Include them in your direct marketing programs. Communicate with them several times during the year. Invite them to special events. If you have enough repeat campers to justify it, invite them to a special event early in the year. Sometime during the event, give them an informal sales presentation. If there are not enough repeat campers to justify a special event, consider inviting them to a regular seasonal event to show them the friendly country club atmosphere and other extras that seasonal campers enjoy. Sometime during the event, make a special sales presentation to them.

Rental Ease

Consider offering special deals to encourage seasonal campers to buy. For example, offer them a discount off their current year's camping fees applied to next season's seasonal fee. If they want to begin during the middle of the season, prorate the fee for the rest of the year. Another possibility is to offer special sales events early or late in the year.

Point of Sale

Repeat campers are regularly registering at your front desk. Train your staff to ask repeat campers, "Would you like to hear about our seasonal program?"

Offer your staff a bonus or commission for every sale they make. If they are not successful, you might approach the campers conversationally within the campground later.

Happy seasonal campers will try to sell their friends on renting a seasonal site so they can be together at your campground. They will also sell other overnight campers.

Rate Determination

Whether you have many or just a few seasonal campers, establishing the best site rate is very important to the financial success of your campground. Two different approaches for determining realistic seasonal site rates are explained, one in which seasonal site rental income is a minor part of total campsite rentals, and also one in which seasonal rental income is a major part of your site rental income.

As a Minor Part of Income

A rationale for determining or justifying a seasonal rate when seasonal site rentals are a small part of total site rental income is as follows:

1. Multiply the occupancy of the average site in the area to be rented (or overall occupancy) times the length of your camping season. Seasonal campers will want to rent your choice sites, so use the occupancy of such sites.
2. Then multiply the result by the daily rate you charge (including hook-ups) for that site. Example: 50% occupancy × 150 days × $20 overnight rate = $1,500.
3. Next, add on some percentage, such as 10 percent, to compensate for the lesser amount that seasonal campers spend in other profit centers, compared to overnight campers. Example: $1,500 × 10% = 150; $1,500 + $150 = $1,650.

Using this method ensures that the seasonal rate will generate the same site rental income as if the site were rented on an overnight basis.

As a Major Part of Income

When seasonal rentals become a significant part of the total site rental income, a different approach from the previous method discussed is appropriate. Let's assume that 20 sites (40 percent) are rented on a seasonal basis. Isn't it logical that the seasonal sites should provide 40 percent of the income needed from site rentals? (See Chapter 21, Realistic Rate Determination, for more insight into this subject).

Suppose that the income needed from site rentals to cover expenses plus payment of Principal is $80,000. Forty percent of this—or $32,000—is the income needed from seasonal site rentals. Divide this number by the number of seasonal sites (20) to be rented, and get $1,600 ($32,000/20 = $1,600), the rate needed to cover those costs.

Of course, any proportion of seasonal to total site rental income can be used. As more and more sites are rented to seasonal campers, the number of sites available for overnight rentals is less, so overnight rental income will be less, unless you expand your number of sites.

Willingness to Pay

The next step in the approach is to consider how much potential seasonal campers and your current seasonal campers are willing to pay. Be sure to consider that a close alternative is the second home, with its related higher costs. Consider all of the activities, security, country club atmosphere, and other amenities in your campground as part of the experience they receive for the seasonal fee.

Seasonal Competition

Observe what others charge for the same quality site and amenities. Why would (did) your customers choose your campground and not somewhere else for a seasonal site? Why would they leave your campground and go to another campground? What price differential would it take? Keep in mind that if you let them build decks, patios, and piers, it's going to take quite an effort to move. These are some of the considerations to ponder in arriving at the best price for your seasonal campers.

As in other pricing and management decisions, you must make the final decision. You are best qualified because you know your campground and your seasonal campers better than anyone else. In general, it has been noted that campground seasonal rates are lower than they may need to be, so you may want to take a chance on being a little too high rather than a little too low.

The Seasonal Lease

Many campgrounds require a written seasonal lease. Tammy and John Heidrick, of Shangri-La RV Park in Yuma, Arizona, use a registration card on which campers sign a statement that they will obey the rules and regulations of the park. Mike Farmer, of Pardee Lake Resort in Lone, California, uses a permit with a "hold harmless" clause.

A written lease can be very helpful in the smooth operation of a campground. The absence of a lease means your state statutes apply that relate to the more traditional types of rentals, such as apartments. Regulations relating to abandonment also apply, which can mean long and complicated lien procedures.

Note: *Much of the information in this section came from the unpublished workshop handout created by James G. Pouros for attorney, O'Meara, O'Meara and Eckert, West Bend, Wisconsin.*

You can avoid misunderstandings and confusion with a written lease. Sit down with the camper and go through the lease point by point, then have the camper sign that he or she has read, understands, and agrees to all the terms included. This removes most of the potential for misunderstandings. Without a written lease, you must rely on what you verbally agreed on as remembered by you and the lessee.

You can design a lease to meet your own specific needs. Of course, you must consider whether anyone will sign it as you decide what to include. Items to consider including in your lease are as follows:

- length of time of the lease;
- lease fee, payment dates, deposits;
- definition of the seasonal camping party, usually father, mother, and dependent children;
- off-season use;
- use or not use as legal residence;
- gate cards, fees for replacement;
- policy for guests of seasonal, overnight and day guests;
- policy for seasonals allowing other families to use the site;
- pet policy;
- use of electricity, meters and payments;
- upgrading of hookups;
- storage sheds—size, design, materials used in construction, placement on site;
- decks—size, materials used in construction;
- screen houses—size, design, materials used in construction;
- fire rings—placement, covered when not in use;
- firewood storage—maximum allowed;
- all storage on site—boats, campers, trailers, vehicles;
- other permanent improvements, trees, shrubs—approval of management required;
- site condition—clean and orderly, mowing of grass, consequences if not kept up;
- moving to another site;
- sale of the seasonal's RV—policy on commission;
- golf carts—licensed drivers, number of riders, lights, horn, vehicle sticker;
- taxes on camping units—owner pays;
- termination of lease—by camper, by management, policy regarding rest of season fee, removal of RV and other property;
- liability and comprehensive insurance for acts of man and nature—understand that campground is not responsible, campground named as coinsured, certificate of insurance to campground annually;
- event of medical/accident emergency—hold the campground, rescue squad harmless and allow treatment; and
- abide by campground rules (attached).

State statutes vary, so check your lease with an attorney familiar with your state. A sample lease from O'Connell's Yogi Bear Jellystone Park Camp-Resort is included in Appendix A of this chapter.

Appendix A

O'CONNELL'S
YOGI BEAR
JELLYSTONE PARK CAMP - RESORT
P.O. BOX 200 - 970 Greenwing Road
Amboy, Illinois 61310-0200
(815) 857-3860 - FAX (815) 857-2916
e-mail: yogibear@essex1.com

EXTENDED STAY CAMPER SITE LEASE

Date_____   Site Number_____

Name_____and/or_____

Address 1 _____ City_____St. Zip_____

Phone 1 _____ Phone 2 _____

Dependent children in school, names & ages_____

_____

_____

Key Card(s) No._____ Issued with this Contract.

Make of Camping Unit _____ Model_____

Year_____ Length _____ Width _____ Air? _____ Awning?_____

Deck size _____ Shed size _____ Storage box? _____ Casita? _____

TERMS AND CONDITIONS

This Lease is herin agreed to by and between O'Connells, Inc., d/b/a O'Connell's Yogi Bear Jellystone Park Camp Resort (herinafter referred to as Camp Resort) and the party(s) signatory hereto (hereinafter referred to as Seasonal Camper). Said Seasonal Camper Herein agrees to all of the terms and conditions of this lease as follows. Seasonal Camper agrees to be bound by the rules and regulations of the Camp Resort on behalf of the parties signatory hereto, as well as for all children, guests and visitors of said Seasonal Camper. All overnight guests and visitors must register immediately upon arrival on Camp Resort Property, and pay all fees as detailed below.

This Lease shall be from_____, 19 _____, to February 28, 20————.

March 1st of each year shall be the annual effective date of all Extended Stay Camper Site Leases.

The Lease Fee for the above period shall be $_____. This is a non-refundable Lease. Campsites may not be subleased.

The terms of payment shall be:

Option 1: _____ Payment in full to be received by Camp Resort no later than March 1st each year. Late payments will be charged a 15% per month (18% annual) late charge for all payments received after March 1st. Fall deposits for the same Campsite for the following year must be received by the Camp Resort prior to October 15th each year, and will be deducted from the balance due on the annual bill. Failure to make and deposit by October 15th of each year shall be construed as a cancellation of the Extended Stay Campsite Lease, and the lease(s) signatory hereto shall pay in full all bills pending, and remove any and all camping equipment and other personal property, leaving the Campsite in clean condition, prior to March 1st.

Deposit of $_____ received, Balance of $_____ due on or before March 1st.

Option 2: _____ Payment of the annual lease fee shall be paid on a quarterly basis with due dates of March 1st, September 1st and December 1st. A deposit of $150.00 shall be held in escrow as surety, by the Camp Resort until the termination of the annual lease, or unless written notice is received by October 15th notifying of cancellation. No interest will be paid on said deposit. Refund of the deposit is based upon all bills being paid in full, all camping equipment and other personal property removed, and the campsite is undamaged and in clean condition. Late payments will be charged a 1.5% (18% annual) late charge for all payments not received by the due date. The deposit will be refunded and mailed upon final inspection by the Camp Resort.

Surety deposit of $150.00 received on _____. Payment schedule as follows. March 1st_____;   June 1st_____; September 1st_____; December 1st_____..

A seasonal Camping Family shall be interpreted to be Father, Mother and dependent Children in this lease.

The Camp Resort is operated as a seasonal business, and not designed or operated for camping on a year round basis. It is our policy to allow" Winter Camping" on an occasional or special event basis only, and Camp Resort Management reserves the right to limit occupancy of any type in the off-season. Full-time winter camping or residency is not allowed.

Campers may not use our P.O. Box number, nor our street address as their legal residence, nor may they register students in our local schools utilizing our address as their legal residency. Campers receiving mail should make arrangements with the local United States Postal Service for a Postal Box in their own name.

One gate pass key will be issued with each site lease. Additional or replacement cards are available for a $10.00 charge. Key cards remain the property of the Camp Resort and must be turned in when terminating this lease.

Guests staying overnight in the camping unit of a seasonal camper must register immediately upon arrival, and will be charged $5.00 per individual or $10.00 per Family, per night.

Day visitors must register immediately upon arrival and either utilize a visitor pass supplied by the Seasonal Camper or pay the current visitors fee. Seasonal Campers may purchase visitor passes from the Camp Resort office for $2.50 per pass. Visitors staying overnight must re-register the next day and pay the overnight camping fee.

Seasonal campers allowing another Family to utilize their camping unit in their absence must first notify the Camp Resort. The Family using the camping unit must register and pay a fee of $20.00 per night, per Family, for the time they will be on the Camp Resort, and agree to abide by all Camp Resort rules and regulations.

Pet owners agree to clean-up after their pets and keep said pets under control from excessive barking and/or bothering other campers, in the event complaints are registered with the Camp Resort Management, after notification to the pet owners, the Camp Resort Management or its representatives may ban the pet from the property.

Each Seasonal Campsite is supplied with an electric meter owned by the Camp Resort. Each Seasonal Camper agrees to pay a monthly equipment rental charge of $7.00 per month. April through October. Monthly bills will be mailed to the Seasonal Camper by the Camp Resort reflecting the equipment charge plus the actual cost of the electrical service as to provided to the Camp Resort by the local power company. All bills are due in full as specified in the monthly statement. In the event a bill is not paid on time, a 1.5% per month (18% annual) late charge will be added to the bill. In the event a Seasonal Camper requires electrical upgrading, it shall be performed by the Camp Resort, and any costs incurred in equipment and/or labor will be paid by the Seasonal Camper requesting same. All equipment becomes the property of the Camp Resort.

All camping units shall be kept in conformity with all national, state, electrical, plumbing and health codes.

One shed is allowed on Seasonal Campsites not to exceed 8' x 8', and must be constructed in a professional manner of wood materials. They will placed on the site only in such locations as allowed by the Camp Resort Management and must be kept in a state of good repair and painted in earthtone or neutral colors.

Decks may be constructed not to exceed the width of the Camping Unit, nor to exceed the length by more than two (2) feet. Concrete decks will be allowed only with Camp Resort approval.

Casitas or Screen Houses shall be allowed only when the size, location and materials used are approved by the Camp Resort prior to installation. In no event shall a Casita or Screen House exceed 13' x 13'.

Fire rings will be placed not to interfere with neighbors, and must be covered when not in use. All fires must be extinguished when unattended.

Firewood storage on site will be limited to not more than two (2) face cords of firewood. A face cord is 16' deep, 4' high and 8' long.

All storage must be maintained so as not to distract from the view of neighbors.

Additional storage of any boats, trailers, campers or other items must be arranged for with Camp Resort Management under separate contract.

Permanent improvements such as trees, shrubs, concrete decks or other, must first be approved by Camp Resort Management prior to their installation and will become the property of the Camp Resort when the Extended Stay Site Lease is terminated.

Site condition is the sole responsibility of the Seasonal Camper. Seasonal Camper shall maintain said site in a clean and orderly fashion, inclusive of mowing and maintaining all of camping equipment, inclusive of decks, shed, and any other camping equipment. In the event the Camp Resort Management determines it is necessary to mow a site, a fee will be charged not to exceed $10.00 per mowing. This fee will be billed with the monthly statement.

Moving on the Camp Resort will only be allowed with the exclusive permission of Camp Resort Management and will be subject to the terms and conditions determined by Camp Resort Management at that time. It shall be, and remains the exclusive right of Camp Resort Management to determine site arrangements. Any cost incurred by the Camp Resort in moving a camping unit will be billed to the Seasonal Camper requesting same, at a rate of $40.00 per man hour, and in accordance with the terms and conditions agreed to at the time arrangements are made.

A Seasonal Camper desiring to sell their camping unit may do so by posting a small picture and description (3" x 5" card) of same on the Camp Resort bulletin board. No "For Sale" signs are allowed on the Camp Resort. The sale of a camping unit does not include the Site Lease, which may be enacted as a separate order of business by the Camp Resort Management. In the event the Camp Resort is involved in the sale of a camping unit, directly or indirectly, it shall be entitled to a 10% commission and/or the terms outlined in a signed Consignment Sale Agreement with O'Connell's RV Sales.

The Seasonal Camper acknowledges that the Camp Resort is a private enterprise. As such, camping units commonly referred to as park trailers (over 8' wide in the towable state) are restricted to sales conducted by O'Connell's RV Sales, a wholly-owned subsidiary of O'Connell's, Inc. Camping units not over 8' wide, such as travel trailers, fold down units, motorhomes, etc., may be supplied by outside dealers.

Golf carts may be operated by a licensed driver only. Seasonal Camper shall carry liability and comprehensive insurance on the golf cart and, further shall furnish a certificate of insurance, which will also name Camp Resort as co-insured. Seasonal Camper shall also allow Camp Resort to make a photocopy of the drivers license of the owner(s) of the golf cart. All golf carts shall have working lights, both front and rear, and an operable horn. Passengers shall not exceed number of seats, and persons must remain seated. Seasonal Camper shall purchase a vehicle permit sticker from Camp Resort which will be displayed in the golf cart. Vehicle permit sticker will show site number, year and expiration date. Seasonal Camper shall enter into with Camp Resort a separate cart Agreement which sets forth the terms, conditions, rules and regulations of golf cart use.

In the event that any governmental regulatory body places taxation of any type upon a camping unit, it shall immediately become the responsibility of the owner of the camp unit to pay such fees and, further, to provide the Camp Resort with proof of payment.

Seasonal Camper acknowledges that this Site Lease is in full force and effective for the term forestated in this document and accepts the obligation to pay in full all monetary obligations for said term.

Seasonal Camper shall have the right to terminate this lease by written notice to Camp Resort Management, and to remove all personal property, including the camping unit within ten (10) days of receipt of said written notice by Camp Resort Management, however, said termination does not remove the financial obligation of the Seasonal Camper terminating this lease. In consideration of said written notice, Camp Resort Management shall attempt to re-lease the site for occupancy immediately upon removal of the camping unit and, if successful, will pro-rate the remainder of this lease.

In the event a Seasonal Camper removes his camping unit from the Camp Resort without proper written notice to Camp Resort Management, the terms and conditions of this Lease shall remain in full force and effect for the term of the lease. Camp Resort Management shall have the right after ten (10) days to declare the site abandoned, take ownership of any and all property remaining on the site, and to lease the site to another camper.

Camp Resort Management reserves the right to cancel or amend this lease. In the event this lease is terminated by Camp Resort Management the parties signatory hereto agree that after written notice of said cancellation, they will remove any and all of their personal property from the Camp Resort within ten (10) days of the date said notice is sent by first class mail. In the event said property is not removed because of termination, expiration or abandonment, the Camp Resort shall have the right to remove said personal property from the site and place same in a storage area and charge for such removal and storage an amount equal to the current daily camping fee for a primitive campsite. The Camp Resort shall not be held liable for any damage incurred in moving said camping unit or personal property, nor for safekeeping. Any item left in storage sixty (60) days beyond the expiration date of this site lease, or from date of notice of termination, mailed first class to Seasonal Camper, shall be offered to public sale without further notice.

Seasonal Camper agrees to carry liability and comprehensive insurance on the leased site to protect against theft, pilferage, fire, windstorm, water damage, hail, vandalism and other acts of nature or man. The Camp Resort cannot, and will not, be responsible for loss of any kind and it is mutually understood that the Seasonal Camper hereby release Camp Resort from any and all liability. The Camp Resort shall be named as a co-insured, and a certificate of insurance issued to the Camp Resort annually.

In the event of a medical emergency and/or accident, permission is herin granted for the term of this Extended Stay Camper Site Lease to allow for emergency medical treatment of the undersigned, and/or our children as listed above. Said permission includes permission to treat for minor injuries and/or to call for emergency services from the Amboy Fire District, the Lee County Emergency Services and Disaster Agency, and to transport to a hospital. Further, to allow for the emergency room of said hospital to administer such treatment as they determine necessary. In consideration of the foregoing, I (We) hold harmless from any litigation and/or cost involved, O'Connell's, Inc. Yogi Bear Jellystone Park Camp Resort, its owners, stockholders and employees or agents; Daniel E. O'Connell, Jr., M. Jane O'Connell and Kevin O'Connell and any other person(s), Fire and/or Ambulance Services; Emergency Medical Technicians or hospital personnel who may render assistance.

I (we) have read the above Extended Stay Camper Site Lease and understand and agree to the terms and conditions set forth herein. I (we) have received a copy.

Accepted

———————————————————/ ————————————————————
Seasonal Camper   Seasonal Camper

——————————————————————————————
O'Connell's Yogi Bear Jellystone Park Camp Resort   WHITE ORIGINAL..RETURN TO O'CONNELL'S
                                                           YELLOW CUSTOMER COPY..KEEP FOR YOUR FILES

Chapter

15

GENERAL CAMPGROUND OPERATIONS

This chapter deals with helpful hints on several areas, including front desk operations, rules and policies, and maintenance and security.

Front Desk Operations

The front desk is the campground headquarters, or the operations center. It's where everyone goes for check-in information, answers to problems, and activity arrangements. It is extremely important that it be operated in a manner that you want reflected in your entire campground. A large part of your campground image is determined there. Anyone who works behind the front counter should be well-trained, neat, and cheerful.

Reservations

The front desk is where the reservations are handled, at least for small and medium-sized campgrounds during the camping season. Campgrounds handle reservations in myriad ways. Choose the method that works best for you. Reservation techniques are discussed at campground workshops and crackerbarrel discussions at campground owners' conventions, workshops, and tours.

Perhaps the main consideration is accuracy—being able to keep track of the reservations with a minimum of errors. Customers with reservations can easily be lost by not having a site available when they arrive or by being relocated to another site.

When starting out, it is good to have a large sheet of paper mounted on a board. On it make a grid pattern. Then list the days of the camping season across the top, and the campsite numbers or other designations down the left margin. Then, with a coding system, identify if the site-day is reserved or occupied at the present time. If space allows, the campers' names can be written on the board.

Another method is to have reservation book with a single page, with all the sites identified on it for each day of the camping season. Yet another option is the computerized system. Thirty-nine percent of the campgrounds in the 1998 National Operations Survey of the RV Park and Campground Industry reported using a computerized reservation system.

The Reservation Form

The reservation form is quite important to you. First, you are required by law, at least in most states, to have on file the names and addresses of everyone in your campground. You need this, regardless of regulations, to be able to identify everyone in your campground in the event of a disaster such as a tornado. You can find an example of a reservation/registration form in Appendix A of Chapter 22. Other information is very useful in conducting your marketing program, as will be discussed in Chapter 22 on market research.

Registration

There are a multitude of ways to conduct registration. A major consideration is to perform the registration efficiently and to get the campers to their sites quickly. A real camper service is to have a staff member guide the campers to their sites on a golf cart or bike. This is especially appropriate if the campsite layout is difficult to describe. It also avoids having campers set up in the wrong places and then asking them to move their equipment.

Some campgrounds have staff stand on the entrance road during busy check-in times to register campers with reservations so that the campers don't even have to get out of their vehicles to register. This doesn't get them into your campstore, however. Staff behavior is very important at the front desk. Please refer to the chapters on managing staff and customer relations for information on staff behavior.

The Registration Form

This can be the same form as the reservation form. Then with duplicates, it only has to be filled out once. The form is nearly completed when a reservation is made, which speeds up the registration at the front desk.

For campers who arrive after your registration desk has closed for the evening, the California Travel Park Association has developed a standard form. It asks such campers to stop the next morning at the registration desk and register. A space to indicate when the office opens is included. In fine print at the bottom, it states that failure to register is a crime and punishable under the California Penal Code.

Registration/reservation forms should be printed so there is a duplicate or carbon attached. It is usually of heavier paper stock, and is the one kept and filed by the campground.

Other Forms

Other forms are useful in operating campgrounds. A car pass has sizeable space for the site number and the departure date. It hangs from the rear view mirror, and it has instructions for the front side to be facing out, so it can be read from the front of the vehicle.

A *visitor pass* is designed like the car pass. It is of a different color, so it can be identified as such at a glance. These are essential for identifying cars that haven't been registered in the campground.

A "Please Stop at the Office" form has space for the site number, and can be hung on a door handle or placed on the windshield. It has check boxes to give reasons, such as phone messages, extra charges, and so on. A "Confirmation of Reservation" form in duplicate has space for necessary information, very similar to the reservation form. These forms are all available from printing companies, especially those that specialize in campground forms, as identified in Chapter 22.

Campground Rules and Policies

Campground operators develop a set of rules and policies over the years, the main purpose of which is to encourage a smoothly running campground and to prevent problems from recurring.

Try to minimize rules. A danger in making rules making is that too many are created. As soon as a problem arises, a new rule is often enacted. Before long, there is a list of rules that even the staff can't remember. Having too many rules for campers makes the campground a less attractive place in which to camp. You need some rules, but don't overdo it.

State rules positively, if possible. When rules are made, make an effort to state them positively. Instead of "Keep off the grass," say, "Please use the sidewalk." Stating signs positively not only makes your campground more user-friendly, the chances of campers complying with the rules are increased.

Many areas require a policy statement. For example, a position has to be taken regarding pets. Do you prohibit them and lose those campers who won't go camping without their pets? Or do you let them run all over the campground, and hope nothing bad happens? Certainly, there is some middle ground. Past research has shown that campers' first preference is to have the pets kept on a leash, followed by pets being the responsibility of the owner and kept in one area. A good policy to meet such camper preferences is to require pets to be kept on a leash and not be left unattended by the owners.

Quiet hours. Campers come to have fun, but within the confines of a campground, they can't be allowed to have fun at others' expense. Therefore, you need a quiet hours policy. You must decide when you want the campground to quiet down for the night, and then enforce it.

Part of the solution to maintaining a quiet campground is to restrict certain types of campers. Large groups of campers is one example; young, unrelated groups is another. Realize that every time you discourage some group, you restrict the number of potential customers for your campground. Also, be familiar with the antidiscrimination laws so that you are in compliance with them. Another solution is to have groups camp in a separate area.

Other rules. There are possibilities for rules concerning swimming, tree damage, off-limits areas, and the pilfering of firewood and rules pertaining to various recreation activities, areas, and site hookups. Whenever you make a campground rule, consider first the impact on campers. Ask yourself, "If I were a camper, would I like that rule, and be willing to follow it?" If the answer is no, you had better take another look at the rule.

Your Maintenance Program

Many dollars can be saved, accidents prevented, and a nicer looking campground achieved if proper maintenance plans and practices are implemented. A few hints on some of the areas of maintenance follow. Not only will you save money, you'll be less liable when accidents do happen, because of equipment failure or malfunction.

The Maintenance Plan

A maintenance plan is a very helpful tool in the campground. It serves as a guide for planning work schedules, writing job descriptions, and for helping the operator/manager learn what needs to be done in maintaining the campground. It should include, for each area of the campground and each piece of machinery and vehicle, what should be done in terms of preventive maintenance. It should indicate schedules of maintenance, with checklists of preventive maintenance examinations and procedures.

Small Engines, Vehicles, and Equipment

Preventive maintenance on small engines, vehicles, tractors, and other equipment will make them last considerably longer than without such care. Tasks as simple as regular lubrication, oil changes, and cleaning pay big dividends. Adult education courses in this area might be beneficial.

Buildings

When you choose materials for surfaces on walls and floors of your buildings, especially the toilet/shower facility, consider the relative cleaning and maintenance costs. What looks like a bargain at purchase may not be such a bargain when adding in relative cleaning costs and early replacement time.

Become informed on products and methods to use for preserving wood, metal, and concrete surfaces. It might be a good idea to take some vocational/technical school courses on this subject. Your state's campground owners' association will likely plan and coordinate such courses also.

Trees and Shrubs

If trees and shrubs are pruned and trimmed properly, they will also last longer and make your campground look better. Again, be familiar with proper pruning procedures. More information on this area is discussed in Chapter 4, Campground Design.

Your Security Program

Security has come to be very important with campers, given the increasing crime and violence in our society.

Theft of belongings and personal safety are areas of concern to campers. Several things can be done to make your campground more secure and to make your campers feel more secure. The most practical measures include front entrance security, lighting, and security patrol.

Front Entrance Security

Several alternatives are available for securing the front entrance. If your front office, store, and other buildings are right at your entrance, their presence is a deterrent to would-be intruders. This may be enough of a security measure by itself.

The entrance gate is another measure that can be used. It can consist of simply a chain suspended between two posts that can be locked with a padlock. It may consist of a gate made of wood or metal, or it may be a wood board or metal bar, pivoting from a post on each side and joining in the center. These can all be secured with padlocks.

There is also the card-operated electronic gate. To open it, a plastic card is inserted in a slot. This activates the mechanism, which opens and closes the gate. There are two considerations to be aware of in deciding on a security gate. One is that you must make it possible for people to leave quickly in the event of an emergency. Therefore, if you lock the gate and that is the only exit people know, you have to give every camping party a key or other means of getting out when no one else is present.

Another consideration is allowing campers to get into your campground after closing time. These may be campers who are camping with you, campers looking for a place to camp, or late arrivals.

Campground operators have stated in cracker-barrel discussions that the mere presence of a gate is an adequate deterrent for uninvited guests. It doesn't matter whether the gate is locked or merely standing there.

Another way to provide a secure front entrance is to have someone stationed throughout the night. This may be practical for large campgrounds, especially at busy times. The staff person may do other things while there, such as handling incoming camper registration late at night. Adequate lighting at the gate is also desirable.

Lighting

Thieves and others with less than honorable intentions do not like to commit their crimes in the light. Campers feel more secure also when there is adequate lighting. Lighting is adequate when campers can clearly see the pathway to the toilet facility, but not when it is so bright that it disturbs other people who are trying to sleep, or when it destroys the aesthetic looks of the campground. A Wisconsin campground had installed a light for security and to assist people who needed to get up in the night—but was a 50-foot utility pole with a huge mercury vapor light, bright enough to conduct a baseball game. Needless to say, it was removed soon after installation.

The lighting should be soft, but adequate. Indirect, low light along paths to the toilets provides adequate light while remaining attractive. Indirect lighting in parking areas and between buildings is also more attractive than bright, direct overhead lighting. The amber and incandescent lights are also more appealing to many than the florescent or mercury vapor lights.

Security Patrol

Security patrols are becoming more popular in these times of increasing concern over security. Many campground operators make a final round through the campground, just before going to bed, when the campground is busy. If they live right on the campground, they can hear if there is a noisy disturbance.

Other campgrounds hire off-duty sheriff's deputies to come in at night and patrol the campground until dawn. They usually wear their uniforms, so people can identify them as security. This makes many campers feel more secure.

Camper Screening

Many campers screen their camper customers and do not rent sites to stereotyped groups that they've had trouble with in the past. This is thought to be easier than trying to deal with them after they arrive, and then having them cause trouble. If you screen campers, make sure you are not in violation of the civil rights laws.

Appendix A

Suppliers of Reservation Forms and Software

Reservation Forms

Jenkins Business Forms
P. O. Box B
Mascoutah, IL 62258
(800) 851-4424, Fax: (618) 566-2404

Executive Services Group
P.O. Box 5578
Auburn, CA 95604
(530) 823-6331, Fax: (530) 823-6331

Computer Systems and Software

Note: Most of the following information is from *Woodall's Campground Management, the Annual Buyer's Guide*, published annually in January. For this and many other sources of campground supplies, contact Woodall's.

Campground Management
139750 West Polo Trail Dr.
P.O. Box 5000
Lake Forest, IL 60045-5000

Bugler Computing Resources
P.O. Box 104
Brunswick, ME 04011-0104
(207) 725-6969, Fax: (207) 729-5388

Digital Rez Software Corp.
P.O. Box 489
Secamous, BC VOE 2VO
Canada
(800) 811-5988, Fax: (250) 836-3560

Fast Tracker/Desktop Solutions
2439 S. Kihei Rd., Suite 203B
Kihei, HI 96753
(808) 874-3610, Fax: (8089) 874-3804

Indiana Cash Drawer Co.
P.O. Box 236
Shelbyville, IN 46176
(800) 227-4379, Fax: (317) 392-0950

Mission Management Systems
5219 Victoria Ave.
Niagra Falls, ON L2E 4E4
Canada
(800) 547-9147, (905) 374-8643
Fax: (905) 374-4493

Sher-Tek Software, Inc.
107, 3-11 Bellrose Dr.,
St. Albert, AB T8N 5C9
Canada
(403) 458-9799, Fax: (403) 458-3237

Systems Development Resource
3702 Socorro Dr.
Grandville, MI 49418-1955
(616) 532-9090

Chapter

16

CAMPGROUND RISK MANAGEMENT

Liability, insurance, and litigation have become household words in camp-ground operator families in recent years. This chapter discusses the back-ground of liability, and takes a broad look at a workable program to manage the entire liability program in your campground, from inspection to dealing with accidents that do happen. It also covers such misunderstood or unknown concepts as assumed risk, business interruption insurance, and waivers.

Legal Background

As soon as you open your campground to the public, a liability is created. Because you charge fees, you make yourself more vulnerable—that is, more liable. Common law doctrine (due care) is the legal basis for liability. This is a set of general principles, as opposed to a set of laws, arising out of statutes passed by governmental bodies, which have resulted from a long series of court decisions (precedents). Because the final interpretation is decided by juries in cases that go to court, it is useful to look at previous similar cases.

Therefore, it is wise to consult with attorneys and insurance profession-als with questions about the liability aspects of your campground enterprise. However, it is also useful to have a general understanding in order to make decisions on facilities, activities, and related management of risks associated with your facilities and activities.

Negligence

Negligence, or failure to provide due care, is the basis for liability. However, one must have been proven negligent before being held legally liable for un-intentional injury to others. Negligence is usually defined in terms of what a "reasonable man" *would* or *wouldn't* do under the same circumstances. It could be the someone omitting to do what a reasonable person would do under similar circumstances, or it could be the act of doing what a reasonable person would not do.

One's ability to anticipate danger is a further gauge of negligence. Therefore, the ability to foresee danger is an important factor in determining liability. This is what makes preventive maintenance and safety programs important in avoiding potential sources of negligence. There are several elements necessary to support a legitimate negligence suit:

- a legal duty or obligation to conform to a standard of behavior to protect others from unreasonable risks;
* a breach of that duty caused by failure to conform to the standard required under the circumstances;
- a sufficiently close causal connection between the conduct of the individual and resulting injury to another; and
- actual injury or loss to the interests of another.

Rights to Possession

Individuals who come into your campground can be classified by their relationships to you as they concern your liability. The person who comes into your campground may be an invitee, a licensee, or a trespasser. An *invitee* is a camper customer or visitor. This person has your permission and pays a fee. You must have your campground in a safe condition for your customers.

A *licensee* enters your campground for purposes of his or her business with the permission or implied consent of you, the campground operator. Your suppliers or vendors are examples. You, the owner/operator, are under no obligation to make your campground safe. Further, you don't need to warn them of concealed, unsafe conditions that are concealed when you know such conditions exist. In effect, the licensee must take conditions as they are.

The law has also recognized social customs as an aspect of liability. If a friend or neighbor comes to call socially, such an individual cannot normally collect for damages unless it was proven that the host was grossly negligent.

A *trespasser* is an individual who comes on to your campground *without* permission. In most states the liability for injuries suffered by trespassers is very slight, but there have been some unusual cases regarding trespassers (Espeseth, 1980).

In regard to liability for children, the *attractive nuisance doctrine* applies. This is very important in the case of campgrounds, because there are so many situations in which it may happen. The attractive nuisance doctrine applies when there is an attraction for children. In such cases, they are no longer considered trespassers, even though you may have the area fenced off or signed. However, if children were drawn by one attraction and were injured in some other way, the liability would probably not apply.

Two dangerous attractions common in campgrounds are water and machinery. Fences or other barriers *and* signs need to be used. The warning signs alone are not sufficient because children may not be expected to know how to read. In cases of equipment, the keys need to be removed so they can't be started by accident.

Your Risk Management Program

The presence of liability implies an exposure to a *peril*, which is something capable of causing or contributing to a loss. This is known as risk. Risks are present everywhere. We are liable—or face risks—all the time. Whether we drive our vehicles or take care of our children, the risk factor is present because it is unknown whether the liability will turn into a loss; and if so, how bad the loss will be. This risk of loss is what you need to manage in your campground.

Risk management involves the identification, evaluation, control, and administration of risk. The most common method used in the management of risk is the purchase of insurance. Because of that, a large part of the risk management process is the constant reexamination of insurance needs and review of maintenance practices, operational procedures, and program evaluations that influence the insurance program for your campground (Espeseth, 1980).

The Risk Management Process

Identification → Evaluation → Methods → Administration

Campgrounds with substantial liability insurance premiums would be well advised to carry out the complete risk management process, especially if there is much labor available. Such campgrounds would then be best able to adopt improved methods for protecting against risk. This assumes that the process hasn't been previously carried out. Smaller enterprises may find it more practical to identify the risks and implement the necessary methods for reducing or controlling their exposure to risk.

Risk Identification

This is where you need to begin your risk management process. You need to identify the exposure to risk faced by you, your campground business, your staff, and your camper guests. This is necessary so that you don't overlook any potential risks, so that you reduce the impact should a loss occur, and so that you prevent loss wherever possible. You have to know what risk exists before you can deal with it.

Dennis Templeton, of Templeton Southwest Insurance, San Antonio, Texas, says the flags (high exposures) that insurance companies look for are:

1. exposure to water, e.g., swimming, boating, and other watercraft, and waterslides in swimming areas;

2. beer and liquor;
3. propane gas sales;
4. horseback riding; and
5. motorized rides, trampolines and special events (Templeton, 1991).

Property risks are the easiest to identify. The recreation equipment, buildings, and vehicles are examples. Is the playground equipment well-maintained? Does the equipment meet (CPSC) standards? Are there bearings that might wear out, as in swing sets? Are there any bolts, pins, or screws loose or missing? Are there any sharp pieces of metal exposed that could possibly injure someone? Are the individual pieces of equipment far enough apart so that a person playing on one piece doesn't get in the way of someone on another piece? Is the ground surface relatively soft so that someone falling on it would not be severely injured? Is it in compliance with CPSC guidelines? Has the sand or pea gravel been worn to a hard surface?

In checking the buildings, are there adequate handrails for people to use when walking up and down the stairways? Are the stairway step surfaces made of nonslip material? Are all electric conduits properly secured? Are there loose power cords on which someone might trip and fall? Are your vehicles safe for your employees to use?

Are there any dead trees on your property that need to be removed? Are there any limbs or branches that have grown out into the walkways? These are examples of situations that should be identified in a risk identification tour. It also serves as the first step in a safety inspection.

For your recreation activities, are there some that expose you to more risk than others? For example, horseback rides, by their very nature, carry a high risk exposure. So does swimming. Is your swimming area properly signed and equipped with the necessary safety equipment? Does your park meet minimal standards in areas where they exist within the park?

The people involved in the survey effort should be aggressive in probing areas where your campground may be liable. They should also make it clear that the purpose of the survey is to discover areas where actions are needed to reduce liability, not to analyze anyone's job performance.

The survey should be written to include information such as the date of the survey, descriptions of the problem areas, and notations of those areas that were found to be of minimal exposure at the time of the survey.

As you may have noticed, the mere identification of your risks is a major step toward managing them, because many can be eliminated. The others aren't so easy; they need to be evaluated.

Risk Evaluation

Evaluating the risk of each activity, piece of equipment, and the camping area is not easy. You need to rank each risk area—to rate it on a probability of an accident occurring, from high to low. Then using a monetary value, a severity rating can be assigned to it.

You can begin by determining the monetary value of the physical property itself. Then you can easily determine the most and least costly in terms of replacement and service value. You need this information in order to select a method to protect against loss of each item. Those with high monetary and service importance should be protected by the best available methods, such as property insurance and preventive maintenance. The others don't need such comprehensive protection and so might be a source of insurance cost savings.

Those risks identified as having a high frequency or probability of occurrence should receive high priority in your risk management program. Those risks having devastating potential should be protected by the use of commercial insurance. Those with lower impact potential can be dealt with through other methods discussed next.

Selection of Risk Management Methods

There are many ways to deal with the risks just identified and evaluated. They include methods to *reduce, eliminate, retain,* or *transfer* risk. For many, the predominant method of protection is insurance, which is a method of sharing risk with, or transferring it to, other people who purchase insurance from the same company.

Risk Reduction

In reducing risks, the goal is to reduce the frequency and the severity of risk exposure. The situations that cause the risk exposure can be changed to reduce the frequency and severity of risk exposure. Doing these kinds of things will reduce the cost of insurance premiums, since the coverage can be reduced.

Risk Elimination

The sure way to reduce risk of loss is to avoid any exposure to it completely. This suggests knowledge of a situation before anything happens. You have to identify such a risk ahead of time, evaluate it, and take the necessary steps to remove it. Examples include the removal of a dead tree, releasing or not rehiring employees who appear accident prone, not leaving vehicles in an unprotected area or with the keys in them, discontinuing a horseback riding enterprise, or removing a waterslide from your swimming pool.

Risk Retention and Control

Sometimes it's better to retain risks and control them to minimize their frequency and severity. This is a form of self-insurance. The deductible portion of an insurance policy is a common example. Retention of losses should be an active and conscious process, but all too often it becomes passive, and the losses occur due to default.

Usually such types of risk are those with low impact or severity and that can be absorbed. An example is collision insurance on an old vehicle that you probably wouldn't fix if it did get damaged. Such items are often dropped from insurance policies. Others that should be dropped are those in which the insurance cost is more than the cost of replacing the items.

Risk Transfer

This method involves assigning the risk to another party. Such transfer can result in substantial cost savings. You have access to expertise to assist you in this effort. Your insurance professional will give you an idea of the exposure and the magnitude of severity. A good share of the insurance premium you pay is based on these factors. Past records can also be useful in evaluating the risks.

The main reason for transferring risk is financial protection. However, other advantages include the auxiliary services available. Insurance companies often offer excellent engineering and safety services to their policyholders. Such services should be included in the written contract. Transferring risk can result in substantial cost savings. Methods of transferring risk include the following:

- leasing in lieu of purchasing property;
- insuring the presence of "hold harmless" and of the "certificate of insurance," indicating a transfer of liability and proof of insurance;
- using surety bonds or performance guarantees to assure contractual obligations and conditions are met; and
- the purchase of insurance policies through companies with an assortment of risk coverages. (Espeseth, 1980)

Which method or methods should you select? Some rules of thumb for deciding are listed below:

- Risk exposures with loss impacts of high severity potentials should be likely candidates for transfer.
- Risk exposures conducive to low severity losses may be reduced or retained.
- Liabilities may be eliminated by selling or disposing of unneeded property, or contracting for services.
- Avoid and control risks whenever possible. If the risk or liability associated with an activity, program, or contract has a potentially extreme budgetary impact should a loss occur, work to avoid the risk or discontinue the program or activity altogether *(Espeseth, n.d., p.12)*.

Your risk management program will be unique to your campground, and will no doubt differ from any other program. The guidelines to build your own program are indicated in the following steps:

Step 1. Your own commitment and direction you give to the program. This is probably the most vital part of any risk management program.

Step 2. Ensure that present risk protection efforts, if any, continue while the identification, evaluation, and method phases are being completed.

Step 3. Begin to generate or gather the necessary records to actively administer the program. Key documents needed for comprehensive planning include:

- an insurance register;
- record of losses;
- checklist of assets; and
- resources and liabilities.

Step 4. Develop and disseminate internal operating procedures to guide internal control and reporting practices. Such common practices include accident reporting, hazard observation and reporting, outside technical assistance, and safety and loss control.

Step 5. Initiate a loss control program by establishing safety and control efforts (Espeseth, 1980).

A good risk management program protects the campground enterprise against severe loss. Although these losses are generally equated with financial cost, a risk management program must first be designed to protect against human loss or injury.

Accident Prevention

Perhaps the best thing that can be done is to prevent accidents from happening. You should do as much as possible to prevent human loss or injury. There are three main components to the prevention of accidents. They are safety programs, preventive maintenance, and adequate supervision. Each is discussed in the following paragraphs.

Safety Programs

The first thing that should be done is to conduct a thorough inspection of your entire campground to identify existing or potential hazards. Then determine methods of eliminating them. These should be written down on cards or forms developed for that purpose. An example form is included in Appendix A at the end of this chapter. Things to be noted include the date of the inspection, who did the inspection, description of the hazard, date of corrective action, costs incurred, and who did the work. The reason for this method is that memory doesn't always provide adequate protection.

Preventive Maintenance

An ongoing preventive maintenance program should be carried out to identify hazards soon after they appear. Then prompt, corrective action needs to be taken to eliminate the hazard. Such prompt, corrective action does more than just correct the situation. It places you in a much more favorable situation in the event of an accident elsewhere. The reason is you may have a difficult time defending against a claim or lawsuit if safety precautions are lacking, even though the lack thereof had nothing to do with the accident for which you are being sued.

Keep a record of the maintenance activities that are performed in your campground. An example is shown in Appendix A the end of this chapter. This log is proof that you have an ongoing safety/maintenance program. Plaintiffs have been known to drop cases when they discover such a practice is ongoing in a campground (William McKnight, personal communication, 1990).

Ongoing Supervision

You need an ongoing program of supervision. It should be more than just noticing a hazard, or reacting if someone else calls your attention to some potential hazard.

Ideally, perform a routine inspection throughout the campground, complete with forms filled out and records of corrective actions taken. For example, after a storm is a good time to make a check. Another good time might be after a major event you coordinated or after a major holiday. At times with so many people, it's difficult to stay on top of everything that goes on in your campground.

Your Campground Regulations

In order to guide campers in the proper and safe use of recreation areas and equipment, you should have regulations posted to provide reasonable safeguards for those who participate.

A map to show visitors where they are allowed to go in the campground, with instructions on what they can and cannot do, is useful. This is important because an operator is basically responsible for injuries caused by camper guests. This responsibility is similar to preventing dangerous conditions from existing.

Water Regulations and Other Safety Procedures

One of the biggest attractions in a campground is water, and the largest hazards are the swimming pool, pond, river, and lake. *Note:* This information is from "Swimming Pools/Water Hazards," from the *Insurance Corner,* by Jim Calfee Insurance Agencies, Inc.

Swimming pools: It is extremely important that your swimming pool be fenced and have a self-locking, self-closing gate. The fence should be as high as your state code specifies and have openings no larger than 2 inches. A cyclone-type fence provides safety and yet allows visibility.

The gate needs to have a padlock on it that is kept locked during nonswimming periods. It should be monitored by an adult. This security is to prevent children from swimming when unaccompanied by an adult. Experience has indicated that unless locked, the gate may be propped open, which nullifies the entire security measure.

Rules for the pool should specify clearly what is and what is not allowed. They should be stated positively, in an effort to be as user-friendly as possible. Rules are more likely to be followed if stated in a positive manner. Signs about rules should also be placed in clear view, such as near the pool entrance gate and inside, as well as outside, the fence. In some cases, your state health department has regulations or guidelines to follow regarding such safety rules.

Lifesaving equipment should be in plain view, especially when there is no lifeguard on duty. A "shepherd's crook," lifesaving ring, and attached rope and lifeline rope should be present. Depth markings should be placed on the side and on the walking surface of the pool.

Water clarity is also important. Ph readings should be taken and recorded daily. The water should be clear enough so the drain in the bottom can always be seen.

Ponds, rivers, and lakes: Ponds, rivers, and lakes have safety hazards different from swimming pools. Warnings should again be posted in clear view of users. Notices of such rules should also be posted. Swimming areas should be clearly marked by roped areas or buoys. Docks should be well-maintained, and depth markings should be placed in clear view of the dock, as injuries have occurred from people diving off docks.

Boats should be kept out of swimming areas. Boat operators should be informed about areas of the lake or river to be used. Maximum speeds should be indicated, and boat operators should also be informed of such rules. Place appropriate signs at boat launch areas.

Swimming beaches are another area for potential hazards to appear. Beaches should be monitored by an adult regularly, cleared of any obstructions, floating or submerged. Fishing should not be allowed in swimming areas. Ponds that are not for swimming should be clearly signed as such and should be patrolled regularly to ensure that people do not swim there.

Swimming and other water sports are very popular recreation activities in campgrounds. In fact, water sports are a major attraction for many campgrounds. The liability hazard that they present can be managed by the use of safety measures to reduce the risks. For more information on swimming pool safety, read *Minimum Standards for Public Swimming Pools*, National Spa and Pool Institute, 2111 Eisenhower Avenue, Alexandria, VA 22314.

When Accidents Do Happen . . .

Part of your overall safety plan must contain an emergency plan. You and your staff should know what to do with a minimum of delay or confusion. Such plans can be simple or elaborate, depending on the size of the campground.

Emergency Preparation

You need to have first-aid equipment and related equipment for dealing with emergencies. Fire extinguishers and other firefighting equipment should be readily available, and staff should be trained in their proper use. A backboard is necessary for persons with suspected back and neck injuries, but don't keep it unless you are EMT qualified. A first-aid kit should be part of the emergency equipment. Training of staff is necessary to have the efficient and effective handling of emergencies. Some regular staff person should be qualified in the Red Cross life-saving course and a CPR course. The person needs knowledge of blood pathogens and proper procedures, as addressed by OSHA.

Being in a rural area means you are not as accessible to rescue service from your local municipality. In order for them be as efficient as possible, it is very helpful if they know where your campground is located and are familiar with your road and major activity centers. In this way, they can be instructed to go directly to the scene of an accident and not have to stop at a front office for directions. It might also be appropriate to meet them at your front entrance and lead them to the accident scene.

Be sure to include them in any public relations and open house activities that you plan. The availability of two-way radios among staff and the front desk is also important in dealing with emergencies.

Emergency Plan Development

The following emergency plan, or something similar, should be in place to deal with emergencies:

1. **Establish the nature of the emergency:** What type of emergency is it? Are fire, rescue squad, and police needed? Can your own equipment or personnel handle the emergency? If there is any doubt, the appropriate emergency personnel and equipment should be called.
2. **Dispatch equipment and personnel to the scene of the emergency:** If outside help is called, tell them you will meet them at the entrance, and direct them to the scene. Dispatch as many of your own personnel to the scene as possible. Proceed to either lock the office or to station someone at the office to take care of possible questions or calls.
3. **Act on the emergency:** Render first aid, if possible. Offer assistance to victims. Make sure the first-aid kit is available for use. Try to see if any medical help is available within the campground while waiting for the rescue squad. If there is a fire, make sure all firefighting equipment in the campground and vehicles are at the scene or on the way. Handle the fire as you are trained.
4. **Secure the area:** As extra help arrives, use them to handle the emergency, if needed. Then use help as needed to keep others away from the scene. Implement traffic control to get people and vehicles away from the area and to open routes for emergency equipment to get to the scene and out again.
5. **Monitor the emergency until it is over:** Stay on the scene until the emergency is over, or until told to leave by outside emergency personnel.

Make sure the emergency is over before releasing any of your personnel. Clean up if needed, and make sure your equipment is ready to go into service again. If necessary, rope off the area to keep people out. Offer assistance to victims.

As soon as everything is secure, write out a detailed report, stating exactly what happened and when it happened, making sure to include all of your actions. If the fire equipment was used, make sure calls are made to see that extinguishers are recharged. Replenish first-aid supplies as needed. If asked about insurance, do not admit to anything. Leave that to the insurance company. *(Wagon Trail Campground's Emergency Plan, 1984)*

Litigation Preparation

There are a few common sense things to do regarding litigation as soon as the emergency is over:

1. **Identify potential witnesses:** Find out who saw the emergency, and get their names, addresses, and phone numbers.
2. **Take pictures of the incident:** As soon as possible, take pictures of the accident scene. Take pictures of anything that will support your written account.
3. **Inform your insurance company and attorney:** The sooner you tell your insurance company and your attorney, the better position they'll be in to help you with your legal defense or offense, as the case may be.
4. **Don't apologize:** Throughout the incident, do not make apologies or in any other way offer any information that could be used in court to make you liable or guilty.
5. **Save any equipment that was involved:** Do not destroy it.

Written Waivers

Many public recreation providers have their customers read and sign a written statement that states that the signee accepts the full responsibility for the risk of the activity. Are these legally binding? The answer is most likely not. People are, however, responsible for their own behavior if your state has assumed risk legislation, which is described below.

However, there is a value in having people sign waivers. For one thing, the participant may, will the action of being asked to read the warning and sign it, be more careful in the activity participation. This reduces the potential for an accident. Further, the participants may *think* they are responsible for their actions and may therefore be less apt to initiate a legal claim against you. An example of a waiver for a horseback riding operation is provided in Appendix B at the end of this chapter.

Assumption Of Risk

Some states have laws that intend "to establish the responsibilities of participants in recreational activities in order to decrease uncertainty regarding the legal responsibility for injuries that result from participation in recreational activities, and thereby to help assure the continued availability in this state of enterprises that offer recreational activities to the public" (Participation in Recreational Activities Act, 1987).

This particular law defines recreation activities to include camping, and almost all activities that would occur within a campground. It further describes the "appreciation of risk" of participants as "accepts the risks inherent in the recreational activity of which the ordinary prudent person is or should be aware" (Participation in Recreational Activities Act, 1987).

It further describes the responsibilities of participants: is to do all the following:

1. Act within the limits of his or her ability.
2. Heed all warnings regarding participation in the recreational activity.
3. Maintain control of his or her person and the equipment, devices, or animals the person is using while participating in the recreational activity.
4. Refrain from acting in any manner that may cause or contribute to injury to him or herself, or to other persons, while participating in the recreational activity. A violation of this subsection constitutes negligence." (Participation in Recreational Activities Act, 1987).

The purpose of such legislation is to prevent "frivolous" suits from occurring. Such legislation in no way reduces the need to take all the safety, risk planning, and related measures discussed previously. Be sure to check in your state to see if similar legislation exists.

Insurance Options

Business interruption insurance is carried to compensate for *loss of income* due to tangible loss of property. While other insurance may compensate you for the damage, this covers lost income.

Key-Man Insurance

This is insurance to cover losses in the event that one of your key persons is lost. It is intended to compensate for losses that occur until someone can be brought up to proficiency in performing the job of the person that was lost.

The Insurance Agent/Company

As stated earlier, your insurance company, through your agent, can be a good source of information and technical assistance to you. The agent can suggest ways to reduce your exposure to liability, and can inform you of the premium costs associated with various activities and situations within your campground so you can evaluate your insurance program and make the most informed choices.

You may think that all insurance companies are interested in is charging the largest premium possible, thereby making the maximum profit possible. However, more profits may be possible in dealing fairly and as efficiently as possible with clients so they'll get several referrals from them. Furthermore, most of the rules that have been set for you have been tested in court.

The following insurance companies specializing in supplying insurance to campgrounds:

Jim Calfee Insurance Agencies, Inc.
9769 West 119th Drive, Suite 3
Broomfield, CO 80020
1-800-525-2060

Evergreen USA Risk Retention Group, Inc.
Programs administered by International Insurance Services, Inc.
P.O. Box 61, 655 Main Street
Lewiston, ME 04240
1-800-343-7900
Fax: 207-783-6778
e-mail: iis@post1.hartfordinc.com

Appendix A

Safety Inspection Form

Date of Inspection	Description of Hazard	Date of Corrective Action	Cost of Corrective Action	Person(s) Doing the Work

Maintenance Log

Date	Description of Maintenance Performed	Person(s) doing the Work	Length of Time and/or Cost

Appendix B

Waiver Sample

Rider is accepted for horseback riding on the condition that rider acknowledges that horseback riding is a hazardous sport, that hazards and obstructions exist in the area, and that falls, local wildlife, and insects disturbing the horses, and kicking and biting horses are common, and the rider accepts the risk of injury incident thereto. If you do not wish to assume the risk of the sport, then do not ride here.

_____

SIGN HERE

Chapter

17

CAMPGROUND STORE OPERATIONS

Many campgrounds have a store as part of their campground operation. Stores vary in size from a few shelves behind the front desk, to a full service merchandise area. Regardless of the store size, you need to operate it as efficiently and profitably as possible. Although you may not be a retail store professional, you can learn enough information to make the store operate as a successful profit center.

Campground Store Advantages

Many campgrounds offer the campground store as a service to campers. Those that are in remote locations have a real chance to offer this service profitably, especially if located 5 to 10 miles or more from the nearest competing store.

Even if the campground store is located close to a supermarket, it can still serve as a convenience to campers. When a camper starts cooking a camp meal and finds that one ingredient is missing, it's a real convenience to go to the campground store and get it rather than drive into town, find a store, purchase the product, and return. In addition, you can offer items needed by campers in your store that are not normally carried in supermarkets.

Labor Force Employment

A store may increase your labor efficiency. The person working the front desk may be able to handle the store check-out duties in addition to working the front desk.

Profit

A campground store can be a profit center for a campground. A profitable store should be an objective of the campground operation. However, it needs to be efficiently managed in order to achieve that objective.

Individual campground operators may have other reasons for operating a store. For example, a campground may have a gas station and convenience store out on the highway, so it is combined with the campground to serve the campers.

Types of Campground Stores

Store Size

A small store would probably carry only emergency and high-volume items, such as milk, bread, buns, ketchup, soda, ice, firewood, and starter fluid. A medium-sized store would carry most grocery and camper items, but with a limited selection of each item. A large campground store would be a complete store, with several choices of high-volume items. Factors that affect the type of store you choose to run are discussed below.

Campground Size

A major factor determining the size of most campground stores is the size of the campground—the more campsites, the more campers; the more campers, the greater the store sales potential. Perhaps the only case where this isn't true, is if the store enjoys a large off-road business. The potential number of Customers is determined by the number of campers and off-road or off-lake/river business.

Space Available and Location

Sometimes the space available may determine the size of a campground store. If there isn't sufficient space for a larger store operation, the cost of expansion may not be justified by increased sales in the store.

How much volume can be generated in a campground store depends in part on the competition. If there is a supermarket just a mile or two away, the campground store would likely be smaller than if that supermarket is 20 miles away.

Type of Campers

The type of camper that predominates in your campground is a size determinant. It is believed among campground operators that seasonal campers don't spend as much in the campground store as overnight campers. They apparently have their regular shopping lists that they take to the supermarket on their way to the campground, along with plenty of refrigerated space for storing food. Destination campers will naturally tend to run out of camping supplies, compared to overnight or weekend campers. It is the opinion of campground operators that camper types can be ranked by how much they spend in the campground store, from most to least, as follows: destination, overnight, and seasonal.

Principles of Store Layout

There are many factors to consider in designing your store layout. These are good to keep in mind when designing a store from scratch, or when considering expanding or upgrading in general. See Appendix A at the end of this chapter for a sample store layout plan.

Product Exposure

The more products people see, the more they will buy. People are used to serving themselves in stores. If they don't see something they want, they may assume you don't have it. Try to get them to visit all parts of the store. For example, place the milk and bread in the rear of the store. Then customers have to walk past many other products to get products most of them need. This concept will be discussed more in the merchandising section.

Key Locations

Always play the winners. Fast-moving products should be given the best locations with sufficient space so they will move even faster. Gifts, souvenirs, postcards, and toys are examples of products that usually enjoy high markups. These should be placed where most of the customers will see them. Such locations are those near the check-out counter, where people stand to check out or register for a campsite.

Impulse products are purchased without much or any previous thought. Examples are chewing gum, candy, popcorn, toys, costume jewelry, and ice cream. These items should also be placed in high-visibility locations.

Shoplifting

Campers are like all people when it comes to shoplifting. It's easier to prevent shoplifting than it is to deal with it after it happens. Dealing with a camper shoplifter usually means the loss of a camper customer. Keep everything wide open, with lots of visibility. Have wide aisles, given the space available. Use fixtures that are low enough to see over. Display small items near the check-out counter, or if possible, buy those products packaged in large containers. Keep the expensive items under glass. This applies to jewelry, expensive crafts, and other gift items. Use convex mirrors or TV cameras to see in aisles that can't be seen from the checkout counter. Just having these things in the store is a deterrent.

The doorway should be in clear view of the check-out counter, so that everyone can be seen coming and going. This may be difficult if you have other profit centers in the same building, such as the game room and laundry, with doors opening into the store area.

Fixture Flexibility

A perfect store layout is hard to achieve. Therefore, experimentation is urged to create the best layout for your individual situation. Some store fixtures need to be easily movable.

Related Items

Placing related items next to each other makes it easier for customers to find the products they want to buy. This is also convenient for stocking shelves and pricing, because you may choose to apply the same markup to the entire line of products.

Related Departments

Related departments should be located next to each other for the same reason you locate related products this way. It makes shopping, restocking, and pricing easier.

An example of a campground store layout (see Appendix A) would include a check-out counter in clear view of the entrance. Assume that the entrance road goes past the store entrance. The glass door and windows on either side of the door make it possible to see vehicles going in and out of the campground. This is important for campground security, as well as store security.

The sale and specials locations should be near the front desk. These are the most valuable locations because they have the highest visibility.

The expensive jewelry counter would be under glass on one side of the check-out island. Candy, an impulse item, would be under the other counter, under glass also. It can be located near the counter and not under glass, but if it's individually wrapped it's good to keep it under glass. Expensive gifts would also be under the glass counter.

The most important items should have the best locations. Ice, milk, soda, and beer should be located in the rear of the store. These are products that people will look for; in the process, they will walk past many other products in the store that may induce them to purchase.

Get ideas from the experts on this subject. Observe the layouts of other retail stores that carry relatively the same products that you carry. Most campground stores are convenience stores, so look in convenience stores. These are found in conjuction with gas stations. Notice the overall layout and where the different kinds of products are located. Also, observe how they have various products on sale or displayed as specials.

Merchandising Decisions

How do you know what products to stock in your store, especially if you are just starting a store operation? Experimentation is one way to find out. It may be a little expensive if big mistakes are made. You certainly want to keep track of what does and doesn't sell so that you can do a better job of ordering merchandise in subsequent orders you place.

After deciding which store items to stock, you need to decide which brands to stock. The answer is to stock those that your campers prefer, not the brands you and your family prefer. Go to food stores in market areas where your campers come from, and notice the brands displayed for sale. These are the brands your camper customers are used to buying.

Sometimes the major newspapers do readership studies for their advertisers to determine the brand preferences of their readers. They will often share this information with you if you request it from them.

Quantities

When starting the campground store profit center, stock small quantities. This is good advice for two reasons. First, it allows you to stock more kinds of products in a given amount of space. It also reduces the risk of ending up with a large quantity of one item at the end of the season. However, for products such as logo items, you may have to order a season's supply.

Capitalize on the convenience nature of the store and the lack of storage space in RVs. You might want to split egg cartons in half and sell them by the half dozen. Also, consider selling potatoes, apples, oranges, and tomatoes individually or two for $.59, and so on. Another advantage of selling smaller portions is that a larger markup can be added to the costs.

Inventory Control

The objective of inventory control is to have enough inventory on hand at all times without being overstocked. Every dollar's worth of unneeded store inventory costs about 25 cents in net profit. There are storage costs and money tied up in inventory that could be earning you money elsewhere, or not costing you money in interest charges.

Generally, the amount to order at any time depends on how much merchandise is selling and how long it takes to get more. It is highly recommended that accurate records be kept. Records should be kept on last year's sales and order quantities by date. Also, keep a written record of customer requests for products. If you don't, you may miss out on good sellers, or stock too much of a product.

Computer Systems

The most sophisticated system is the computerized inventory system, which is what most supermarkets use today. As merchandise is rung up at the cash register, the computer program automatically deducts it from the inventory. Thus, you can refer to a computer printout at any time to determine order quantities. This system is only cost effective when you have a fairly large store volume.

Check-In/Check-Out

Another inventory system is the "check-in/check-out" system, also known as the "perpetual inventory" system. In this method, as merchandise is received, you make a note of the volume on a record form, then as the merchandise is taken out of the storage room, the appropriate notation is made on the same form.

Another method is to note the change in inventory level as the merchandise is sold, either by using the sales slips or by keeping track of stub tickets or tags removed from the products when they are sold. This may be practical in small stores only.

Shelf Inventory

Regularly checking the shelves is a system that can be used. In this system, most or all of the inventory is stocked on display shelves. A label is placed on the shelf with one number indicating the number below which you should order more of the item. An adjacent number indicates the order quantity. In this way, you can go through your store with a merchandise list on a clipboard and make out your order by checking the shelves. This is probably the most efficient method for small stores.

Volume Discounts

Volume discounts can save you large amounts in purchasing costs, provided you can resell the quantities required for the discount. Some merchandise items have a regular schedule of sales. Learning when these occur and taking advantage of them can be very cost effective. Be sure you can sell the quantity that you buy, because if you have considerable inventory left at the end of the season, the cost of such inventory may be as much as you gained by taking advantage of the discount.

Craft fairs are a good source of wholesale craft items. The fairs are held throughout the country. Your nearby craft wholesaler can give you information on the fair schedule in your area.

Logo Items

These are items with your campground logo imprinted on them. Selling them promotes your campground and generates store profit. Often, such logo items as T-shirts, windbreakers, sweatshirts, and caps can be big sellers. Because these items are personalized, it usually takes considerable time to get delivery after you've ordered them. In many instances, they are only ordered once per season, such as at the campground owners' convention trade show.

Seasonal Changes

Your store sales volume fluctuates with your camper volume. Your order quantities must fluctuate correspondingly. It is important that you keep records throughout the season each year, so you can look back in time and establish trends in store sales as related to camper volume, both for annual levels, and for order quantities within the camping season. Plan to have a minimum inventory at the end of the season.

Group Buying

Some campground operators have found it cost effective to get together with neighboring campground operators and buy as a group. In this way, you can each enjoy the benefits of quantity discounts. Conversations at campground workshops have indicated that six is the maximum number of campgrounds to make group buying effective. Someone in the group has to order the merchandise, pay for it, collect the money from the other campgrounds, and deliver the merchandise to the respective campgrounds. It does involve considerable paperwork and coordination. The success of group buying depends on the personalities of the members in the group—namely their willingness to cooperate.

Consignments

Local crafts people may be willing to have you sell their craft items on consignment, which saves you the cost of the inventory. You don't have to pay them until a product sells. The campground should receive 35 to 40 percent of the sale price, with the crafts person receiving the rest.

Campground Store Pricing

One of the big decisions you make in operating your store is the pricing decision. How do you know how much to price each of many products? The answer is very similar to that of pricing campsites. You can base your store merchandise prices on your cost of merchandise and markup, what others charge, and what you think your customers will pay. Here, as in campsite rate determination, a combination of the above is recommended.

Markup-Based Pricing

In this method the selling price is based on some level of markup over the cost of the merchandise. This is perhaps the most misunderstood concept in campground store operations. Let's use an example to explain this concept. Assume that we buy a product for $3.00 and sell it for $4.00. The difference between our cost and our selling price ($1.00) is the markup.

Selling price	$4.00
Cost	−3.00
Markup	$1.00

The above markup is stated as a dollar amount. It can also be stated as a percentage. The percentage markup can be based on the selling price or the purchase cost, but most of the time it is based on selling price.

Markup Based on Cost

The markup based on cost is computed by dividing the dollar markup by the cost, which in this example is 33.3 percent.

$$\textbf{\$1.00/\$3.00 = .333 = 33.3\%}$$

Markup Based on Selling Price

The markup percentage based on selling price is computed by dividing the dollar markup by the selling price. In this case it is 25 percent.

$$\textbf{\$1.00/\$4.00 = .25 = 25\%}$$

Conventional retailing practice uses this latter method. Unless otherwise stated, assume that this is the method intended to be used.

The difficult part is determining a selling price when all you know is the cost you paid and your desired markup percentage. Let's compute a selling price for that $3.00 item, with a desired markup percentage on a selling price of 25 percent. First, subtract the desired markup percent from 100 percent, which is 75 percent or .75 (100% – 25% = 75%).

Next, divide the cost by 75 percent and get $4.00, the selling price ($3.00/ .75 = $4.00). This is the selling price based on markup of the selling price.

$$\textbf{100\% – 25\% = 75\% = .75}$$
$$\textbf{\$3.00/.75 = \$4.00}$$

Always Divide, Never Multiply

Do not confuse this method with calculating the selling price with a markup based on cost. To demonstrate why, refer to the above example, and notice that the selling price computed from a desired markup on selling price is $4.00. To compute a selling price based on a desired markup on cost of 25 percent, we have the following:

$$\textbf{\$3.00} \times \textbf{.25 = \$.75 = markup}$$
$$\textbf{\$3.00 + \$.75 = \$3.75 = selling price}$$

Notice that the markup based on cost is $.25 less than the markup based on selling price. Therefore, your selling price is going to be less than was intended if you use the markup based on cost when the markup based on selling price should be used. This can amount to substantial amounts of foregone store profits.

Selling Price Calculation

With pocket calculators, this is a relatively easy procedure to use. Just enter the cost, press the divide key, subtract the desired markup percent from 100 in your head or on a piece of paper, enter the result, press the "equals" key, and read the resulting selling price. Many calculators are designed so that after you've made one division, you can simply enter the new number to be divided, in this case the cost. Press the "equals" key, and it will perform the division over again, giving you a new selling price with the same desired markup as used previously.

There are electronic calculators available with markup keys designed for calculating selling price by the markup procedure. With these calculators, all you need to do is enter the cost, press the markup key, then enter the desired markup percent, press the "equals" key, and the result is the selling price.

How do you know what markup percentages to use? Often the manufacturer will suggest it. In fact, some manufacturers place a suggested retail price right on the package. Sometimes your local distributor will recommend one. Unless stated otherwise, these markup percentages are intended as markups on selling price. Your local distributor may not understand this markup concept.

Suggested markup percentages for products commonly sold in campground stores are as shown in Table 17.1.

Table 17.1

Suggested Markup on Selling Price for Selected Items

Merchandise Item	Markup on Selling Price
Postcards	60%
Souvenirs	50
Toys	50
Bumper stickers/decals	50
Novelty items	45–50
Hats and beach wear	40
Logo imprinted t-shirts and sweatshirts	35–45
RV accessories	35–40
Hardware	35v40
Camping supplies	35–40
Film	30–35
Housewares and cleaning supplies	30
Picnic supplies	30
Candy and snacks	25–33
Groceries and dairy items	28
Health and beauty aids	28–30
Beer and soft drinks	25
Cigarettes	25
Magazines and paperback books	20
Frozen meats	20
Pizza and TV dinners	20

You'll want to apply the same markup to entire product lines, not each item individually. In this way, you can be much more efficient in your pricing efforts.

Competition-Based Pricing

Most campground stores are convenience stores. You are providing a convenience, the same as the 24-hour mart and self-serve gas station. Therefore, these are the prices with which you should compare yours, rather than with the prices of large supermarkets. People will be willing to pay a little more, knowing it's a convenience. Of course, when prices get too high, they'll go to their home supermarkets for their camping supplies.

It is important to consider the nearby supermarket or convenience store, if there is one. Repeat and seasonal campers will become familiar with those prices, as well. The distance of that store from your campground is also a consideration.

Willing-to-Pay-Based Pricing

One consideration is how sensitive you are to being known as a high-priced convenience store operator or a competitively priced store operator. Campers will let you know by complaining and not buying your merchandise if they feel your prices are too high. If, on the other hand, they think your prices are bargain prices, they'll buy your products but won't tell you that your prices are too low. You must determine your prices based on your own judgment, in relation to the objectives you have set for your store.

Promotion and Merchandising

Your store sales volume depends to a large extent on how much and how well you promote your store and merchandise your products. A practical approach to promoting and merchandising your store is to let campers know that you have a store as they plan their camping trip, get them into the store when they're at your campground, and then sell them lots of merchandise when they're in your store. Information about your store should be included in your brochure, newsletter, and ads. Statements to this effect could be: *We have a complete store, We can supply all your camping needs,* or *Our store features competitive prices.*

Maria Baptista of Acres of Wildlife in Steep Falls, Maine, has a bakery as part of her campground store. She promotes her bakery and her country store in her newsletter and activity schedule. In the newsletter she lists the available store items, including her popular bakery items and their prices.

There are many ways to get campers back into your store once they have checked in. First, your store should look attractive from the registration counter, as well as from the outside of the building. As campers register, you can give them fliers featuring store specials for the weekend or week. Your staff can be instructed to tell campers during registration that you have a complete store, give the hours of operation, and mention one or two items that are on sale. Free coffee (one cup per person) until 10:00 a.m. is a good way to get people into your store in the morning.

Discount coupons can be a part of the flyer that you hand out at registration. A free ice cream cone, a two-for-one sale on some items, and a free mini-golf pass are examples (the mini-golf is sold in the store). The mini-golf pass might be for children only. Then when the parents bring their children, they'll probably play mini-golf also. Or once there, the group will probably play more than one round, thus expanding mini-golf sales as well.

This sales approach can also work with ice cream cones. If you give children one single dip cone, the parent may then also have an ice cream cone and be exposed to many store products in the process. If you have a lounge, you might try a free bag of popcorn to get them into the lounge. In all of these examples, the objective is to increase sales in the store or lounge.

Another way to get people into your store is to establish an information area in the store. A word of caution is advised here: such an information area takes up valuable shelf space and display areas. If you have plenty of room, it may be a good idea. If you don't have such ample space, you may not want to use the space in that way.

Sales Techniques

Suggestive selling. Train your employees to suggest items to customers. Instead of training your staff to ask, "Will there be anything else?" train your staff to make specific suggestions on products that complement what campers have already purchased. Some examples are:

Item Purchased	Suggestion
eggs	bacon or sausage
hot dogs	buns, potato chips, catsup
Bread	butter or oleo
	sandwich meats, spreads
ice cream	toppings for sundaes
beer	chips, nuts, pretzels
wine	cheese and crackers

You might feature some type of camper appliance with a fairly high price or markup to justify the effort. Your staff could say to customers, "Have you seen our new popcorn popper? It's great for campfire corn popping." Display the popper close by.

Display the merchandise. Displaying merchandise is one of the most important parts of store merchandising. The store fixtures you use should be attractive and efficient. If shirts, windbreakers, and sweatshirts are to be sold, they should be hung in an attractive, easy-to-examine setting. Placing them on shelves is not a good idea, because customers want to hold them up to check the size and appearance and then put them back on the shelves. As a result, the shelves usually become messy and unattractive. Hanger racks can be obtained that are free standing or fastened to a wall.

Items for different age groups should be displayed at the appropriate eye level for the intended customer. Items for adults should be placed on the higher shelves, and the children's products should be on the lower shelves. Men's products should be a little higher than women's products.

Always keep the shelves full, as customers tend to buy more when the shelves are fully stocked. This suggestion can be disregarded at the end of the season when the inventory is intentionally reduced for the off-season.

Always display impulse items—items bought with no previous thought or planning—in conspicuous places. Check your local supermarkets and convenience stores to see where they place the impulse items around the check-out counter and on the ends of the shelves.

Provide information. Do everything you can to make it easier for the customer to make the buying decision. Appropriate signing on the aisles to direct customers to the products they are looking for, is an example. Descriptive labels on the merchandise are also beneficial. If they have a question about a product, they may not want to go to the effort to ask about it, and they may put the product back on the shelf and forget about it. Tags should also be located on the products that can be easily seen and read.

Offer specials/leaders. There is nothing like a perceived bargain to make people buy. Bargain shopping is definitely a leisure and recreation activity. You need only consider all the garage, yard, and rummage sales and the popularity of discount malls and factory outlet stores to know this is true. Heavy customer activity is a very strong pull to other customers.

Observe again how the supermarkets conduct specials. Holidays, school openings, and store anniversaries generate specials in retail stores every year. You can do similar promotions. (Coordinations with local community events can also be done to promote your store.)

Campground Store Financial Analysis

A financial analysis is used to measure how your store is performing. An operating statement for the store should be generated and should take the following form:

Operating statement

For the year (month) ending ____

	Gross sales	-	Cost of sales	=	Gross profit	Markup
Groceries	$____	–	$____	=	$____	% ____
Beer	____		____		____	____
Ice	____		____		____	____
Wood	____		____		____	____
Other	____		____		____	____
Total	____		____		____	____

Operating expenses (store)	$____
Wages	____
Payroll expenses	____
Maintenance/supplies*	____
Insurance*	____
Licenses	____
Utilities*	____
Miscellaneous*	____
Total operating expenses	____
Net profit before debt service and depreciation	$____

* Share allocated to campground store

Cost of sales computation

The cost of sales can be determined as follows:

Inventory, beginning of period	$____
Plus merchandise purchases*	+ ____
Equals goods available for sale	= ____
Less ending inventory	– ____
Equals cost of goods sold	= $____

---

*Subtract the amount of any returned merchandise from this amount plus amounts taken for personal use. Include any shipping and delivery costs.

233

Gross Profit/Gross Margin

The gross margin or gross profit is a useful indicator of store performance. It is the difference between the selling price and the cost of goods, and is the effective markup. You can compute the gross margin for each merchandise category. If you divide the gross profit by the gross sales, the result is the effective markup percentage on selling price for the entire store. If you do it by merchandise category, you get the effective markup percentage for each category. This is the percentage in the previous store financial statement example, and its use is highly recommended.

The management value comes from comparing the effective markup percentage with the desired markup you used in your pricing decisions. If the effective markup is lower than your desired markup, it could be due to one or more of the following:

- Spoilage or shrinkage;
- Customer or employee theft;
- Family use;
- Inaccurate records;
- Mistakes, errors; or
- Discounts/sale price reductions.

This management tool is a red flag to look further into the cause of any problems.

Operating Expenses

Operating expenses may be too high for profits to be earned in the store. One of the major expense items is for labor and related payroll expenses. You may want to examine your scheduling of store hours and assign staff to other tasks. Or, you might add a profit center that could be operated by the same staff person who runs the store.

Net Profit

The net profit is your bottom line and tells you how your store is doing as a profit center overall. Watching this from period to period, and comparing it with the same period last year and the year before, is an excellent indicator of your store's overall performance.

Appendix A

Campground Store Layout

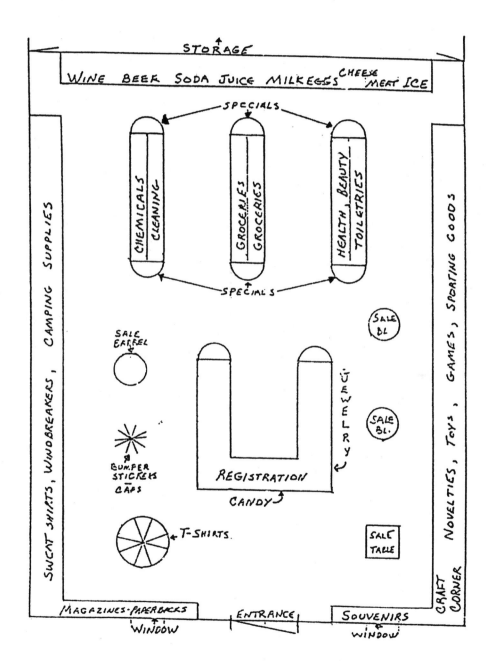

Part

III

Marketing Your Campground

Most campground operators will agree that the major constraint on campground profitability is business volume, generated by the marketing efforts of the campground. This is true for all campgrounds; large and small, old and new. In fact, it is generally true for the entire free enterprise business community.

It is agreed by most that it takes at least three to five years from start-up to reach the maximum level of campground business volume. But it's also true that this volume never really reaches the maximum level that is desired.

For most people going into the campground business, marketing is a new field. They bring little, if any, background training or experience to the campground business.

A Unique Marketing Situation

Campground marketing, along with tourism marketing in general, is unique in that the customer has to travel to the campground to consume the product—the camping experience. It can't be purchased in a store and taken home. It can't be obtained through a mail order system, nor can it be delivered by any delivery vehicle. The camper party must use some means of conveyance and travel to the campground to consume or enjoy the camping experience. Further, they usually bring their camping equipment with them. Because of this feature, marketing efforts have to be planned accordingly.

Further, the "experience" includes not only the camping experience within the campground, but also the planning, the anticipation, the packing, the trip to the campground, the return trip, and the reminiscing, along with the unpacking, after reaching home. Your main concern is with their experience at your campground, of course, although you may also influence their anticipation and their reminiscing, or their savoring of a wonderful camping experience.

The Marketing Concept

Marketing experts have, in the last few decades, proclaimed the marketing concept as the proper approach to business marketing management. In this concept, the entire business operation is carried out with the needs of the customer as the main concern. The product design (the camping experience) and all other activities—including marketing, personnel management, and so on—are designed and carried out to satisfy the needs of the customer. The Ten Commandments of Good Business follow:

1. A **customer** is the most important person in any business.
2. A **customer** is not dependent on us—we are dependent on him or her.
3. A **customer** is not an interruption of our work—he or she is the pur pose of it.
4. A **customer** does us a favor when he or she calls—we are not doing him or her a favor by serving him or her.
5. A **customer** is part of our business—not an outsider.
6. A **customer** is not a cold statistic—he or she is a flesh and blood human being with feelings and emotions like our own.
7. A **customer** is not someone with whom to argue and match wits.
8. A **customer** is one who brings us his or her wants. It is our job to fill those wants.
9. A **customer** is deserving of the most courteous and attentive treatment we can give him or her.
10. A **customer** is the life blood of this and every other business.

This has not always been true. A famous case in point is Henry Ford's statement, "They can have any color of car they want, as long as it's black!" And then along came GM. It was quite common in the past for manufacturers to make a product and then figure out how to sell it. Now, extensive research is carried out to find out what customers want, then a product is created to fulfill those wants.

The same applies to the campground industry. Campground operators should use extensive efforts to find out what campers want, then provide it for them. This concept carries through all of the campground operations, including staff behavior, campground rules and policies, and quality service facilities and amenities.

Practical Approach of This Section

This section is organized in a practical manner to show you how to approach the marketing area of campground management. It follows the "what," "who," and "how" of marketing, that is:

- *What* are you selling? (your campground product)
- *To who* are you selling? (your potential market)
- *How* do you invite them? (your marketing program)

Other chapters address related marketing subjects, including rate determination and market research.

Chapter

18

PRODUCT AND MARKET IDENTIFICATION

How can you effectively market a product if you don't know what you are selling? This chapter discusses many aspects of the campground experience that are useful in planning and conducting an effective campground marketing program. The campground industry is getting more competitive every day, so it is vital for marketing to be successful. Keep in mind the question, "Why would anyone want to camp at my campground rather than someplace else?"

Identifying Your Product

What are you selling? Is it a campsite, mini-golf, swimming, snacks, drinks, groceries, or camping supplies? Or are you selling the benefits of camping at your campground and the total camping experience: fun, relaxation, excitement, socialization? This chapter makes a strong argument for the latter.

Certainly you want to sell campsite reservations, groceries, camping supplies, and articles from other profit centers. But in the marketing of your campground, are you going to reach prospective campers with grocery ads, camper supply ads, and food and drink ads? It makes more sense to sell the ingredients of a happy camping experience: the relaxation, socialization, and satisfaction of the needs and wants of campers you want to attract.

You have the opportunity to sell whatever you want to sell. However, you can't sell everything or every type of camping experience. You can try to sell a wide range of camping experiences, but you may fall short in several different areas. As the saying goes, if you try to be all things to all people, you'll probably end up being everybody's second choice.

For example, if you decide to run a family campground, your campground won't be as attractive to golden agers because the wants and activity needs of these two groups are quite different. The marketing program you develop would have to be geared to two very different groups.

You must decide which type or types of camping experiences to offer, and then develop your campground and marketing program accordingly. You must sell the idea to camping parties that they are wanted and so that they will be pampered. Why? Simply stated, so they'll have a super camping experience. Then they'll come back, tell others, and bring others with them.

Product Analysis

In order to evaluate your campground or resort product, rank the following list of items as follows:

5   We're doing great
4   We're doing pretty well
3   We're about average
2   We could do better
1   We need a lot of improvement here

Circle your ranking for each item below. Be honest.

Product: What Are You Selling?

(Just rate the items that you want to offer, and add any you think are unique to your campground.)

5 4 3 2 1 The overall quality of the experience you provide.

5 4 3 2 1 Relaxation.

5 4 3 2 1 Socialization/being with friends.

5 4 3 2 1 Fun and excitement.

5 4 3 2 1 Family togetherness.

5 4 3 2 1 Solitude/quiet/communing with nature.

5 4 3 2 1 An overnight stopover, just a place to park.

Physical Features: Rate the Quality of Each Feature

5 4 3 2 1 Highway signs.

5 4 3 2 1 Access: easy to drive in, plenty of room to park.

5 4 3 2 1 Front entrance sign: attractive, easy to read, reflective of your image.

5 4 3 2 1 Front entrance: well-landscaped, good lighting, attractive, uncluttered.

5 4 3 2 1 On-premise signs: attractive, adequate, and effective so things are easy to find.

5 4 3 2 1   Entry roads: free of dust and potholes, wide enough to pass if two-way traffic.

5 4 3 2 1   Landscaping: good sod cover, weeds cut, trees and shrubs pruned, diseased and dead trees and branches removed.

5 4 3 2 1   Store: good layout, bright, attractive, inviting.

5 4 3 2 1   Laundry: machines adequate, work properly, sufficient number of them, attractive-looking room.

5 4 3 2 1   Public telephones: well-maintained, attractive, easy to find.

5 4 3 2 1   Toilets: adequate number, well-lighted, attractive walls, ceilings, floors, screened, ventilated, clean at all times.

5 4 3 2 1   Showers: good controls, adequate hot water, plenty of hooks, private changing area, place to sit, adequate ventilation, heated in cool weather, kept clean.

5 4 3 2 1   Septic/sewer: free of odors, prompt pumping service, dump station—easy to use, well kept.

5 4 3 2 1   Campsites: well-marked, large enough, well-drained, some with shade, privacy with vegetative barriers, grassy, graveled or paved.

5 4 3 2 1   Hookups: water pipes well-supported, backflow preventers in place, in close to RV pad on left side of parking space, in good condition, proper amperage in electrical hookups.

5 4 3 2 1   Picnic tables: recently painted /stained, do not tip easily, no rotten boards, sliver free, one at each site.

5 4 3 2 1   Fire rings: attractive, can't be moved, cleaned after each use.

5 4 3 2 1   Trash containers: sufficient number, proximity to sites, recreation hall, playground, store, etc., attractive looking.

5 4 3 2 1   Lighting: soft colors, pathways to toilets easy to see at night, enough for security purposes, but not too much to be unattractive.

5 4 3 2 1   Roads: materials used to avoid dust and mud, free of pot holes.

5 4 3 2 1   Presence of safety equipment.

5 4 3 2 1   Facilities for the physically challenged.

Maintenance: Evaluate the Success of Your Maintenance Program

5 4 3 2 1   Grounds in general.

5 4 3 2 1   Store, front office.

5 4 3 2 1   Campsites.

5 4 3 2 1   Bathrooms.

5 4 3 2 1   Laundry.

5 4 3 2 1   Signs.

5 4 3 2 1   Recreation hall.

5 4 3 2 1   Pool.

Appearance: Evaluate the appearance of You and Your Staff

5 4 3 2 1   Are you and all your employees an asset to your business?

5 4 3 2 1   Do you and your employees dress appropriately for your roles?

5 4 3 2 1   Are you and all your employees readily identifiable by guests? Do you wear identifying shirts or uniforms?

5 4 3 2 1   Do you and all your employees look well-groomed (neat, tidy, hair trimmed and attractive, well-shaved, etc.)?

Hospitality: Rate the Management's Success at Providing Hospitality

5 4 3 2 1   Overall service attitude.

5 4 3 2 1   Friendly, prompt, and informative handling of all inquiries.

5 4 3 2 1   Friendly demeanor (smile frequently and easily).

5 4 3 2 1   Courteous to guests at all times.

5 4 3 2 1   Listen attentively to guest concerns.

5 4 3 2 1   Free of annoying habits (gum or tobacco chewing, smoking, etc.).

5 4 3 2 1   Knowledgeability of the campground/resort and surrounding area.

Hospitality: Rate the Employees' Success at Providing Hospitality

5 4 3 2 1   Friendly and informative handling of all inquiries.

5 4 3 2 1   Friendly demeanor (smile frequently and easily).

5 4 3 2 1   Courteous to guests at all times.

5 4 3 2 1   Listen attentively to guest concerns.

5 4 3 2 1   Free of annoying habits (gum or tobacco chewing, smoking, etc.).

5 4 3 2 1   Knowledgeable of the campground or resort and surrounding area.

Recreation: Rate the Success of Your Campground

5 4 3 2 1   Variety of activities available for market segments targeted.

5 4 3 2 1   Number of activities available on-site and off-site.

5 4 3 2 1   Activities suitably managed and directed.

5 4 3 2 1   Rainy day activities and facilities adequate.

5 4 3 2 1   Organized activities for children, teens, adults, intergenerational groups (depending on type of camper served).

5 4 3 2 1   Special events: well-organized, wide appeal, well-attended.

How did you do? On which side of average (3) did you rank your campground? Areas that need improvement should be clear to you. List and prioritize them. Correct as soon as possible those that are inexpensive problems. For the expensive areas, develop a three- to five-year improvement plan to update your campground.

If you don't continually upgrade your campground, it will go downhill and you'll lose your business in a few years. Further, it becomes more difficult to acquire loans, sell your campground, or even leave it to an heir. If you worked through the previous self-evaluation and found many areas hard to evaluate, try having someone else do it for you who knows your campground and who can give you an honest appraisal.

Camper Desires

The famous department store retailer Marshall Field is quoted as saying, "Find out what the ladies want, and sell it to them." Likewise, you should find out what the campers want, and sell it to them. This is not as easy as it may seem.

Past studies have shown that what campers say they want in choosing a campground and what campground operators say their campers want are not the same. For example, "good facilities" were much more important to campers as operators thought. "Cleanliness" was twice as important to campers than it was to operators. "Accessibility" was many times more important to campers. "Good customer relations" was more than twice as important to campers, whereas "recreation" was more important to operators.

"Ads and promotions" was many times more important to campers than to operators. This may indicate a lack of incentive to advertise on the part of campground operators. In summary, campground operators grossly underestimated the importance of their facilities, location relative to camper markets, advertising and promotion, and cleanliness

As a former frequent camper parent with four children, it is clear that having my children like the campground was paramount. That meant having plenty of things to do in a friendly atmosphere.

Image Projection

Are you really selling what you think you are selling? Does your average camper perceive the same experience at your campground as you think you are offering? The answer deals with image. As shown previously, there is no guarantee that your campers see your campground and the experience you offer in the same terms as you see them. In fact, it is quite likely that there will be differences. And what's important to you is the image your campers have, not yours. They are the ones who provide your income. The product self-evaluation exercise shown earlier in this chapter can be used to help identify your image.

The Experience

An old marketing adage says: "Sell the sizzle, not the steak!" In the campground business, the sizzle is the benefits—the things that satisfy the wants of campers. What are these want—satisfiers that will cause campers to have such a good time that they'll come back, tell others, and bring others with them? Some examples follow:

- family togetherness;
- fun, excitement, action, adventure;
- socialization, being with friends; and
- nature, solitude, nature study.

Remember when planning your marketing program that the phrases used to describe these want-satisfiers become the copy (written portion) of your ads and brochures. People will pay for what they want. When you find out what they want, provide it for them and charge them for it. Of course, there are some physical facilities that are necessary to offer such experiences. For example, if you want to offer family togetherness, you need facilities for families, such as playground equipment, mini-golf, and shuffleboard. The organized recreation activities should be intergenerational so that families can participate as a unit.

If you want to offer socialization, campsites should be laid out to accommodate groups, and activities should include mixer-type events to get people introduced to each other quickly. If it's back-to-nature, the campsites should be spaced further apart than normal, with much vegetative growth between them. Nature trails should be developed and interpretive activities offered.

Differential Advantage

In the competitive camping market, each campground needs to have a differential advantage. In other words, you need to be unique, to offer something in a camping experience that no or few other campgrounds offer. You need a positive answer to the question, "Why would anyone want to camp at my campground, rather than going someplace else to camp?"

For example, Ray Hoekstra, of Yogi Bear's Jellystone Park in Fremont, Wisconsin says he wants his campers to think "Wow!" when they enter his park. His campground recently won the Park of the Year award from the Jellystone franchise.

How can your campground be unique? A different, or better, camping experience is an answer. This can be accomplished through better facilities. For example, offer higher quality campsites—level, spacious, well-drained, sunny in the morning, and shady in the afternoon. Offer higher quality service buildings and facilities. Offer more and higher quality recreation activities. High-quality hospitality skills from you and your staff are a must in every campground, but they will set yours far above the average. Making your campground something special depends on the segment or segments of the camping market that you plan to attract.

Service and Hospitality

One of the most important ingredients of a satisfying camping experience, and, therefore, a key to repeat business, is a high quality service attitude and hospitality program. Making your guests feel important, wanted, that you care about them, and that you want to see them at your campground are critical to a successful camping operation. Many average physical characteristics in a campground can be overcome with such a high quality program.

Market Identification

Who are the campers to whom you are selling? Where do they live? The answers to these questions are important, because campground marketing is expensive and you want to be as efficient and effective as possible in your marketing program.

Market Segmentation and Analysis

The first logical step is to list all the possible segments into which the camper market can be divided. With the following segments, some comments will be included that are relevant to the potential of each.

By Age and Family Status

Married couples with children younger than 13 years and teen families have been the mainstay of the camping market in the Midwest. Now these "traditional" young families are becoming a smaller percentage of the total market, because there are fewer of them in the population. Census figures show that married couples with children have decreased. High divorce rates, later family formations, and unrelated people living together are factors that have reduced the proportion of such families in the population. In addition, the post World War II baby boom generation is getting past this part of the family cycle and people are living longer.

Married couples with children in their teens have competing uses for their summer vacations, such as summer jobs, which are often service jobs that include evening as well as weekend schedules. Also, they have summer camps, including scout, church, athletic, and other special interest camps. Summer school is also a competitor for camping time.

Empty nesters, married couples whose children are grown, have more discretionary income than younger couples, because they are nearing the peak in their earning cycles and have lived past most of their children's expensive needs.

Golden agers and retirees have the leisure time to travel and camp. They also may have ample discretionary income. The fixed retirement income is becoming less significant in this group, as retirement plans are becoming more geared to cost of living increases, with increased income possible through investment income. However, these people have much experience at spending wisely, and they expect to get value in their purchases. This segment is not a homogeneous group. They have a wide range of interests and activity preferences.

Young people usually camp in groups. They may camp by themselves or with chaperones or counselors, through church, Y, 4-H, or other organized groups. The group leaders are the ones to reach, perhaps in direct mail advertising.

Young singles are young adults (18 and over) who camp in groups of the same sex or mixed groups. Some campgrounds try to discourage these groups because of past experiences, such as noisy partying. Others handle them well.

Married and unrelated couples without children will probably prefer adult facilities and activities. Single parents are usually female heads of families, who desire services such as babysitting, supervised children's recreation activities, and assistance in setting up their campers. They are more concerned than average about security. This is a growing segment that offers increasing potential. Few campgrounds really pursue this segment.

By Type of Camping Equipment

Campers can be segmented by type of camping equipment preferred. This information is useful in marketing planning. For example, RV owners can be contacted via RV dealerships and RV brand-specific camping clubs, who often travel in caravans. They should also be informed that you provide adequate sites with adequate hookups.

By Type of Stay

Most of the discussion in the marketing section is geared to the destination camping market. For overnight or transient campers, listings in camper directories, adequate outdoor advertising, and a location on a main interstate highway are useful. Also, listings or information at the local information booth, Chamber of Commerce, service stations, and restaurants can be good for one-nighters. With destination campers who make their stay a weekend or longer vacation, marketing efforts become more elaborate.

By Recreation Activity

Campgrounds can develop reputations for providing excellent facilities for certain recreation activities, or for being near an attraction or an area known for such activities. Amusement parks, natural beauty, and nearby historical sites are a few attractions that draw campers. Sport fishing is a popular attraction in many areas of the country. It's a good idea to advertise the area and the activity that goes with it.

By Special Interests

Some campgrounds are successful in catering to RV clubs, square dancers, and other special interest groups. It is necessary to have adequate accommodations for large groups. To reach these groups, you would most likely use direct marketing methods.

By Physical Abilities

People with disabilities represent a growing segment of the population. This market segment has special needs, and there are regulations regarding some of these needs already. Special groups can be reached through word-of-mouth and direct mail lists.

By Origin

It's necessary in your marketing planning efforts to segment your camping market by origin—or where they live. This tells you the cities in which to place your ads, which sport shows to attend, and where you can distribute brochures. Your market may be closer to you than you think. Studies have shown that, on average, people travel less than 100 miles out of town to spend a weekend camping in the outdoors.

In trying to determine the origin of potential guests, contact the local Chamber of Commerce or other tourism promotion group for information on studies that may have been conducted on origin of tourists in your area.

Market Segment Selection

Given the product or recreation experience you've decided to provide and sell, decide which market segments you wish to attract. Start with your present clientele. Analyze your guest registration forms to determine the profiles of the current campers. It is probably sufficient to analyze several years' forms.

Determine the party size, type of camping equipment, origin, and anything else on the cards that you think would be useful. Refer to the chapter on how to do your own market research for more information on this important matter.

The rationale for developing these camper profiles is that it's probably easiest to attract more campers like those already camping with you. The same principle applies to origin. It's likely easier to attract more customers from origins from which substantial portions of your campers are already coming than it is to attract them from other areas.

If you're starting a new campground, choose those major market areas within 250 miles and where known tourists are coming from beyond that distance. Also, choose them in the direction from which tourists have historically traveled.

Chapter

19

ADVERTISING AND PROMOTION

How do you invite campers to come to your campground? This invitation is the key to successful marketing and consequent successful campground management. Sounds easy, doesn't it? Then why is there concern about the difficulty in getting people to come to your campground? The answer is that it isn't all that easy, especially when you have a limited marketing budget. Add to this the competition for campers' leisure time and discretionary income, as well as an increasing supply of high-quality campgrounds. An advertising adage states "Spending money on advertising is easy. Spending it smart is hard" (Fitt-Peaster and Fitt-Peaser, 1989).

Marketing Objectives

What is it you really want to accomplish in this next camping season? What are your marketing objectives? If you have a written business plan, your marketing objectives and a complete marketing plan should be a part of it.

The marketing objectives should be derived from your overall financial or business objectives. Given a financial objective of a certain profit level, your financial plan should require a certain gross income, and a proportion of that would have to be generated from campsite rentals. Considering income generated from other profit centers based on camper volume, the number of desired campsite rentals can be calculated.

You might have a goal of a 10 percent increase in campsite rentals. This can be further broken down into seasonal and overnight rentals, which can then be broken down by season, such as peak season and shoulder (off-season). For example, in the snowbelt, operators often try to expand business in June, late August, and September.

Another possible objective is to attract a certain number of new campers and repeat campers. Because of normal attrition of business, you should probably strive for 25 to 35 percent of your camper parties as new campers, and the remainder as repeats. Table 19.1 may help you analyze your situation.

Table 19.1

		Peak Season		Shoulder Season		Total	
		Last Year	Next Year	Last Year	Next Year	Last Year	Next Year
Overnight	New						
	Repeat						
Seasonals	New						
	Return						

Remember that the more specific you make your objectives, the more specific you can make your marketing budget and marketing program. If you're just starting out in business, decide what you need to do to generate the income for your business plan budget, because you don't have a track record on which to base your objectives for next year. If you purchased an operating campground, the previous owner's records probably aren't of much value to you in planning, unless it was operating quite successfully and just as you plan to operate it.

The Marketing Budget

There is no magical amount to spend that will make your campground successful. However, it may be helpful to know what others spend. Spending on marketing, as well as other operating expenses, is usually stated in terms of an operating ratio, or a percentage that the expense category is of gross sales.

If you're just starting out and have no gross figures on which to base an advertising ratio, the above ratios can only be applied to your projected or budgeted gross sales figure in your business plan. You should spend more than the above, because when starting out you need to advertise much more in order to make people aware of, and start camping at your campground. You should spend what you think it will take to accomplish your occupancy goal.

Marketing Methods

How do other campgrounds market their campsites and other profit centers? What are the possibilities? A list of the more common marketing practices campgrounds employ include:

- business (calling) cards, stationery;
- brochures, fliers;
- outdoor advertising—advertising, directional and front entrance signs;
- direct mail—newsletter, answer inquiries, and so on;
- sport, travel, and mall shows;
- directories, listings and ads;
- media ads;
- web page on the Internet;
- personal selling;
- on-site promotions;
- cooperative efforts through local, county, regional, state, and national campground owners associations;
- packaging with other businesses in your area;
- promotions with RV dealers;
- cooperative efforts with municipal, county, state and national parks; and
- publicity and public relations in the local newspaper/community.

Experience indicates that brochures, outdoor advertising, the answering of inquiries, and directory listings (state and national) are used by most campgrounds. Many, but not all, use direct mail, sport shows, directory ads, and the Internet. Some do a better job of personal selling than others. Fewer still take advantage of the rest.

With this fist of possibilities—and not being an expert marketer—how do you decide what to do, and how and when to do it? If you're already in business, you've probably tried some of these. Experience is the best way to find out what really works for you. However, you need a way to evaluate the various marketing programs that you try to implement. These methods are described in Chapter 22, Market Research.

If you're new in the campground business, learn as much as you can by reading books, going to workshops, campground owners' conventions, and by talking to other campground owners/operators. Study others' ads, brochures, and sport show booths. Other campground operators are generally very willing to share their knowledge and information. They realize that they're better off being near other good quality campgrounds rather than poor quality campgrounds, on the principle that if campers go to one campground in an area, they'll tend to judge all campgrounds by the one experience they have, good or bad. After gathering your information, decide what you need to do to achieve the marketing objectives you set for yourself earlier.

A Sample Marketing Plan

A typical abbreviated marketing plan for the first year might look like the following:

Brochure. Five thousand brochures at $.30 equals $1,500. Distribute these at local and area tourist information centers, local gas stations, restaurants, and RV dealers. Send these in response to inquiries.

Letterhead stationery. Two thousand sheets at $.10 equals $200. Use this for answering inquiries and for other campground correspondence.

Outdoor advertising. Road signs, advertising, directional, and front entrance signs should be part of your capital investment. The estimated cost is $5,000.

Newspaper advertising. Choose a few suburban and small town weekly newspapers in communities that have great potential, and place ads in the spring and early summer. The estimated cost is $2000 to $2,500.

State/county/local campground owners' associations. Join these groups, if they exist in your area and state, and buy modest ads in their directories. The estimated cost is from $250 to $500.

Local Chamber of Commerce or tourism promotion association. Join these groups and get involved. Make sure campgrounds are well represented. The estimated cost is $350 to $1,000.

Publicity and public relations. Hold a grand opening or open house. Invite your local community, especially those who are likely to come in contact with campers looking for campgrounds. Invite the local news media. Take pictures for them to use if they don't take their own. Take pictures and write news releases for your own campground's special events. Always be ready with your camera if you're holding a special event in your campground. The estimated cost is $200 to $500.

Sport shows and mall shows. This is beneficial if the booth and initial set-up costs are reasonable. The estimated cost is $750 to $1,000.

Campground directory ads. The estimated cost of placing these ads is $1,500 to $5,000.

Word-of-mouth. The cost is nothing.

The entire cost adds up to $11,750 to $17,200. Notice that this is higher than the $6,750 shown earlier, as quoted in the national survey. Remember that the $11,750 to $17,200 is for a new campground just starting. You don't need to do all of these things every year. For example, your outdoor signs will last many years and just need repainting and rent paid regularly. Also, you don't need to hold an open house every year. Further, your stationery and brochures may last into the next year. Your actual marketing plan should be much more detailed than the above, stating exactly how you plan to carry out each of the marketing strategies that you plan.

The First Year

Let's suppose you're just starting out in your campground business. The following is a checklist of marketing tools you can use, with discussions of how to implement them.

Campground Name

The campground name is very important because it reflects the image of your campground, the quality of camping offered, and the type of camping (rustic, family, etc.). In short, it's what you're trying to sell. The name should be easy to read, pronounce, spell, and remember. When choosing a campground name, look through campground directories to see what others have named their campgrounds. You'll find a wide range of different names.

It's important to have the name help sell your campground. If you're going to sell the area in which your campground is located, you might use the area name as part of your campground name. For example, Mt. Rushmore Campground, Valley Forge Campground, or Wisconsin Dells KOA.

If you want to sell to RV campers, include "RV Park" in your name. If you want to sell a resort camping atmosphere, name your campground with those words in it, such as Yogi Bear's Jellystone Camp-Resort. If you want to appeal to families, you might name your campground something like Pine Acres Family Campground.

Unique Attributes

To be unique is to be different from all the others. Your campground may be unique in its location or some other category. You cannot assume the public knows about your uniqueness until you tell them about it.

Logo

This is the symbol, design, or drawing that goes on your brochure, letterhead stationery, and your business calling cards. It may well include your campground name. It's important because it also reflects the image that you want to communicate to others. It is advisable to go to a commercial artist to have this created, unless you have artistic skills yourself. The cost shouldn't be prohibitive.

Outdoor Advertising

There are two general types of outdoor advertising. One is outdoor billboard advertising, and the other is the directional signing showing campers the way to your campground. There are regulations specific to each kind regarding location, size, and placement. Your regional or district highway engineer or office can provide you with the regulations pertaining to state and federal highways. Your county highway engineer or office can provide information on regulations for county highways.

Roadside signs also reflect the image of your campground. The message, of course, is limited to what a motorist can see driving down the highway. At 60 miles per hour, a motorist covers 88 feet per second. In five or six seconds drivers come within good reading range and pass most smaller highway signs and outdoor advertising. Outdoor advertising must therefore be visible, legible, and organized for rapid understanding if it is to be effective. A roadside sign should have high visibility to attract attention from a greater distance than it can be read. Size, shape and color determine such visibility. A sign should be legible from 250 feet in areas where traffic moves about 30 miles per hour, and at least 500 feet where speeds are around 60 miles per hour. As a guide for the amount of message and the size and thickness of letters that can be read at various distances, two outdoor poster distance scale viewers are shown in Appendix A at the end of this chapter (from the Institute of Outdoor Advertising, 485 Lexington Avenue, New York, NY, 10017).

Because the reading and viewing time is quite limited, the message on the billboard must also be limited, probably to the campground name, a phrase or two that identifies your camp ground type, and one or two common activities, followed by distance and highway location. Bright, warm colors are advised. Study other outdoor advertising to get an idea of what is effective.

Directional signs should be placed at intersections directing campers from major highways to your campground. If in doubt about whether or not one is needed at a particular intersection, put one there. They also reflect your campground image.

Directory Ads and Listings

Placing ads in camper directories can be quite effective, because the readership of such directories is comprised mostly of campers. These companies have substantial distribution of their respective directories. The ads you place in them must be designed to apply over the entire camping season or even several seasons, as campers sometimes use a directory for more than one season.

Brochures

Nearly all campgrounds have brochures. There are perhaps as many types of campground brochures as there are possible ways of designing a brochure. How do you design a brochure? Should you design your own? Where can you go for help? Who can you get to do it for you? The answer depends on your skills and your marketing budget. Unless you have some special skills along this line, you're better off to hire someone to do it for you. Often your local printer will help you with the design. Be careful, though, because this person may not possess the necessary skills either. Contact ad agencies that have brochure design experience. The following discussion will help you understand what is involved in brochure and ad design.

The Message

There is a logical series of steps to follow in the selling process, whether it's an ad, a brochure, or personal selling. The names of the steps may vary depending on the jargon, but they usually follow the same approach as the following practical AIDAS model:

Attention. You have to get a person's attention before you can communicate, or sell.

Interest. The next step is to capture the interest of the person being sold.

Desire. You say or write things that cause the person to desire the product-the camping experience—that you offer.

Action. All of the above leads to action, or making the sale. It's also known as the close, of asking the person to purchase or make a reservation.

Satisfaction. Build satisfaction into the transaction. Make campers feel they're getting value for their camping fees and other expenditures they make in your campground. It's a real must for repeat business.

An ideal advertising message is one that incorporates all the above, although in practice it's hard to accomplish. The message content should cause the camper to make the site reservation. How this appeal is stated is called the theme, idea, or unique selling proposition. These appeals were discussed when the camping experience was described earlier. The camping fun, family togetherness, relaxation, and solitude, are examples.

In addition, anything that makes your campground unique should be used in the message. A rational appeal can be used to appeal to the camper's self-interest. Emotional appeals can be used, including love, joy, fun, humor, or pride. Last, a moral appeal can be used, such as family camping, being a clean, wholesome family outing.

Brochures

The front page or panel must capture the camper's attention. There may be many other brochures on the rack and many other things at which to look. Your brochure should stand out from the others. It should send an alluring visual message of your campground image.

The Front Panel

Make your brochure cover headlines similar to newspaper headlines. They should be as big as possible, clean, and printed in very dark ink. It should never be necessary to unfold the brochure to completely read the headline. The main illustration should show campers enjoying camping. Vitally interesting points should appear in the beginning, even if this means repeating the information inside."

A few phrases describing the appeal—your unique appeal or selling proposition—should do it, along with artwork and/or a picture. Using a four-color process is good but not an absolute necessity. Your campground name and logo are good identification. The cover must gain sufficient attention to get campers to look inside.

The Inside Panels

You create and develop the interest and desire of the AIDAS model inside your brochure. The inside should answer the question, "Why should we go to this campground rather than anywhere else?" Explain the benefits that they will gain if they come to your campground.

A second headline should appear on the inside, and subheads should be used on the inside and on the back page. The inside headline isn't set in all capital letters, and it should be of smaller type size than the main headline. Pictures in the center spread are very important; this is the place for shots showing different features and points of interest.

Photos are good for painting the picture of the message. They should have campers in them. Intersperse them with the story. Short blocks of copy will more likely be read than solid continuous print, especially if highlighted. Don't worry about using complete sentences; bulleted lists may be adequate. These are short phrases often presented in bold print, prefaced by dots, stars, or asterisks, and will catch attention. The inside should continue the image of the cover, that is, the image of your campground.

It is commonly said in marketing that the big three advertising appeals are fire, water, and sex. Examples of using these in your ads might include:

- people sitting around a campfire with a tent or RV in the back ground;
- families roasting marshmallows over a campfire;
- pictures of the swimming pool, beach, or people boating or water skiing;
- a couple holding hands on a pier, watching the sunset over the lake; or
- an older couple holding hands while walking along a nature trail.

The Reservation Panel

The message should be aimed at the whole point of the brochure—making the sale. The interest and desire bring the camper to the close, when the sale is made, which in this case is a reservation. You're not there in person to ask them to make a reservation, so you put it in print with such phrases as:

- Make your reservation today!
- Reserve your site now!
- Be an early bird—reserve your favorite site now!

Closing statements such as these make it easier for campers to make their reservations. Use one panel of the brochure for a reservation form to be filled out, torn off, and mailed in. Be careful not to have information on the other side that they'll still need, such as directions to your campground. Leave your phone number in bold print for them to call in a reservation.

Your instructions on how to make a reservation should be clear, concise, and simple. The reservation deposit should be stated clearly. Your rate schedule should also be included. Rate information should be put on a separate page the size of one of the brochure panels. With a separate rate panel you can change your rates the next year and only need to print a new rate panel. In

this way your brochure is still usable. You can also have only enough brochures printed up for one year. Then simply change the rate panel in the
brochure, and have another year's supply of brochures printed.

The Back Panel

The back page should contain subheads, a guarantee (if any), testimonials,
and a closing sales pitch. Testimonials can add important weight to the presentation. Pleased customers are the best sources. Quotes from pleased campers should be saved for this purpose. Permission is needed before quoting
from letters or using comments. Celebrity testimonials should be from celeb-
rities of the same general age as the customers.

Exaggerations

A word about exaggerations in your brochures. The tourism industry is not
without fault in this regard. Do not overstate the benefits and claims you make
in regard to your campground. If you do, it will only make things worse for
you in the long run, as people will come with expectations that your campground cannot fulfill.

Photographs

Photos are excellent tools for creating an image of your campground. You are
selling a pleasurable camping experience. Photos of people having a good time—
playing games, relaxing, laughing, or catching fish—can be very effective in
enhancing such a word picture.

Do *not* include pictures without people in them. Remember you're not
selling the facilities, but rather the experience. Include photos of people of the
ages you want to attract. If it's young families, include pictures of young families. If it's retiree clientele, include pictures of retirees. Even if you have a
million-dollar view of a natural resource, put some people in the foreground
of the view.

Do *not* use old pictures that are out-of-date. Such photos create the image
that your campground is outdated also. Use high-quality photos. The quality
in the brochure will not be better than the quality of the photo print. Pictures
must be sharply focused, or in the brochure the will also be blurred or fuzzy.

Unless you are really good at photography, you should hire a professional to come out for a day on a busy weekend to take pictures. Decide ahead
of time the pictures you want to put in your brochure. Don't expect someone
else to know what will work best for you.

Get a signed release from people who are clearly identifiable in your
brochure or ad photos. Without such approval you are violating a person's
right to privacy. The release should simply state that it's all right to use their
photo for promotional purposes. Suggestions on brochure distribution are included in the following chapter.

Fliers

Some campground operators like to have an inexpensive promotional piece to hand out at sport shows or other events at which potential camper customers attend. In these cases they produce a flier.

The selling message is by necessity even shorter than in a brochure, but should have all the steps of the AIDAS formula included, unless you have a purpose in mind other than selling your campground and getting a reservation. The attention should be captured at the top of the panel. This should be followed by the interest and desire part of the message on that same side of the panel. The other side should include the close, with information on how to make a reservation and a reservation form, which can be torn off and mailed along with the deposit check.

Newspaper Advertising

Most campground operators restrict their media ads to newspapers. Radio and TV are usually too expensive, unless the campground is very large or there is a good-sized RV sales operation for which to advertise. Listening audiences do not contain a large enough proportion of campers to justify the cost.

Newspaper Selection

Advertising in large metropolitan newspapers is also too expensive, unless done by a large campground, promotional association, or a cooperatively sponsored ad.

Suburban weeklies are often good places to get a return on your advertising dollar. The ad space costs much less than in the large dailies, and the audience may contain a high percentage of potential customers. Trial and error is probably the best way to find out what works for you.

Advertise in small town weekly newspapers where many of your campers live. These newspaper ads are relatively inexpensive. Weekly shoppers' guides may work for you also. Some campgrounds advertise in the classified sections of these newspapers.

Be Aware of Your Market

Where in the paper do you place your ad? It depends on your audience and who makes the decision to go camping. Experience indicates that the decision is most often made by adults.

Therefore, place the ad where the adults read, especially the adult male. Your ad may do better if placed in the sports and business sections of the paper. If the paper publishes a travel section, that is also a good section in which to place an ad.

Be Aware of Timing

Ideally the ad should be in the paper when campers make the decision to go camping. When are such decisions usually made? Past studies show that the trip decision is made anytime from more than two months to less than a week before the trip. However, over half make the decision a month or less in advance.

Therefore, in order to have your ad in front of your campers when they make the decision to go camping, you should have your ads running from about two months before your season begins to about a month before it is over. Then, if you want to run ads to increase your shoulder season business, you should run such ads about a month before shoulder seasons begin, up through most of such seasons. The odds are that the decision is not made as far in advance for shoulder seasons. This is based on the fact that campgrounds are usually not full during such seasons, and reservations are not required as often as in the peak season. Also, campers during those seasons may not be as likely to be working at jobs for which vacation scheduling is necessary.

Internet Web Page

An excellent place to advertise your campground is on the Internet. You can create a web page and place your advertising message on it. It has the capacity to display much more information than a brochure.

The advertising message should follow the same approach as described earlier for a brochure. To do this, go to a computer sales or consulting service that has an Internet provider service. They should have a web page designer. They may also have a marketing person that can help design the marketing message.

Fees for this service run around $75 to $100 per hour. In addition, there is an up-front charge of $75 or more and about $35 per month for the Internet.

Effectiveness Measurements

It's good to measure the effectiveness of ads, especially when trying something new. There are easy ways to do this. For example, when designing an ad for a particular paper, code it by varying the address you ask readers to respond to. Just add, for example, "Dept. A" after your rural route or box number. Then count the inquiries that arrive to that particular address. When someone calls in for information or to make a reservation, ask them how they heard about your campground, and record their answers.

To really find out what each ad produced in terms of income or reservations, keep track of the reservations that resulted from those inquiries. If you divide the cost of the ad by the number of reservations, you'll get the cost per reservation from the particular ad. Such tracking makes future advertising decisions easier.

Appendix A

A Guide to Road Sign Visibility

To see how an actual bulletin design will appear at various distances:

- Hold viewer at arm's length. Frame artwork in rectangle.
- Read distance for opening used.
- Clear area outside rectangle shows limits for extensions or embellishments.

Outdoor Bulletin Distance Scale Viewer

<u>9.5' × 21.5'</u>

Source: *Institute of Outdoor Advertising, 485 Lexington Ave., New York, NY 10017.*

To see how an actual bulletin design
will appear at various distances:
Hold viewer at arm's length.
Frame artwork in rectangle.
Read distance for opening used.
Clear area outside rectangle shows
limits for extensions or embellishments

Note: This viewer is designed for use with
artwork in the proportion of $1 \times 3\,^1/_2$, since
most painted bulletins measure 14' × 48'.

500'

400'

300'

200'

Source for viewers: Institute of Outdoor Advertising

500'

400'

300'

200'

100'

To see how actual poster design
will appear at various distances:

Hold viewer at arm's length.
View artwork so
copy area fills entire opening.
Read distance for opening used.

9.5' × 21.5'

Chapter

20

DIRECT MAIL ADVERTISING AND OTHER PROMOTIONS

Direct mail can be the most effective method of advertising. It is also one of the more complex forms, which is why it is being discussed in a chapter apart from other forms of advertising. Direct mail is so effective because it can be aimed at people who have a very high potential to be camper customers. Because of this, more expense per mailing piece can be afforded to convey the sales message.

Direct Mail List Sources

The following section should provide you with ideas on where to obtain mailing lists.

Inquiries

Requests for information from anyone who goes to the effort of writing or calling your campground makes him or her a potential new camper. Therefore, such inquiries should be responded to promptly and effectively. Campground operators often send a brochure and schedule of events for the current season. Some also send a personal note, handwritten or typed. The more personal you can afford to make it, the better. A follow-up phone call in a week or 10 days after the mailing might also be cost-effective. People who make inquiries should be placed on your regular direct mail list.

Former Campers

People who have previously camped at your campground constitute an excellent mailing list for a direct mail campaign. Three years is probably as far back as its cost-effectiveness reaches. The list is generated from your camper registration forms, which underlines the necessity of accurate and legible registration form information. Your staff should be trained to make sure the information is legible and complete when campers register. Computers are very efficient in developing mailing lists and in addressing labels and envelopes.

Sport, Travel and Mail Shows

People who sign up for prize drawings, more information, and so on at sport, travel, and mall shows are another source of direct mail lists. Such lists may have less potential than the sources discussed above, especially if people walk through the show just to sign up for prizes. On the other hand, if they come to your booth and ask you questions about your campground or in some other way sound interested in camping, they are probably potential camper customers.

Direct Mail List Brokers

Many companies are in the business of selling lists for direct mail purposes. In the recent computerized information explosion, such lists are abundant and reasonably priced. A list of such companies is located in Appendix A at the end of this chapter.

Additional Sources

Camping clubs are sources of names for direct mail advertising. These are helpful mostly for group camping events. In some states, the Department of Natural Resources or Conservation Commission may give you names of campers who have camped in their respective parks. The same may be true for county, town, and municipal campgrounds in your area. Caution should be exercised to make sure such campers aren't looking for a camping experience quite different from what you offer.

Fishing, hunting, and boat license holders are also ideal direct mail recipients if such activities are popular in your area. You can often obtain them from the state agencies that issue them. Usually the charge is no more than what it costs to run a printout of them.

Senior citizen clubs, scout groups, churches (especially those that don't have their own denominational camps), and 4-H clubs are all potential sources of group business. They offer potential for expanding your shoulder-season business. Lists may be available from their respective state offices.

Community directories, Chambers of Commerce, and local tourism offices are potential sources of lists. They receive inquiries for information on your area, and may be able to give you just those inquiries related to camping. Usually they will share names and addresses with you.

You may get lists of recent buyers of RVs from local RV dealers and RV dealers in your market areas. This might work especially well if you offer a free weekend of camping, or something similar, to the dealer for him or her to use in making sales.

Lastly, if your state or regional tourism promotion organization receives inquiries as a result of their promotional programs, such inquiries might make good quality mail lists. Their success depends on how specifically they define the inquiry, as to preferred destination, time preferred, and type of lodging (camping, resort, or motel).

You have to decide which of the above sources of names offer you the best potential. For example, if you want to attract the nature lover who wants a quiet, secluded camping experience, then the campers who have camped at those types of parks would be your best sources. If you feature an RV park, perhaps lists of RV purchasers or RV clubs would be good sources.

Your Direct Mail Package

You may want to send different messages to potential repeat customers and potential new customers. For example, to repeat customers you might send a folksy message about your family, members of your staff, and so on. These are topics they can relate to, because they've been to your campground before. In any case, your message should be as personalized as possible.

For potential new customers, you may want to concentrate on describing your campground in terms they can relate to, using images of fun, excitement, and relaxation in a rewarding camping experience. This should be conveyed in all messages.

Forms in which to send your selling message include a personal letter, newsletter, brochure, schedule of events or activities, rate sheet, holiday greeting card, and/or a reservation form. Some operators employ a tabloid (small newspaper) newsletter format filled with interesting news-type articles featuring their campground and their families. It may include the history of the campground, a calendar of events, features on new amenities, news of major improvements in facilities, and so on.

You probably wouldn't mail out all of these at once. A schedule for a direct mail series might be laid out in this manner:

Christmas season. Many campgrounds mail a holiday greeting to former campers and seasonal campers. It often consists of a warm greeting in the form of a brief newsletter, informing them of what happened in the campground over the past year. Major improvements completed or that are in progress make interesting news to campers. Also, any family events you'd like to share with your campers may be of interest. Any major events you've got planned for early season (snowbelt campgrounds), such as a clean-up weekend or a winter party, could be announced.

March. Mail out a brochure and newsletter. This newsletter could again discuss the campground improvements and concentrate more on early season activities and events. Any events outside the campground could also be promoted. The brochure should have a reservation form and rate sheet in it.

April/May. Again, send out a brochure and newsletter. This newsletter could concentrate on the grand spring opening, opening of fishing season, or some other event, such as Memorial Day weekend festivities.

June. This is a reminder mailing, with a brochure and newsletter that highlight the rest of the summer. It could also promote some shoulder-season activities.

Early August. This is the time to highlight your Labor Day celebration, plus your fall events.

In any of the above mailings you could feature any specials that require quick reservations to provide incentives for campers to make reservations immediately. A general cover letter introducing yourself and your campground, and mentioning the other information included in the mailing, seems appropriate for any of the mailings. The above is for a campground in the snowbelt. Others may vary depending on the season opening.

Your Message

The need to be as personal as possible in all of your messages was discussed earlier. This is an advantage you have as a small tourism business. Any message you send must appeal to the basic human needs of the camper customer. Examples of such needs are:

Fun. This includes the travel, the outdoor camping experience itself, and all of the many recreation activities in and near your campground.

Family togetherness. This can be a very strong appeal to camper families. An intergenerational family experience is something for which many families will pay dearly.

Individual/family wellness. Providing a setting for exercise and wholesome outdoor recreation is very attractive to many.

Socialization. Many social needs can be met in the community-building process. Campgrounds are generally known as more friendly places than other public places. In fact, the recent trend toward seasonal camping is explainable, in part, because of the socialization potential being realized in camping experiences. Some families living in cities don't know their neighbors very well, but next-door seasonal campers at your campground can be very close friends.

Status. This is acquired through specific status symbols such as a new RV, car, pickup, or boat.

Economy. The camping vacation is one of the most inexpensive vacations available.

The message you send should appeal to at least one of these needs, possibly two or three of them. Your message should be warm and friendly and should carry through all of your advertising messages. The AIDAS model discussed earlier applies to direct mail advertising also. Your message should stimulate interest in your campground and what you have to offer. It should describe how one or more of the above basic human needs can be met, in terms with which your campers can easily relate. Examples are:

Enjoy a fun-packed weekend swimming in our new olympic pool!

Enjoy the serene, quiet solitude of the northwoods at our campground.

Most importantly, your message should ask for the sale. It should lead to the action of the camper making a reservation with you. Ask for such action and hasten it. Tell your campers exactly what to do and when, such as:

Send in the attached reservation form with your $20 deposit today!

Give your family a real treat by sending or calling in your reservation today!

You can hasten action by offering a discount that only lasts a short time. Examples are a free day of camping in the off-season, or if they bring in another new camping party, they get one campsite free. The offer then runs out at some date in the near future. Watch what other advertisers are doing in the media to sell their products.

Be natural throughout your message. Write your copy the way you talk. If it sounds like you, it will be more effective, especially to those who know you.

Remember, in order to sell people anything, you must make them want *it* more than the money they spent for it. And, in the case of camping, they must want to spend the time camping at your campground more than participating in any other leisure activity.

Publications

The quality of your direct mail materials is a direct reflection on the quality of your campground. Choosing appealing paper and attractive colors doesn't mean that you must pay for the very best there is, however.

To stand up in a rack, your brochure needs to be of at least 60-pound paper. Explore the use and cost of two or three colors of ink. Four-color photo separations that you pay for are your property—be sure this is clear with your printer.

Get bids from at least three printers. It doesn't hurt at all if they know you are getting other bids. The more brochures you have printed, the lower the cost per unit, but make sure you don't print a lot more than you'll use. Have a clear understanding about any print overrun, who pays for it, and who owns it.

Ask your printer for samples of other brochures the company has printed. You can then see examples of the quality of their work, as well as get ideas for your future brochures, fliers, and other direct mail pieces. Paying for professional artwork may seem expensive, but if you can use it again, it may well pay for itself.

Brochure Distribution

Brochures are only effective when they reach your potential camper customers. We've already discussed sending them out in direct mail programs in answer to inquiries. Other places to distribute them include the following:

- Travel, sport, and mall shows. You can have your own booth at these events, or you can often pay someone to do it for you. There are people who make a business of distributing brochures for lots of tourism businesses like yours at sport shows. Your campground association may also distribute them for members.
- Local tourist information centers (TIC's), Chambers of Commerce, gasoline stations, and restaurants in your area.
- Hire a brochure distribution service. These companies will distribute your brochure in display racks that they maintain. For example, Ad-Lit Distributing Company distributes brochures to displays in 600 locations throughout the Midwest. They boast over 75 accounts. Full service includes rack service daily and weekly, up-to-date inventory reports, free year-round brochure insurance coverage, and free off-season brochure storage. They also offer assistance in brochure design. (Contact the Ad-Lit Distributing Co., Inc., P.O. Box 24, Pioneer Drive, WI Dells, Wisconsin 53965.)

Sport/Travel/Mall Shows

Some campgrounds attend sport and mall shows heavily, up to 25 or 30 of them in one season. Others don't attend them at all. Many go to a few of them annually. Currently, there is no research to evaluate their effectiveness.

Sport Show Objectives

A sport show allows you the opportunity to conduct personal selling activities. You can often sell reservations at the booth. This one on one sales presentation can be very effective. How to conduct personal selling is described later.

The location probably affects the effectiveness of sport and travel shows. For example, being located fairly close to a major metropolitan market area could justify such promotional activity. Also, attendance at mall shows in suburbs and small cities where major portions of your campers live, could prove to be an very effective use of money, time, and effort.

The Booth

The booth you use at shows should, like all your promotional pieces, reflect the quality and image of your campground. It should look attractive, and should include your logo and campground name on a large, easy-to-read sign.

You need a counter on which to display materials such as your brochure, pictures of your campground, and cards and pencils for people to write their names and addresses for drawings, more information, and so on. Your pictures should include campers having fun while participating in the activities you are selling. Some campgrounds invest in automatic slide or cassette tape equipment, whereas others show videotapes; many have photo albums containing pictures of campers in their campgrounds.

You can also provide information about your campground that may not be in your brochure. Likewise, you can create awareness and visibility for your campground. You can also greet former campers.

Sport Show Behavior

Not only is your booth on display, but you and anyone working in your booth are on display also. Therefore, you need to be well-groomed, and wear neat and casual clothing, preferably what you wear when working in your campground.

Avoid distracting habits such as gum chewing, smoking, eating in your booth, and so on. If you get tired, get someone to take over and get yourself some rest. If you don't, you're only defeating the purpose of being there.

On-Site Promotions

If your customers have a good experience camping at your campground, there is a high probability that they will come back at a later date. Why not promote future events to those who are already camping at your campground?

One strategy is to get them back during the shoulder season. Ways to do this include promotions of special events during those seasons. You might have posters printed and locate these on your bulletin boards and anywhere else campers would be likely to see them, such as the insides of the doors on toilet stalls. Place a flier inside the information you give them when they check in. Naturally, you and your staff can promote by word-of-mouth at the front desk, and at other convenient places and times.

Packaging

Packaging is a strategy that some campgrounds use very effectively. Packaging is making arrangements with other recreation providers to offer camping at your campground, plus several activities at nearby locations—such as pond fishing, golf, and so on, along with a meal at a supper club—for one overall price.

Some operators offer a package that includes camping at their campground, golf at an area golf course, dinner at a supper club, admission to an area attraction, and sometimes even transportation to the attraction. This takes cooperation and effort in coordination. You need to contact the other recreation providers, ask them to cooperate, and find out the charge for their activity or service. Then add them all up, along with your camping fees, and promote your package. The total package price can be less than all of those activities purchased separately, because any one party probably won't participate in everything. Also, it will increase business volume if successful.

Appendix A

Sources of Direct Mail Lists

Bulk Mailing Lists and Related Services

The Mail Room
P.O. Box 1945
Borrego Springs, CA 92004
(760) 767-5407,
Fax: (760) 767-0491

Camping Equipment Dealers and Others

Zeller and Lettica, Inc.
15 East 26th St.
New York, NY 10010
(212) 685-7512

Marine Mailing Lists
P.O. Box 62
Springfield, IL 62705
(217) 529-1909

Subscribers: Trailer Life

Market Compilation and
    Research Bureau, Inc.
11633 Victory Blvd.
North Hollywood, CA 91609
(213) 877-5384

RV Manufacturers and Dealers

Network Lists and Data
400 Halstead Ave.
Harrison, NY 10528
(914) 835-5353

Alvin B. Zeller
475 Park Ave.
New York, NY 10016
(212) 689-4900

RV Owners

American Business Lists, Inc.
230 Hillcrest Building
P.O. Box 27347
Ralston, NE 68127
(402) 331-7169

Gish, Sherwood, and Friends, Inc.
2 International Plaza,
    Suite 511
Nashville, TN 37217

S & G Business Associates, Inc.
P.O. Box 302
Elkhart, IN 46515
(219) 295-1500

Woodall's Magazine Lists

List House East/West
130 Lyons Plains Rd.
Weston, CT 06880
(203) 227-6027

Chapter

21

REALISTIC RATE DETERMINATION

Are you charging realistic campsite rates? Are your rates the best possible rates for your particular situation? How can you logically determine the best rates for your campground? No single decision is more critical to the profitable management of a campground than rate determination. There is no easier means of increasing net profit than by charging the best possible rates.

Prices are always rising due to inflation. Costs of the essentials you need to operate your campground increase also. If you don't do something to offset or recover them, such cost increases will come right out of your profit. You should always try to keep costs as low as is feasible by implementing energy-saving practices, by using labor-saving equipment and practices, and by efficiently purchasing supplies and repair materials.

One way to recover some of these cost increases is by attracting more campers. There are several ways of doing this: strengthening your marketing program, lengthening your season, and so on. It may be, however, that you are doing your best in all these practices, and you still end up with a lower than desired profit picture—unless you take a long, hard look at the rates you are charging and raise them. This chapter deals with how to evaluate your rates and how much to charge campers to operate more profitably. It also deals with fees for recreation activities.

Realistic Rate Determination

There are at least four practical approaches to use to arrive at rates. They are based on: (1) what others charge, (2) demand, (3) costs, and (4) a combination of the other three.

According to Others' Rates (Competition)

Find out what others in your area are charging, and set your rates at approximately the same level. If everyone did this, all of the rates in a given area would be similar. Of course, everyone could end up charging rates that are too low or too high, which would result in lower profits for everyone. This method does not take into consideration differences in the quality of campgrounds or differences in the related camping experiences. We all know that such differences exist.

According to Demand

This approach considers your camper customers. It hinges on what you think is the maximum they'll pay, and then charging that amount. This is very difficult to do. The major problems in establishing rates based solely on what you think your guests will pay are (1) if your rates are too low, few campers will tell you, and (2) if they are too high, they won't tell you because they won't be around to tell you.

A few campers leave your campground without renting a site and tell you your rates are too high, but most won't come to your campground and you won't know why. They may not come for a combination of reasons, such as the quality of your campground or disinterest in the attractions in your area. Other factors, none of which you can do anything about, may play a role, such as weather, illness, or death in a camper's family.

According to Costs

In this approach, a rate is determined by adding up the costs of operating your campground. Estimate the number of site nights that you plan to rent, and divide the result into the estimated costs. This gives the minimum rate you need to charge in order to cover such costs. Maybe this rate, along with a desired profit, is in line with what others charge or what your campers are willing to pay, but maybe it isn't. You won't know this unless you also use the other approaches.

According to a Combination

By using a combination of the above three approaches, the advantages of each can be achieved. Using any one of the above methods alone may result in rates that are not the most desirable when considering the other two approaches.

Remember when we discussed your objectives in operating your campground? Why are you in this business? This chapter assumes that one of your main objectives is to earn some level of net income or profit. Unless you have another source of income, your campground must earn some level of profit, or eventually you'll be forced out of business.

Practical Rate Determination

The overall procedure of rate determination begins when you list your total financial needs (costs) and then subtract from them the income generated by all other sources in the campground. (Seasonal rental income will be treated as nonsite rental income at first, then seasonal rate determination will be treated separately later on.) Next, divide the income needed from site rentals by the estimated number of site rentals to figure the average rate needed to cover those financial needs. This rate is then adjusted based on what others are charging and what you think your guests are willing to pay.

Cost Approach

The intent of this approach is to make your site rental income cover all costs as you want them to cover. Let's begin with the cost method by working through an example of a hypothetical 100-site campground. The following hypothetical operating statement will be used in the example. First, let's look at the annual costs that must be paid. These costs don't have to be calculated exactly for the purpose of this example, but they should be good estimates when applying this approach to your records.

Review your financial records, and estimate your costs for *next* year based on your management plans and anticipated inflation. A worksheet is provided here for you to follow. You will find another blank worksheet like it for your use in Appendix A at the end of this chapter.

Table 21-1

Hypothetical Operating Statement for a 100-Site Campground

Estimated Revenues	Dollars	% of Gross Income
Site Rentals	$130,000	65.0%
Overnight	80,000	40.0
Seasonals	50,000	20.0
Day guest receipts	4,000	2.0
Groceries	16,000	8.0
Beer/wine	10,000	5.0
Vending machines	4,000	2.0
Souvenirs	10,000	5.0
Mini-golf	6,000	3.0
Equipment rentals	4,000	2.0
Came room	8,000	4.0
Wood and ice	6,000	3.0
Laundry	2,000	1.0
Total gross income	200,000	100.0
Cost of sales	40,000	20.0
Gross profit	$160,000	80.0%
Operating Expenses		
Salaries/wages	$26,000	13.0%
Payroll taxes/benefits	3,000	1.5
Operating supplies	10,000	5.0
Vehicles operating expense	5,000	2.5
Maintenance supplies/repairs	12,000	6.0
Utilities	10,000	5.0
Telephone	2,400	1.2
Advertising and promotions	10,000	5.0
Dues/subscriptions	1,000	0.5
Licenses and permits	1,000	0.5
Legal/accounting/computer	2,600	1.3
Office expense	3,000	1.5
Property taxes	10,000	5.0
Insurance	10,000	5.0
Miscellaneous	4,000	2.0
Total expenses	$110,000	55.0%
Net income	$50,000	25.0%
(Before income taxes, debt service, depreciation)		

To continue with the cost calculation, you may want to add an amount for family income, if it isn't already in your operating statement. Remember to include everything that you want to get out of your business in this statement.

Let's assume that you would like a family income (owner's draw) of $40,000. Adding this income to the total expenses will give us a total of $150,000 in costs.

Cost Calculation Worksheet

Account Title	Hypothetical 100-site Campground	Your Figures
Salaries/wages	$26,000	_____
Payroll taxes/benefits	3,000	_____
Operating supplies	10,000	_____
Vehicle operating expense	5,000	_____
Maintenance supplies and repairs	12,000	_____
Utilities	10,000	_____
Telephone	2,400	_____
Advertising and promotions	10,000	_____
Dues/subscriptions	1,000	_____
Licenses and permits	1,000	_____
Legal/accounting	2,600	_____
Office expense	3,000	_____
Property taxes	10,000	_____
Insurance	10,000	_____
Miscellaneous	4,000	_____
Family income (draw)	40,000	_____
Other _____	_____	_____
Other _____	_____	_____
Total Costs	**$150,000**	_____

Income Other Than Site Rentals

Let's take a look at sources of income other than site rentals. This income will be deducted from the total costs to determine the amount that needs to be recovered from site rentals. These figures should be realistic. Use your own figures if at all possible. If you're generating a projected income statement for your business plan, use the operating ratios in Chapter 9 for those profit centers you plan to have in your campground.

Other Income Worksheet

Gross Sales	Example	Your Figures
Day guest receipts	$4,000	
Groceries	16,000	
Beer & wine	10,000	
Vending machines	4,000	
Souvenirs	10,000	
Mini-golf	6,000	
Equipment rentals	4,000	
Game room	8,000	
Firewood & ice	6,000	
Laundry	2,000	
Other	0	
Other	0	
Total Gross Sales	70,000	
Less Cost of Sales	- 40,000	
Net Income other than site rental	**$30,000**	

Subtracting the cost of sales of $40,000 from gross sales of $70,000 gives a net income of $30,000 from sources other than site rentals. The total costs of $150,000 less $30,000, or $120,000, represents the amount that must be generated from site rentals in order to break even and cover your costs, including family income.

Seasonal Rental Income

If you rent to seasonal campers (renting a site to one camping party for the entire camping season), you need to subtract that income also before you compute the break-even rate for daily or overnight rates. Let's assume for our example that we rent out 10 seasonal sites at an average rate of $1,500. This will generate $15,000. Subtracting it from $120,000 gives us $105,000, the amount needed from daily and weekly site rentals to break even. Seasonal rates will be considered later.

Occupancy

Next, we need to estimate the level of occupancy in order to determine the number of site nights needed to cover the costs. A site night is one campsite rented for one night. An occupancy situation for a 100-site campground in the snowbelt is shown in Table 21.2. A blank worksheet is provided in Appendix B at the end of the chapter so you can estimate your occupancy rate. In this example, we're assuming 10 seasonal site rentals. This leaves 90 sites available for overnight rentals. With the hypothetical occupancies shown, we estimate a total number of overnight site rentals of 4,300.

Please do the same for your campground for next year. If you were in business last year, go through your guest registration records, if you haven't already done so, and add up the total number of sites rented. Then adjust it for the coming year on the basis of any factors you think will change it, such as new and improved advertising or facilities.

Table 21.2

Occupancy Example

For a 100-Site Campground (10 Seasonals)

Month	Number of Sites		Days in Month		Potential Site Nights		Occupancy Rate %		Site Nights Rented
May	90	×	31	=	2,790	×	5	=	140
June	90	×	30	=	2,700	×	20	=	540
July	90	×	31	=	2,790	×	65	=	1,815
August	90	×	31	=	2,790	×	50	=	1,395
September	90	×	30	=	2,700	×	10	=	270
October	90	×	31	=	2,790	×	5	=	140
		Total Estimated Site Nights							4,300

Break Even Rate

If we divide $103,000, the cost to be recovered from site rentals, by 4,300, the estimated total site nights of occupancy, we get $24.42. This is the average rate necessary just to cover the costs indicated, with the occupancy of 4,300 site rentals.

$$\$105,000/4,300 = \$24.42$$

Payment on Debt

If you have a mortgage, you have to make debt service payments. To compute an overnight site rate that would cover a $10,000 annual debt service payment, add $10,000 to the $105,000, the cost to be recovered from site rentals to get $115,000. Dividing this by 4,300 site nights shows that $26.74 is the rate necessary to cover a $10,000 debt service payment. Notice that each dollar increase in the rate generates $4,300, the number of sites rented.

$$\$105,000 + \$10,000 = \$115,000$$
$$\$115,000/4,300 = \$26.74$$

Return on Investment

You have some equity in your campground business (campground value less debt). If you sold your campground and got out of the campground business, you would theoretically receive that much money, and could invest it, and earn a return on it. Consider this as one of your costs, and try to charge a rate that will cover it. To compute this rate, take the equity you have in your business, multiply it by the rate of return you think you could earn on it by putting it in the bank or somewhere else. Add that amount to the cost figure that you divide by the number of site nights rented. The result is an overnight rate that will give you the return on the equity you have in your business. Let's say, for example, that your equity in your campground is $100,000 and you want to earn 10 percent, or $10,000. Add $10,000 to the $115,000 to get $125,000, and divide by 4,300 site nights to arrive at an average rate of $29.10 to cover your return of equity.

$$\$115,000 + \$10,000 = \$125,000$$
$$\$125,000/4,300 = \$29.10$$

Profit Calculation

Let's assume you want to earn a little more from your campground operation, say $10,000. Add that to the $125,000 from above, divide by 4,300 to get a rate of $31.40.

$$\$125,000 + \$10,000 = \$135,000$$
$$\$135,000/4,300 = \$31.40$$

Notice again that if you raise your rate by one dollar, your gross site rental will increase by a number equal to the estimated number of site rentals. Compute a hypothetical rate using various levels of costs, desired profits, and occupancies. Observe the resulting rates. Now we will combine the other methods with the cost approach.

Competitor-Based Rates

Look at the rate that gives you the desired return, and ask yourself how it compares with what other campgrounds in your area, other areas of the state, and even campgrounds in other states are charging. Look at campground directories, or any other sources you can find to see what others are charging.

Using this method, try to compare the quality of camping you offer with campgrounds of similar quality. If your calculated rate is lower than what others are charging, don't automatically assume that your costs and occupancy are out of line. Just decide how close to the other campground rates you should set yours, and how much additional profit to earn at the end of the year. If your calculated rate is higher than the others are charging, you may have a problem. This is discussed in the next section.

Demand-Based Rates

Campers are not as concerned about rates as most operators tend to be. What really concerns many campground operators is how much business will be lost if rates are raised by a certain amount. Maybe the answer is not as much gross income as you think. Sure, you'll lose some, but you'll also gain new guests with your marketing efforts and your area's, county's, and/or region's marketing programs. For example, the situation described in Table 21.3 may exist.

Table 21.3

Possible Demand Schedule

Average rate	Sites rented	Gross income from site rentals
$20	5,000	$100,000
22	5,000	110,000
24	5,000	120,000
26	5,000	130,000
28	4,750	133,000
30	4,600	138,000
32	4,450	142,400
34	4,200	142,800
36	4,050	145,000
38	3,900	148,200
40	3,750	150,000
42	3,550	149,100
44	3,350	147,400
46	3,150	144,900

Notice that even though the number of site nights rented decreases as the rate increases, the gross income increases up to an average rate of $40.00, then it slowly decreases beyond that rate. Aren't you really more interested in the size of your gross income than you are in the number of sites you rent?

This situation is hypothetical. However, there are many reasons to believe that such a relationship exists in the camping market. One reason is that the total amount of fees paid on a camping trip compared to the total expenditures for the trip is quite small. Why then would a few more dollars spent on camping fees make much of a difference in the total trip budget? As another reason, campers in the same survey indicated that they are looking for recreation, clean and adequate toilet and shower facilities, and security when choosing a campground. These campers are looking for value received on their camping dollars and are willing to pay for it.

Campers' attitudes toward site fees in public parks may be different than in the above discussion. A possible reason is that campers may feel they have already paid for part of their camping fees when they paid their taxes.

In the previous example, gross income goes up as campsite rates go up, because the percentage change in the rate is larger than the corresponding percentage change in number of sites rented. (When the percentage change in quantity of a product purchased is less than the percentage change in price, such a relationship is known in economics as price inelasticity of demand.) A very useful concept relating to the price/quantity relationship is that the price can be increased by 50 percent and the number of site rentals can decrease by 33.3 percent, and still produce the same gross campsite rental income. *Note:* This concept was contributed by Larrie Isenring, Blackhawk Ridge Recreation, Sauk City, Wisconsin.

The next example shows that the price can go up from $15.00 to $22.50 (50 percent) and site rentals can drop from 10,000 to 6,667 (33.3 percent), and still produce the same $150,000 gross site rental income.

Site rate	$20	$30	50.0% increase
Number of sites rented	10,000	6,666	33.3% decrease
Gross income from site rentals	$200,000	$200,000	

Over 3,000 site rentals is a lot to lose in the average campground without lowering the gross site rental income. You must also consider gross income from other profit centers such as grocery sales, bait sales and boat rental income, which is likely to decrease as the number of site nights rented decreases. On the other hand your operating costs will also probably decrease as the number of site nights rented decreases. Such costs as time to clean the service building(s), costs of operating supplies, energy costs for heating water for showers, and so on will be less.

Therefore, you need to know how the *net* profit would change as campsite rates change. The table 21.4 shows the possible effect of incremental rate increases on gross campground income. Rates increase from $22 to $37. The number of site rentals decreases from 8,500 to 6,494. Changes in income other than site rental were computed to change by the same percentage as changes in site rental volume. Gross site rental income is the highest at a rate of $34, while total gross campground income is the highest at $31. Table 21.4 shows the effect of the reduction of campers on other profit centers.

Table 21.4

Possible Effect of Rate Increases on Campground Income

Rate	$22	$25	$28	$31	$34	$37
Percent increase		13.6	12.0	10.7	19.6	8.8
Sites rented	8,500	8,500	8,250	7,800	7,215	6,494
Percent decrease		0.0	2.9	5.5	7.5	10.0
Site income	$187,000	$212,500	$231,000	$241,800	$245,310	$240,278
Other income	$75,000	$75,000	$72,825	$68,820	$63,659	$57,293
Total income	$262,000	$287,500	$303,825	$310,620	$308,969	$297,571

These figures are hypothetical to illustrate the effect of a rate increase, and consequent lower camping volume on sales and total gross income. Try going through your camper list from last year, and set up a schedule of rates. Begin with your rate from last season, and increase the rate. Then estimate the number of campers you'll have at each rate. Multiply the site rate times the number of site nights you think you'll rent, and see what happens to your gross income at each rate level.

If your break-even rate is higher than the rates being charged by others, you may want to ask yourself if your customers will be willing to pay it. Go back to your rate and site nights rented schedule to see how much business you have estimated at that rate. This is the method of rate determination based on demand, or what you think your customers will pay. If the number of site nights that you estimated at your break-even is about the same as the number of estimated site rentals on your occupancy table, there is no problem. If they are way out of line, you have either estimated incorrectly or you have a serious problem.

If the latter is true, you must ask yourself if you can increase your occupancy with better methods of advertising and promotion, by adding some extra income centers, or by finding some other factor that will change your situation so you can get more business. The possibilities include having better facilities, better services, treating your customers better, and reducing your costs. If none of these seem feasible, the consequence is operating at a loss or not operating at all.

Use all of these methods, plus any other information you can gather, and decide what rate is best. You are in the best position to make the decision. Remember that if you gain or lose customers based on the rate you decide to charge, you are *gaining or losing gross revenue from site rentals, but also gaining or losing from the other income centers such as your store, equipment rentals, and so on.* Also, charging a rate below your break-even rate will cause you to lose money.

The Search for The Best Rate

In working through the computations so far, you may have come up with some rates higher than those you are now charging. Deciding on what rate to charge is up to you, the operator. No one knows your campground operation, or your guests, better than you. You are the expert. You want to charge the best rate, that is, the rate that results in the highest profit or net income. How many times have you shopped for a product and had the feeling that the most expensive item had the highest level of quality? The same is true for campers. Campers tend to feel that the best camping experiences are those that cost the most. They may not always want the best, but they tend to feel that way.

Why would a camper think the quality of camping is any better than you think it's worth by the price you place on it? People feel that goods and services are generally worth about what they pay for them. If you place a low rate on your campsites, people will think your campground is of low quality.

Site rates also affect the image of the campground. As was discussed in the chapter on image, it is very important to the overall value perceived by the camper customer. Closely associated with the perceived image, and an important determinant of image, is the site rate. Again, this is another reflection of the price/quality relationship.

Seasonal Rate Determination

A rationale for arriving at, or increasing a seasonal rate when seasonals are a minor part of gross site rental income is as follows:

1   Multiply the average occupancy of the site in the area to be rented (or overall average occupancy) times the length of your camping season in days.
2.   Then multiply the result by the daily rate you charge (including hookups) for that site.

Example: **50% × 125 days × $25 = $1,562.50**

3.   Then add on some percentage, such as 10 percent, to cover the lesser amount that seasonal campers spend in other profit centers, compared to weekend campers.

Example: **$1562.50 × 10% = $156.25; $1562.50 + $156.25 = $1,718.75**

The discussion so far has assumed that seasonal rental income is a minor part of total site rental income. When it becomes a significant part of total site rental income, a slightly different approach than the previous method is appropriate. Let's assume that 40 percent of the sites are rented on a seasonal basis. Isn't it then logical that the seasonal sites provide 40 percent of the income needed from site rentals?

In the previous example, the income needed from site rentals to cover operating costs and payment on principal is $120,000. Forty percent of this, or $48,200, is the income needed from seasonal site rentals. Divide this number by the number of seasonal sites to be rented, and you get $1,200 ($48,000/40 = $1,200). Then vary the amount you want to recover from seasonals, and see what happens to the computed rates.

Of course, any other proportion of seasonal to overnight site rentals can be used. And at the same time, remember that the overnight site rental income only needs to cover the remaining portion of the income needs of the campground. Also, the number of sites available for overnight rentals is fewer as additional seasonals are rented. The total overnight occupancy will also therefore be less.

Rate Determination and Profit Centers

What if you have a major profit center that produces a major share of your gross income? It could be a marina, store, or restaurant. Shouldn't such a profit center share the cost of the overhead with the site rental operation?

What is the best way to allocate overhead costs? First, the best way is to determine what it actually is, if possible. For example, if your insurance company representative can break down your insurance premium by building, activity, and so on, use those amounts. If your electric company would meter separate buildings for a period of time, have them do it for you, or perhaps you can do it by some other means.

When the above option fail, overhead can be assigned to various profit centers based on the proportion of gross income earned in that building or area of the campground. Another possibility is to allocate heating costs based on the proportion of total floor space each profit center operation occupies. Lastly, it may be necessary to simply estimate proportions, such as one-fourth, one-third, or one-eighth. Consult with your CPA if you have problems with the allocation of overhead costs. Allocate the overhead in the best possible manner, then follow the same steps as described earlier in the rate determination process.

Rate Strategies

Do you quote your rates on the basis of the camping family, the camping party, the individual, or the campsite? All these strategies are used. Do you charge the same rate for all sites in your campground, the same on holiday weekends as other times, or do you practice some form of differential pricing? Remember, how you charge the rate will encourage some campers and will discourage others.

There are many camping market segments. Many of them are listed below. As you read through the list, think of how the campers in each group would react to the campsite pricing strategies listed above.

- age, family cycle;
- occupation, income;
- purpose of trip;
- geographic location;
- activity, interest;
- destination, overnight;
- traditional families;
- single parent families;
- couples without children;
- empty nesters;
- retirees;
- singles;
- teenagers;
- adult couples;
- adult men and women; and
- groups or clubs.

You have the opportunity to develop a strategy to attract the market segment you want in your campground. In order to get this into perspective, let's look at a motel rate example in Table 21.5 and apply various strategies to it. In the process, examine campsite pricing strategies and the impact of such strategies on the camping market. The target is to generate an average room revenue of $60.00.

Table 21.5

Impact of Motel Pricing Strategies

Alternatives	Segment Attracted
$60.00 per room	Large groups, families
$56.00 for two people, $8.00 each for extras	Couples, small families
$60.00 for parents, kids free	Large families
$35.00 per person	Single travelers
$70.00 per night, 7th night free	Week-long stays
$66.00 per night, discounts for senior citizens, business persons	Senior citizens, business travelers, groups
$52.00 per single, $64.00 per double $8.00 per extra person	Singles, some couples

Now let's go through the same process for campsite rates. In this case, the target is $28.00 average site revenue.

Impact of Campsite Pricing Strategies

<u>Alternatives</u>	<u>Segment Attracted</u>
$28.00 per site	Large families, parties, groups
$12.25 per person	Small parties, small families, single campers
$24.50 for 2 people, $3.50 per additional person	Couples
$14.00 per adult, $5.25 per child	Single adults, single parents with small children
$26.00 per family, $3.50 per extra person	Families
$35.00 per site, 20% discount for senior citizens, Good Sam groups	Groups of senior citizens Good Sam groups

The above examples of strategies, and resulting segments of campers attracted, gives you an idea how the two are related. Now let's discuss more specifically a few of the more common pricing strategies.

Family/Party-Based Rates

The most common strategy throughout much of the country is to charge by the camping family or party of two adults and one, two, three, or more children. Then others pay extra, for example, extra adults pay at $2.00 to $5.00, and children at $2.00 or $4.00.

This method works fine until a group of adults with no children arrives, such as two adult couples who want to camp on the same site. The two extra adults, normally a camping party by themselves, get to camp for only $2.00 or $5.00 each. Furthermore, large families with four, five, or six kids have to pay more. They may use more hot water and so on, but they also spend more money in your profit centers.

In addition, you may have policies of charging extra for TV, air conditioning, additional cars, vehicles, or tents and RVs. You may also charge based on whether they require an extra large site or an additional site. These other charges, however, can get complicated and hard to explain over the phone or on your rate sheet.

Adult-Based Rates

Many of the above complications can be avoided by basing the camping fee on the adult camper (18 and over). Simply divide your average site rate by two if your average camping family usually has two adults in it.

With this method it doesn't matter how large the family is, the fee remains the same. That is, large families pay the same as small families, assuming families have two adults with all children under age 18. If you don't want to encourage large families, charge a per-person (including children) fee. Simply divide your average camping party size into the revenue per site that you want to generate.

If Uncle Joe, Aunt Martha, and Grandma want to come along, they pay accordingly. If Jane wants to bring her 10-year-old girlfriend along, the policy still applies. When camping parties need two sites instead of one, that's fine too. You still get your desired average site rental fee, because there are so many people that their fees add up to your average fee for both sites together.

Site-Based Rates

Another method is to base the fee on the individual site. Campers can bring as many tents, trailers, cars, and so on as they can fit on one site. If they have so many people or equipment that they need two sites, they pay for a second site. On the average, you may not get as much site revenue with the per-site method, because many campers may try to crowd onto a single site.

Group-Based Rates

Some campgrounds attract many camping groups, such as YWCA, YMCA, Scout, and church groups. The normal rate, especially the family rate, does not apply very well. Often these groups want to locate by themselves and in an arrangement that does not conform to your developed sites, so they often camp in an open field or overflow area. They frequently do not require hookups, since they camp in tents much of the time.

A special rate is therefore appropriate, such as a per-person fee, which may be lower than the usual per-adult fee. In these situations, you may want to decide how much you want to gross from the entire group, and then divide by the number in the average group to arrive at a per-person fee. Your price needs to be quoted on a per-person basis, because someone will probably need to collect it on that basis, either you or the group leader, preferably the latter.

Many campgrounds give a discount to such nonprofit organizations, at least until they've had a bad experience with them. The above rationale will handle such a discount. The lower rate can be justified on the grounds that they camp on land not normally used for camping, at least not on developed sites. It can be good public relations for groups coming from nearby communities. A word of caution: groups may use more than their share of the bathroom facilities, hot water, and so on.

Hookups

Pricing of hookups is handled in a variety of ways. Many include water and electric with the base rate, with an additional amount for a sewer hookup, TV, and so on. Whatever fee policy you have, it is highly advisable to do it in such a way as to get your investment back from the installations in a reasonable time, especially those 50 new sites you just developed, for example. Divide the total cost by the number of times you plan to rent them over the next few years—the number of years over which you want to get your investment back. This will give you the amount you need to charge in order to recover your investment. These hookup charges need to be considered as part of your over-all rate determination process.

Furthermore, such charges should be collected when the sites are rented, whether or not the campers say they intend to use them. Experiences shared at cracker-barrel discussions suggest that the campers use them regardless of their stated intentions. Therefore, if the rate is based on the camper family, it should be high enough to cover the hookup charge. The same is true of the per-adult, per-person, or per-site fee.

Differential Rates

The term "differential rates" means charging different rates for different sites or different times of the season, usually based on differences in site quality or camper preference. Every campground has some sites that are better than others, be they waterfront, shaded, or having features that make them more attractive. These desirable sites are easy to identify, as they are preferred and reserved first by campers.

If people prefer such sites, why not charge a little extra for them? This extra charge can be handled the same as the hookup charges. It can also be added to the per-person charge. What this means is increased gross income with no related cost increase. For example, suppose a modest 100-site campground has 30 sites that are of unusual quality and are usually the first to be reserved. With an average occupancy of 50 percent, the occupancy of these choice sites would probably be at least 75 percent. Therefore, if you charge an additional $2.00 for these sites, the additional gross income would be as follows:

$2.00 × 30 sites × 120 day season × 75% occupancy = $5,400

The public is used to this policy in other areas of their lives. Motels charge extra for poolside rooms and honeymoon suites. Sports fans pay more for seats on the 50-yard line or at ringside. Theatergoers pay more for better seats in the theater. Then why not charge a few dollars more for those waterfront sites? If the extra charge were $4.00, the additional gross would be $10,800!

Special Holiday Prices

Holiday weekends are very important because your sites are in greatest demand at these times of the year. Some campgrounds charge more for holiday weekends. Many campgrounds ensure at least the regular fee for such weekends by requiring the full fee in advance to guarantee the reservation. Others require one day's fee in advance with the reservation, and hold the site only until a certain time on the first night of the weekend. Then if the campers don't show, the site can still be rented out for the weekend.

Some think it is bad for customer relations to charge more for holiday weekends and to require more payment with the reservation than usual. It may turn a few people away that may not even come back at nonholiday times in the future. You have to weigh one side against the other and decide what you think is best for you.

An unfavorable attitude toward differential rates may be defused by a considerate explanation. For example, you might explain that not every camper who wants to will be able to camp at your campground because you have to turn away many campers every year. Therefore, your price policy allows those who are willing to pay a little extra a better chance of getting a reservation for those weekends. What will it gain you? Let's suppose you have 200 developed sites, that you are full on the three holiday weekends, and that you charge an extra $3.00 per site over the usual fee. The result is:

200 sites × $3.00 per site × 9 holiday nights = $5,400!

These ideas may be new to you. For some it may be a little different slant on something you've thought about before. Give some thought to them as they relate to your individual campground operation. Your situation is unique, so you must decide what is best for you!

Weekend Rates

Some operators charge higher rates for weekend that weekdays. For this the rationale is the same as for special holidays.

Rates for Recreation Activities

Rates you charge for recreation activities are important in building total campground income because you are usually constrained by the number of campers you can attract.

If the recreation activity is a major income producer, the same approach can be used as was discussed previously in site rate determination. That is, add up the costs that need to be recovered, estimate the number of users, divide the latter into the former, and then consider what the users are willing to pay (demand) and what others charge (competition). Then decide what the best rate is for you.

Appendix A

Rate Determination Worksheets

Expenses Worksheet

Salaries/wages	$ _____
Payroll taxes/benefits	_____
Owner's draw	_____
Operating supplies	_____
Vehicles operating expense	_____
Maintenance supplies/repairs	_____
Utilities	_____
Telephone	_____
Advertising & promotions	_____
Dues/subscriptions	_____
Licenses & permits	_____
Legal/accounting	_____
Office expense	_____
Property taxes	_____
Insurance	_____
Other	_____
Miscellaneous	_____
Total expenses	$ _____

Other Income Worksheet

Revenues $ _____
Day guest receipts   _____
Groceries   _____
Beer and wine   _____
Vending machines   _____
Souvenirs   _____
Mini-golf   _____
Equipment rentals   _____
Game room   _____
Firewood and ice   _____
Laundry   _____
Other   _____
Other   _____
Total gross sales   _____
Less cost of sales $ _____
**Net income other
than site rental** $ _____

Appendix B

Occupancy Calculation Worksheet

Just fill in Column 5 if you have records from last year, adjusted for what you estimate will change next year.

Column 1: Number of sites (omit seasonal sites)
Column 2: Days in the month
Column 3: Potential number of nights rented
Column 4: Occupancy rate (omit seasonals)
Column 5: Site nights rented

	Column 1	Column 2	Column 3*	Column 4	Column 5**
January	___	× 31 =	___	× ___	= ___
February	___	× 28 =	___	× ___	= ___
March	___	× 31 =	___	× ___	= ___
April	___	× 30 =	___	× ___	= ___
May	___	× 31 =	___	× ___	= ___
June	___	× 30 =	___	× ___	= ___
July	___	× 31 =	___	× ___	= ___
August	___	× 31 =	___	× ___	= ___
September	___	× 30 =	___	× ___	= ___
October	___	× 31 =	___	× ___	= ___
November	___	× 30 =	___	× ___	= ___
December	___	× 31 =	___	× ___	= ___

Total estimated site nights rented _____
*Column 1 × Column 2**
Column 3 × Column 4

Chapter

22

MARKET RESEARCH

The campground industry is getting more competitive as it grows and as campground management becomes more sophisticated. For this reason, every campground operator needs to advertise effectively and spend his or her advertising dollars as wisely as possible.

In order to do so, a campground operator needs good market information—and the best source of such information can be found right in your own campground. Such things as your guest registration cards, sport show, camper overflow, and inquiries and referral records provide information that can improve your marketing effectiveness tremendously. Let's take a look at some of these sources.

Camper Registration Research

Are you one who considers your guest registration cards a nuisance? Do you use them and keep them on file only because it is required by law? Or do you use guest registration forms as a very important tool in the operation of your campground? The following discussion explains what can be gained from using the information on guest registration forms and what a good registration form should contain.

Mailing List Information

First and foremost, many campground operators realize the practical use of the name and address of the campers as a mailing list for newsletters, brochures, activity schedules, and other direct mail promotions of the campground. No campers are better prospects for future camping than those who have already camped at your campground and had a good experience.

Origin Segmenting Information

Knowing where your campers come from is extremely important in deciding where to advertise and what sport shows to attend. Such information is available from your registration cards. Most of your customers hail from a few areas. Without any other information, it seems logical that it would be easier to get more campers from those areas than to attract them from areas where fewer or no campers are presently originating.

You may have a general idea where your guests are coming from simply from working in your campground, visiting with campers, and observing license plates. Knowing specifically, by zip code within metropolitan market area, where they come from allows you to advertise in the suburban weeklies and small town weeklies rather than in the less efficient large city dailies.

You may think the circulation of such large city dailies justifies the added cost, but also consider the large portion of the readers of those dailies who may not even be in the camping market at all. Another advertising possibility is the weekly shopper's guide. Most households receive at least one, if not more than one. Thus for zip code information, the origin information can be very helpful.

Shopping Information

You may wonder how stocking your store is related to guest registration cards. Determine the origins of your campers by major metropolitan market area. Find out what the leading brands are in those areas of the popular items you carry in your store. These are the brands you should stock.

Common sense tells you to buy the brands for your store that your campers prefer. This brand information can often be determined from the major newspapers in the metropolitan areas in which you are interested. Large newspapers regularly conduct consumer surveys of their readership, and among other things, determine the brand preferences of their readers. This information assists them in selling advertising for their papers. Since you are a potential advertiser, they will normally share it with you also.

Another way to get this brand information is to ask your campers. You can do this by developing a short survey form, and distributing it to your campers at registration time.

Still another way to get brand information is to go to the cities where your campers live and shop in their stores. Note the brands that have the largest display space, because these are usually the ones that sell in the largest volumes.

Party Size/Age Information

Information on party size by age group gives you general knowledge of the activity interests of your campers. Are a large portion of your camper families those with young children, with teenagers, or about equal numbers of each?

Are they mostly empty nesters or retirees? This information can help a great deal in planning activities to meet their needs. Plan your advertising message accordingly. In planning new recreation facilities, this information is a helpful guide in knowing what to provide.

This information is especially useful when you compare it over the years to indicate trends in your camper market profile. Is your average camper party getting older, younger, or staying about the same age? If the average age is gradually increasing, it might be that a growing portion of repeat campers is gradually getting older. If the average age decreases, it means you have many young families being attracted to your campground. This information is useful in developing your long-range marketing objectives, and consequent promotional programs.

By the way, it's good to have a considerable portion of young or new campers. This is because you'll always tend to lose repeat campers over the years, for a number of different reasons. Thus, you need to replace them gradually with new campers.

Length-of-Stay Information

Knowing how long your average camper party stays is important for several reasons. One reason is to help increase the average length of stay. Site rental income, along with other profit center income, is a direct result of the number of site nights rented and the average site rate. The number of site nights is the result of the number of camping parties multiplied by the number of nights they stay. Therefore, increasing the length of stay is the same as getting more camper parties to come to your campground and increasing gross site rental income, as well as increasing gross receipts in your other profit centers. Monitoring campers' average length of stay is therefore very important in managing your campground.

How can you increase the average length of stay? Offer more activities so that campers will stay busy longer and want to stay longer. Raising the overall quality level of your campground may encourage campers to stay longer and to return. Such campers will tell their friends about your campground also.

Offering a discount to encourage a longer stay has been successful for many operators. Many offer a free day with a week of camping or with camping over a weekend. Caution should be exercised in the use of discounts, as you may defeat the original purpose of encouraging longer stays. The free day of camping presumes campers will spend more in other profit centers, thus justifying the free day. For example, more groceries will be consumed with longer stays, thereby increasing store sales.

Increasing the length of stay is difficult, as is encouraging mid-week business. The major limiting factor may be campers' inability to get away from the workplace. Perhaps the greatest potential lies with campers who don't work during the camping season.

If weekends dominate camper use, it is important to concentrate on weekday check-ins. You can offer a commuter package, wherein the camper family camps Sunday through Thursday (five nights) for the price of four nights, and the wage earner commutes daily and joins the rest of the family every night.

Occupation

Knowing the occupations of your camper parties will give you an idea of their general income level and consequent ability to spend money in your campground. Knowing if one or both spouses work is equally important, as it greatly increases household income. The majority of our nation's households now have two major incomes. Occupation may also be an indicator of activity interests. Families in the professional occupational group will likely have different activity interests than families in the low-skill occupational group.

Trip Decision Information

Knowing who in the camping party decides where to camp is useful in designing and placing ads. Is it the adult male, the adult female, teens, young children, or a combination? The advertising message, as well as where it is placed in the paper, should vary accordingly, as discussed in Chapter 19. You need to know who makes the location decision in your camping parties.

Decision-Timing Information

Your ads should be placed during the time when your campers are deciding when and where to go camping. A past camper survey found that over 57 percent of the camping parties made the decision to go camping a month or less in advance, whereas 19 percent made the decision one to two months in advance About 18 percent made the decision more than two months in advance. This means you should probably start advertising about six weeks before your camping season begins, and continue until about a month before your season ends.

Ad Location Information

Knowing where campers saw your advertising gives you an idea of the relative effectiveness of your advertising efforts. If many campers remembered your brochure from a sport show, it tells you the brochure and those sport shows were somewhat effective. This may be a crude measure of effectiveness, but it's much better than nothing.

People may not be sure of what sold them on your campground, so it's good to ask them where they noticed the advertising. Give them a list of places, and ask them to check as many as apply. The responses should be recorded by market area in order to adequately judge the effectiveness of your advertising. All your campers have seen your front entrance sign, but not all have had a chance to see your newspaper ad.

Use Information (First Time versus Repeat)

Also important in planning your advertising program is the number of first-time versus repeat campers you have. Repeat campers come largely through reminder types of ads and direct mail advertising you send to them. These efforts trigger memories of previous trips to your establishment. New campers come because of your promotional efforts or being told by a friend.

Trip Purpose Information

Knowing *why* your campers made the trip is helpful. Did they come for relaxation to enjoy an activity such as fishing, or did they come to get away from home and the usual routine? This information helps you plan the facilities and activities you offer. It also helps you design your ads and brochures, as well as your newsletter.

One campground operator does a slide presentation several times a week on the attractions in the area. By doing this, he makes visiting these attractions easy and pleasurable for his campers. They have a more satisfying trip, and they are more likely to come back and to tell others. They may stay longer as well.

Occupancy Information

You can compute your occupancy rate from the information on your guest registration cards. However, it may be easier to calculate this from the reservation records you use at your front desk. Occupancy rate is the number of site nights rented, divided by the number of sites available for rent during some time period. Do not count seasonal sites or seasonal rentals. Simply add up all the site nights rented from the registration cards, for the time period for which you want to calculate the occupancy rate. Next, multiply the number of sites you have available for rent by the number of days in your camping season to get potential site nights. Then divide the number of site nights actually rented by the number of potential sites available for rent. The resulting decimal is the occupancy rate. Move the decimal point two places to the right to get your occupancy percentage. The occupancy rate is useful for comparing your campground performance with previous years, with the rest of the industry, and for deciding when it is time to expand your campground.

Overflow and Referral Information

When you must turn campers away because you're full, try to get their names and addresses so you can get them on your direct mail first, unless they have camped recently at your campground and are already on your list. Such campers have great potential to come back in the future.

Also, keep track of how many overflow camper parties you turn away. Keep this by date, as it is very important in making the decision to expand. If you rely on your memory for this information, the number you turn away may seem much larger than it actually is, and you'll invest in additional sites before your business justifies such expansion.

Registration Form Design

The questions found in Appendix A will generate the information previously discussed. Not all of the information would go on one registration form. Rather, you may choose some questions for this year and one or two others for the following year. Another possibility is to have half the questions on one form, and the other half on another, each form being a different color. Then alternate them as you register campers. In that way you'll get the information you need. Also, some of this information might be better obtained from a special survey you conduct among your campers. A sample of registration card information is given in Appendix A; it should give you the information needed from all campers.

Some companies specialize in printing reservation/registration forms used in campgrounds. One is Jenkins Business Forms, P.O. Box B, Mascoutah, IA, 62258. Another is Executive Services Group, P.O. Box 5578, Auburn, CA 95604. They will design the type of form you specify. Care should be taken so that the form doesn't take too long to complete, because your campers will get frustrated, and it will cause congestion during busy check-in times. Also make sure you and your staff see that the registration forms are fully completed and legible. When the registrant asks "Why do you want to know all this stuff?" your staff response should be, "By knowing about you, we can do a better job of serving you."

Camper, Sport, Mall Show Research

When you go to a sport or mall show you have an opportunity to obtain information about your potential campers. You can use this information to identify potential new campers and to gauge the effectiveness of your sport show participation. To get such information, you need to get campers to tell you who they are and give their addresses for direct mail advertising. A sign-up for a drawing is a possibility. A list for those requesting to be placed on your mailing list is another. Simply asking prospective campers if you can send them future information on special events is still another option.

After you get this information, place the names and addresses to which you want direct mail advertising sent on mailing labels. Then code such mail by placing an identification on the camper reservation form. Color code it, or in some other manner identify it, so that when the reservations are sent in, you can count them and measure the effectiveness of that particular show.

Test Ad Effectiveness

When you place an ad, it's an excellent idea to test the effectiveness of the ad and its placement. Then you'll know how to improve your promotional program in the following season. The ad can be coded by adding a department letter or number on your return address that you put in the ad. You can increase the response of inquiries by including a cut-out coupon for campers to fill in and return to you. This coupon can offer further information and/or be a campsite reservation form.

When the inquiries come in, respond to them promptly, and file them either manually or on a computer database. Then when the reservations come in, or when the parties come to camp, record this information as well. In this way you can determine how much (percentage of) business you received from the ad or the media placement. This is known as a conversion study.

Customer Reaction Surveys

Why not take a tip from the lodging industry and find out from your campers what they like and don't like about your campground? Most of the motel and hotel franchises leave a customer reaction form in their rooms. Restaurants often have them on the dining tables. Appendix A contains a list of possible questions you might want to ask, in order to provide a better camping experience for your campers.

Another way to get this kind of information is through the use of a suggestion box, prominently located and marked as such. It probably won't get as much response as the survey form, but those who do respond should be taken seriously.

Research Tabulation

All these research activities require keeping track of numbers, names, and addresses. If your operation is small, you can do it by hand, but if you have considerable camper volume, you'll want to use a computer. An excellent source of information on how to tabulate research can be found in the book, *The First Practical Guide to Campground Marketing*, by Bill Fillman, published by Sagamore Publishing (the publisher of this book).

If you don't have a computer, consider using the memory feature on a cash register. The newer electronic cash registers have increased memory capacity and are capable of market research applications. One major application is the price look-up (PLU) feature. Jim Robinson, of Wagon Trail Campground, found this to be very useful in processing the information from his guest registration cards.

The PLU feature on the cash register allows retail stores to change prices without changing the prices on the products. For example, if a person buys a carton of milk, the clerk simply rings up the code number for that carton of milk, and the price is recorded in the cash register and appears in the cash register window. The price can therefore be changed just by reprogramming the cash register. The feature is not necessary in Robinson's little camp store, but it is useful in doing his market research.

The information that they use from their guest registration cards is:

- type of camping equipment;
- number in camping party;
- type of camping party (family, couple, or other adults);
- length of stay;
- origin of camper, by zip code; and
- how they heard of Wagon Trail Campground.

With the electronic cash register, a code number is assigned to each category in the survey. For example, number one on the PLU key is *tent*, number two is *pop-up*, number eight *is one person per party*, and number 43 *is people heard about Wagon Trail through Woodall's*. Using this code, the clerk takes a registration card and rings into the cash register the code numbers corresponding to all the categories under which the camper falls. The registration card is then filed. When the information is needed from the cash register storage, the register is rung out as is done at the end of a day for sales totals.

Robinson rings out the PLU key three times a year: spring (up to July 1), summer (July and August), and fall (September through November). This gives market information based on camping seasons. He also completes an annual summary at the end of the year. His office staff enters guest registration form data during times when the office is not busy. He uses this information in determining timing and placement of ads, in deciding when to add more sites, and in determining rates. The information is also useful in tracking year to year changes in his camper market.

Secondary Sources of Data

With all this discussion about doing your own market research, don't overlook research information that others have conducted. Keep in touch with your state Cooperative Extension Service, Department of Natural Resources, the U.S. Forest Service, ARVC, and the Recreation Vehicle Industry Association. These agencies conduct various types of research, which may at times be useful for your needs. Much of this information is reported in Woodall's *Campground Management* and in the ARVC newsletter. ARVC also publishes the *National Operations Survey of the RV Park and Campground Industry*, usually every other year.

Appendix A

Sample Registration Form Information

Name: last, first
Address: street, route, city, state, zip code
Phone: home, work
Children: number 12 years and under, number 13 through 17
Number of other adults 18 years and over
Vehicle license number, state
Unit license number
Type of camping equipment: tent, pop-up, motor home,
    trailer, pickup, van, fifth wheel (use silhouettes)
Hookups needed: electric and water; electric, sewer
    and water; none (tent); TV; phone.
Electric heater, air conditioning? Pet? (specify)
How did you hear of us?
    Campground directory
    Friends
    Highway road signs
    Camping shows
    Phone directory
    Newspaper ad
First visit, return visit?

Other information you may not need from every camper, but want to place on alternate registration forms or obtain in a survey, as discussed earlier, includes:

Occupation:	*When was this trip decision made?*
male head of household,	within the last week
female head of household	1 to 2 weeks prior to trip
Who made the trip decision?	2 to 3 weeks prior to trip
male head of household	3 to 4 weeks prior to trip
female head of household	4 to 6 weeks prior to trip
teens	6 to 8 weeks prior to trip
children 12 and under	8 to 12 weeks prior to trip
combination of adults	over 12 weeks prior to trip
combination adults and children	*First trip to this campground?*
	Yes No

Please Help Us

Instructions: Please help us provide you with a better camping experience by answering the following questions. Mark the appropriate answers by placing an "X" indicating- Excellent, Very good, Average, Fair (below average), or Poor.

	Excellent	Very good	Avg.	Fair	Poor
1. How would you rate our campground overall?	___	___	___	___	___
2. How was your campsite?					
- Hookups?	___	___	___	___	___
- Ease of parking and setting up?	___	___	___	___	___
- Picnic table?	___	___	___	___	___
- Fire ring/grill?	___	___	___	___	___
Additional comments, if any?	_____				
3. Toilet/Shower facilities?					
- Cleanliness?	___	___	___	___	___
- Adequacy?	___	___	___	___	___
Additional comments, if any?	_____				
4. Check-In					
- Efficiency?	___	___	___	___	___
- Courtesy of staff?	___	___	___	___	___
Additional comments, if any?	_____				
5. Campground store?					
- Product selection	___	___	___	___	___
- Price range	___	___	___	___	___
6. How do you rate the value we provided for the price you paid?	___	___	___	___	___

7. We would appreciate any comments that you wish to make on your stay. (Use the reverse side if necessary). _____

8. If any members of our staff were especially friendly or responsive to your needs, please let us know who they are so that we can show them our appreciation.

Name _____
Position /comments _____

Your name and address:
Name _____
Street _____
City, state, zip _____

Thank you very much for your cooperation. We sincerely appreciate it.
Please turn this in at the front desk or mail it to us. (This survey form can be given out at registration.)

Chapter

23

A WORD ABOUT SELLING CAMPSITE RESERVATIONS

Importance of Personal Selling

Personal selling is a very expensive form of selling, with salesmen out on the road making calls, each call often many miles apart. In campground personal selling, customers usually come to the campground front desk, the sport show booth, or call. Perhaps the most common situation is when the customer makes a phone inquiry directly to the campground. Considerable sums of money are often spent in marketing efforts to generate a camper inquiry. It is logical that a reasonable effort be made to convert that inquiry into a sale—a campsite reservation.

Countless books have been written, college courses offered, and extensive training programs taught to increase the effectiveness of personal selling. Shouldn't you, the campground operator, make efforts to train yourself and your staff to be more effective in converting inquiries into reservations?

Getting Ready to Sell

Know your goals. Know your goals and tell your staff about them. Are you in business to make a profit? How much profit? How much increase in profit over last year can be translated into gross campsite rental income and occupancy?

Are you in business to entertain your friends and relatives? The answer makes a big difference in how you approach the handling of inquiries, as well as the rest of the campground management functions.

Know your campground product. Know what you are selling in order to be more effective at selling reservations. What specifically are the kinds of camper want-satisfying needs you can meet in your campground?

Your staff should be very familiar with your campground before taking over the important task of selling reservations over the phone, and behind your front desk. They should know the campsite layout in relation to the service facilities, the playground, the swimming pool, and other amenities. They should know where the tent sites are located, the sewer sites, and the water and electric sites. Staff members should not be given front desk responsibility until they've worked in your campground long enough to become thoroughly familiar with it.

Believe in and identify with your campground. You *and* your staff need to believe in and identify with your campground. Have pride in it; be proud of it. Project the feeling that you can't wait to tell others about your campground and the many positive features you have to offer. That may be easy for you, the owner, but not so easy for your employees, so you need to instill that feeling in your staff.

Know your camper customers. For starters, know the type of campers you plan to attract, based on your marketing plan. They may be family campers, empty nesters, retirees, or RV campers and tent campers. Put yourself in their shoes. Try to feel what they feel in terms of camping expectations, and potential frustrations, and anxieties related to their camping experiences.

Try to call your repeat campers by name. Know what their needs are from previous visits. Do they want to be near the playground or the service facilities?

Know your competition. Be familiar with the local competing campgrounds so that you can answer questions about them or handle objections concerning your own campground in relation to others. Know what facilities, amenities, and general quality levels they offer.

Sell Yourself First

Get your attitude in shape. Be friendly and positive. Greet people with a smile. Call them by name, if possible. Get yourself psyched up for selling your campground. An old saying applies here: "It's your *attitude*, not your *aptitude*, that determines your *altitude!*"

Look and act successful. Most people prefer to deal with successful people. Be well-dressed and well-groomed. It's important to look sharp. You tend to behave the way you look.

Make eye contact. You may find it natural to make eye contact when you talk to people, but some of your younger staff may have to learn to make eye contact when they talk to customers. Select staff who normally make eye contact, or train them to do so.

Be attentive. Listen when customers talk. Give them your undivided attention. What they have to say may seem trivial to you, but it's the most important thing on their minds at the time.

Be yourself. Behave in a way that makes you feel comfortable and relaxed, and you'll be the most effective in making your sales presentation. If you're tired because an emergency kept you up all night, get someone else to work the front desk or the sport show booth for you.

The Sales Presentation

There are many approaches to use in making a sales presentation, any of which may be successful. The AIDAS (Attention, Interest, Desire, Action, Satisfaction) approach presented in Chapter 19 will be described again here as it applies to selling a campsite reservation.

Attention. If campers call you or walk into your front office, you should have their attention, unless something such as a fussy child is distracting them. Use your opening to let them know who you are and especially that *you* are the person they want to talk to.

Also, try to find out if they are a repeat campers, spokespersons for a large group, persons interested in renting a seasonal site, or persons who read your listing in a camping directory and have never seen your campground.

Interest. You need to develop interest in your campground. Ask campers what they are looking for in a camping experience. Are they looking for family camping, group camping, or wilderness camping? Ask what kinds of activities and amenities they prefer. You might even go so far as to ask them to describe their perfect camping experience: "If you could have any features in a camping holiday, what would they be?"

These are the unique selling propositions (USPs) that you can use in your ad copy as well as in your sales presentations. Try to write down several of these, so you can refer to them while making your presentations.

Desire. The next step is to tell them about the kind of experience they'll have at your campground, in word picture phrases similar to what they told you earlier were their camping preferences. Want-satisfying needs, or USPs they told you about earlier can be paraphrased and repeated back to them. This isn't as difficult as it may seem, because these descriptive phrases will fall into patterns. Many of them will be identical to the descriptions you used in your ad copy on your brochure. You must be honest in this, or it will lead to disappointment, frustration, and complaints from campers if they don't receive the camping experience promised them.

Action/Close. Sales psychology states that you should get the customer answering positively to a series of questions. Then when you "close," or ask for the sale, it is easier for them to answer positively again. The action you are seeking is for campers to make a reservation. Therefore you need to ask for it. This may be difficult for some. In fact it's probably the main reason many sales people fail. You may not need to ask directly, "Would you like to make a reservation?" You may instead ask a question or two, leading to the reservation:

"When are you thinking of coming?"

"Would you like electric and water hookups?"

"Will you be arriving before 6:00 p.m.?"

"Would you like to send a check, or give us your credit card number as a deposit to hold your reservation?"

By the time you ask four or five questions such as these, and the answers are positive, you've already sold the reservation.

Satisfaction. Very critical in building repeat business is the satisfaction step. This includes the follow-up activities occurring after the sale, up to the campers' stay at your campground. Campers need to have a chance to say everything is OK or if something needs attention, as the case may be. It is part of the service component of campground management.

Handle their objections. There are several ways to handle objections, and after you've worked the front desk for a period of time, you'll learn how to handle objections. Four ways to deal with objections are as follows:

Turn them into a reason for buying. For example, if campers suggest that your rates are too high, describe a few outstanding features of your campground and conclude that, dollar for dollar, you offer more value per fee dollar at your campground.

Admit to the objection. Sometimes it's perfectly all right to admit the truth of an objection. Then follow up with a logical explanation of why things are a certain way and what your plans are to correct the situation if necessary.

Ignore the objection. Some people just like to criticize. Once they've gotten it out of their systems, they may go right ahead and make the reservation.

Deny the objection. Other times you'll want to calmly deny the objection, immediately followed by a positive statement to the contrary, and go on with the presentation. In all the above situations you want to attempt to close, or to get the reservation. With experience, you'll discover how to handle common objections.

Qualify the customer. Often the caller immediately asks about the rates. This is the time to qualify campers to see if they would really be happy at your campground. When they ask the rate, ask them what kind of camping equipment they have, site qualities they are looking for, size and makeup of camping party, and anything else you think will help qualify them.

By this time, you may think they do not match up with your campground. If so, it's better to tell them and recommend another campground than it is to make a reservation for them and have an unhappy camping party. If they are a good match, you've found out what they want in a campsite, and can proceed with the sales presentation in an effective manner.

Sell other profit centers. Once you've sold the reservation, you can take the opportunity to sell other profit centers in your campground. These should be profit centers where there is a substantial fee involved and/or where reservations are also required. It may be a canoe outing on a nearby river, which includes transportation and a picnic lunch, for example.

Get their name and address. If you fail to make a reservation, try to get their names and addresses, explaining that you'd like to send them information on your campground and a copy of your special events schedule for the rest of the season. They did make the effort to call, so they are still potential customers, even though they didn't reserve with you this time. That is, of course, unless they are looking for a completely different camping experience from what you offer at your campground.

Suggestive Selling

While selling the reservation, you might want to sell some other features in your campground. For example, you might want to tell them that you have a complete store, so they won't need to bring every single item they'll need on their trip. Or, if people are coming through the check-out with certain food items, you can suggest other companion items such as buns with wieners, butter and spreads with bread, and so on. This was covered in detail in Chapter 17, Campground Store Operations.

Assume the Sale

Lois Strauss, of Papoose Pond Resort, Maine, teaches her staff to assume that inquirers want to make a reservation. She reasons that, in having called, campers have done enough research to find your name and number to call. They are obviously looking for a place to go. Further, they really want to make a decision (reservation) and get on with their other activities of the day. This attitude, according to Strauss, is much more effective than thinking that maybe they want to come.

Sell from the Top Down

Sell from the top down. Start with the highest priced campsites. Don't assume campers want the cheapest site in your campground. Often they want the best that you have. In this way you can build your gross.

High- or Low-Pressure Selling

Whether to use high pressure or low pressure depends on your personal style and how you want to run your operation. Most campground operators probably prefer to use low-pressure sales practices.

Negative Selling

You might try negative selling, which would be used to impress people with the superior quality of your campground as reflected in your rate structure. If someone doesn't want to pay for the high quality of camping you offer, you might suggest that they go to a nearby campground with low-quality facilities, which is reflected in their rates.

Listen to Yourself

Ever wonder what you sound like when you talk over the phone in answer to an inquiry? Turn on your cassette recorder when the telephone rings, and listen to it at a later time. This should provide excellent insight into your sales presentation and give you tips on how to improve it. Do the same with any staff who work your front desk.

References

Albrecht, F., (1980), Unpublished handout used at Campground Owners' Short Course. Madison, University of Wisconsin - Extension

Arimond, G., Cooper, R., and Silva, D. (1991). *Wisconsin Camper Survey*. Madison, University of Wisconsin-Extension.

Bureau of the Census. (1989). *Statistical Abstract of the United States*. Washinton, DC: Bureau of the Census.

Bureau of the Census. (1997). *Statistical Abstract of the United States*. Washinton, DC: Bureau of the Census.

Busch, M. (1990). "Linking Smart Planning to the Management of People." *The Annual of Developing Human Resources*.

Cooper, R., Novak, R., & Henderson, C. (1980). *Wisconsin Camper Survey*. Madison, University of Wisconsin-Extension.

Espeseth, R. D. (1988), *Site Planning in Park Areas*. (North Central Regional Extension Publication 290.) Champaign: University of Illinois.

Espeseth, R. D. (1980). November/December. *Illinois Parks and Recreation*.

Espeseth, R. E. Unpublished monograph. Office of Recreation and Park Resources. Champaign: University of Illinois.

Falvey, J. (1982). "To Raise Productivity, Try Saying, Thank You." *The Wall Street Journal*.

Fetterman, M. (1991). "New Numbers Show a Changing Society. Homeowners, Wed Couples' Numbers Dwindle. *USA Today*.

Fillman, B. (1990). *The first practical Guide to Campground Marketing.* Champaign: Sagamore.

Frechtling, D. C. (1987, June). "Five Issues in Tourism Marketing in the 1990s." *Tourism Management*.

Harrison, Gerry. 1989. *Northeast In-Sites*. Wilbraham, MA: Northeast Campground Owners Association.

Hultsman, J. C., Richard, R., & Hultsman, W. Z. (1998). *Planning Parks for People* (2nd ed.). State College, PA: Venture.

Hultsman, W. Z. (1990, June). "Variety is the Spice of Recreation Programming." *Woodall's Campground Management, 21(6).*

Januz, L. (1982, October). "Direct Marketers Should Put Best Effort Into Their Brochures." (Direct Marketing Memo.) *Marketing News.*

Kotler, P. (1990). *Principles of Marketing.* Englewood Cliffs, NJ: Prentice-Hall.

Lawrence, L. (1982). *Suggested Markup on Selling Price for Selected Items.* Santa Ana, CA: Associated Campground Systems.

Marshall, K., and Crompton, J. (1991). *How Winter Texans Spend their Time in the Lower Rio Grande Valley.* College Station, TX: Texas A & M.

McEwen, D. (1989). *National Economic Survey of Private Campgrounds.* Washington DC:National Campground Owners Association.

McEwen, D. & Mitchell, C. (1991). *Fundamentals of Recreation Programming for Campgrounds and RV Parks.* Champaign: Sagamore.

Meek, J., & Kingsley, R. (1984). *How to Organize Your Business.* (Business for Profit Series.) Ames, IA: Iowa State University.

Montville, F. E. (1983). *Operating and Managing the Campground Store.* Orono, ME: University of Maine-Cooperative Extension Service.

National Foundation for RVing and Camping. (1998). *National Operations Survey of the RV Park and Campground Industry,* Vienna, VA, National Foundation for RVing and Campground Industry P. 29.

National Spa and Pool Institute. *Minimum Standards for Public Swimming Pools.* Alexandria, VA: National Spa and Poll Institute.

Olmi, A. M. *Selecting the Legal Structure of Your Firm.* (Management Aids Number 6.004.) Albuquerque, NM: Small Business Administration.

Participation in Recreational Activities, Section 19, 895.525, Wisconsin Act 377 (1987).

Penaloza, L. (1988). "Campers in State and Private Campgrounds." In *The 1987 Wisconsin Camper Survey.* Madison, Wisconsin Department of Natural Resources and the University of Wisconsin-Extension.

Pouros, J. G. (1980) *The Seasonal Lease,* (Unpublished workshop handout.) West Bend, WI: O'Meara, O'Meara, and Eckert.

Rose, C., Cooper, R., and Schink, D. (1986). *Financial Analysis of Wisconsin Privately-Owned Campgrounds.* University of Wisconsin-Extension.

Schink, D. (1990). (Unpublished workshop handout.) Chartwell Business Planning. *Financial Management.* Fort Atkinson, WI.

Schneider, M. (1990). (Unpublished workshop handout.) Kenosha, WI.

Seppi, E. (1980). Presentation at the Colorado Campground Association's Fall Convention, Colorado Springs, CO.

"Steps in Incorporating a Business, Small Business Administration." *Management Aids for Small Manufacturers, No. 111.*

"Steps in Starting a Business." (1981). (Bank of America newsletter) *Small Business Reporter.*

"U.S.A. Adult Participation Data and Projections for 2000." 1986. Northbrook, IL: Simmons Market Research Bureau, Inc.

Whitemarsh, Brian. (1985, May). *Ownership/Membership Forms of Campground Development—History/Issues.* (Unpublished paper.) Madison, University of Wisconsin-Extension.

Wise, C. A. *Test Your Success Characteristics.* (Survey.) Hartford, University of Wisconsin-Extension.

Woodall's Campground Directory. (1991). Lake Forest, IL: Woodall's Campground Management.

Woodall's Campground Management Buyer's Guide, Vol. 30, No. 1.

Index